SUPERIOR CUSTOMER VALUE

Strategies for Winning
and Retaining Customers

Third Edition

SUPERIOR CUSTOMER VALUE

Strategies for Winning and Retaining Customers

Third Edition

ART WEINSTEIN

CRC Press
Taylor & Francis Group
Boca Raton London New York

CRC Press is an imprint of the
Taylor & Francis Group, an **informa** business

CRC Press
Taylor & Francis Group
6000 Broken Sound Parkway NW, Suite 300
Boca Raton, FL 33487-2742

© 2012 by Art Weinstein
CRC Press is an imprint of Taylor & Francis Group, an Informa business

No claim to original U.S. Government works

Printed in the United States of America on acid-free paper
Version Date: 20120127

International Standard Book Number: 978-1-4398-6128-8 (Hardback)

Library of Congress Cataloging-in-Publication Data

Weinstein, Art.
    Superior customer value : strategies for winning and retaining customers / Art Weinstein. -- 3rd ed.
        p. cm.
    Includes bibliographical references and index.
    ISBN 978-1-4398-6128-8 (hardcover : alk. paper)
    1. Customer services--Management. I. Title.

HF5415.5.W442 2012
658.8'12--dc23   2011047970

Visit the Taylor & Francis Web site at
http://www.taylorandfrancis.com

and the CRC Press Web site at
http://www.crcpress.com

As always, to Sandee and Trevor, with love.

Contents

SECTION II DESIGNING A SUCCESSFUL CUSTOMER STRATEGY

SECTION V   CUSTOMER VALUE CASE STUDIES

Preface

Designing and providing superior customer value are the keys to successful business strategy in the 21st century. Value reigns supreme in today's marketplace and marketspace. Customers will not pay more than a product is worth and will reward excellence. Consider the remarkable success of Apple, Amazon.com, Citrix Systems, FedEx, Google, IKEA, Intel, JetBlue, Lexus, and Target—these companies truly know how to maximize customer value!

The American Marketing Association and the Chartered Institute of Marketing (United Kingdom) have updated their recent definitions of marketing based on value creation.[1] According to the Marketing Science Institute, managing customers and understanding customer experience and behavior, developing customer-focused organizations, and delivering value through enhanced media/channels are top-tier research priorities through 2012.[2]

I have been researching, writing, consulting, and speaking about customer value for more than 15 years. In addition, I have developed and teach the definitive MBA course on the subject. My work has convinced me that developing the right value proposition (service, quality, image, and price, or S-Q-I-P™) must be a top priority for management.

A customercentric culture provides focus and direction for the organization, ensuring that exceptional value will be offered to customers. This, in turn, results in enhanced market performance. Unfortunately, caught up in the daily economic and competitive pressures of running complex and fast-changing businesses, managers may lose sight of customers' desires. And customer experiences often fall far short of expectations. Great companies delight and amaze customers.

This book benchmarks the best companies and shows you what it truly means to create world-class value for customers. *Superior Customer Value*, 3rd edition, is assembled from the latest thinking from the business and academic communities. Building on a three-pronged approach to the study of customer value—concepts, applications, and cases—the book provides a comprehensive, integrative, and highly practical marketing management resource. It explores key marketing planning issues that emphasize relationship management strategies to keep customers happy. Best practices on customer retention, market-driving behavior, organizational responsiveness, pricing, service quality, and the value proposition are featured.

New, hot topics added to this edition include business models, cocreation of value, corporate entrepreneurship, customer experience management, image, metrics, social media, and process innovation.

Superior Customer Value was written to provide marketing practitioners, executives, and scholars with an informative, state-of-the-art guide to designing, implementing, and evaluating a customer value strategy in service-, technology-, and information-based organizations. The material appearing in the book has been discussed at length in our MBA course, *Delivering Superior Customer Value*.[3] In addition to the more than 10,000 students who have learned these ideas, thousands of managers have benefited from my interpretation of the customer value paradigm via executive seminars, presentations, and trade and scholarly articles.

Superior Customer Value is organized into five sections. Section I, "Customer Value—The Building Blocks" (Chapters 1–3), is the foundation material. This section examines critical business issues such as the importance of creating value for customers, market orientation, and value-creating processes. Section II, "Designing a Successful Customer Strategy," is offered in Chapters 4–6. This section features a chapter on building business models and value propositions as well as chapters on the core offerings (service and quality) and the communicators (price and image). Section III, "Excelling in the Marketspace" (Chapters 7 and 8), explains how to develop an e-commerce strategy and effectively use integrated marketing communications, including social media. Section IV, "Retaining Customers—Analysis and Strategy" (Chapters 9–11), wraps up the text/concepts portion of the book with important material on customer loyalty and retention, relationship marketing, and customer value metrics. Each chapter includes useful figures, tables, customer value checklists and insights, and end-of-chapter discussion questions. Reference material can be found in the Notes section at the back of the book.

Section V, "Customer Value Cases," provides six detailed, hands-on examples of how successful organizations create value for their customers. This section opens with a framework for analyzing business cases via the Customer-Value Funnel approach. The Enterprise Rent-A-Car case is new. Popular, revised cases from earlier editions of the book include FedEx, Grateful Dead, Harrah's Entertainment, Publix Super Markets, and StatePride Industrial Laundry. Each case explores a major customer value theme (e.g., customer intimacy, loyalty, market-driving, value chain analysis, etc.) and offers end-of-case questions to guide the analyses. The cases provide excellent learning opportunities to model effective customer value practices.

I look forward to learning more about your customer value marketing experiences. Feel free to contact me: (954) 262-5097, art@huizenga.nova.edu, www.artweinstein.com, www.linkedin.com/pub/art-weinstein/9/b47/613. And, for related information about the book and my work on customer value go to http://www.facebook.com/pages/Superior-Customer-Value/113613565405735 or visit Facebook and search Superior Customer Value.

Acknowledgments

Many individuals provided valuable input toward the preparation of *Superior Customer Value*, 3rd edition. First and foremost, I thank Rich O'Hanley, publisher at CRC Press, for believing in *Superior Customer Value* (again). Lara Zoble, associate editor, provided sound guidance throughout the book development process.

Second, I must recognize William C. Johnson, coauthor of the first two editions. While Bill reluctantly passed on writing yet another textbook, he graciously contributed two case studies (Harrah's and Publix), prepared a checklist on e-Service Quality, and critiqued the chapter on e-Commerce (Chapter 7). Furthermore, much of what I know about process management, service quality, pricing, and relationship marketing I learned working alongside Bill.

Third, Hilton Barrett and I have worked together on research for 15 years. Our collaboration has resulted in twenty publications in leading marketing, management, and entrepreneurship journals and conference proceedings. Hilton wrote the StatePride case as well as developed innovative value chain models, market orientation frameworks, and ideas on corporate entrepreneurship that are found in Chapters 2 and 9. He also reviewed Chapter 2, "Be Customer Driven and Market Driving." With more than 25 years experience as a "practicing manager," Hilton has influenced my thinking on how to create value and excel in business.

Fourth, eight other colleagues provided key contributions to the book:

- Barry Barnes wrote the interesting and insightful Grateful Dead case. Barry is a management theorist on strategic improvisation as well as a rock music aficionado.
- Jerry Johnson's FedEx case provides a solid application of the Customer Value Funnel, which is presented in Section V of this book.
- Bahaudin Mujtaba, a former Publix executive and management professor, coauthored two case studies for the book (Enterprise Rent-A-Car with Patience Rockymore-Turner and Publix with Bill Johnson).
- Shane Smith coauthored Chapter 11, "Customer Value Metrics."
- Ben Verschuur prepared a detailed checklist on social media marketing and offered useful insights in Chapter 8, "Integrated Marketing Communication and Social Media."

- R. J. Trasorras, a Tampa-based private investigator and a customer retention scholar, offered valuable insights on social media and e-mail marketing as well as reviewed Chapter 10, "Customer Loyalty and Retention."
- Frank Jamieson was responsible for bringing the marketing automation material to the book. In addition, Frank reviewed Chapter 9, "Creating Value through Relationship Marketing."
- Jacob Morgan provided an innovative framework on social customer relationship management.

Fifth, I acknowledge the following people for their insightful customer value examples. In alphabetical order, thank you: Steven Cates, Nancy Domenichelli, Mark Flaherty, Brett A. Gordon, Pam A. Gordon, Linda Hamburger, Alan Hess, Estuardo Jo, Alex Osterwalder, and Jeff Rohrs. In addition, I truly appreciate the excellent chapter reviews/feedback offered by Margaret Britt, Matt Kenney, Paul Knapp, Bill Lowe, and Joel Rodgers. Dana Cocchiara and Trevor Weinstein ably assisted me with computer graphics and technical issues beyond my grasp. Jason Pruitt made me look good in the videos.

Sixth, I have to mention Randy Pohlman, former dean of the Huizenga School at Nova Southeastern University. Randy challenged me in the mid-1990s to think about customer value in a new light. And, I have been thinking about it ever since. My NSU colleagues supported this project by granting me six months without teaching to dive deeply into writing the book. Thanks for the much-needed faculty research sabbatical.

Last, it has been a true pleasure teaching my customers—the MBA, undergraduate, and doctoral students and marketing/business executives—everything I know about customer value. These learning laboratories are a tremendous help to me in sculpting and fine-tuning my message. *Superior Customer Value* is yours—enjoy the educational experience!

Art Weinstein, Ph.D.
Professor of Marketing

About the Author

Art Weinstein is a professor of marketing in the Huizenga School of Business and Entrepreneurship at Nova Southeastern University, Fort Lauderdale, Florida. He earned his PhD in 1991 from Florida International University. Dr. Weinstein is the author of *The Handbook of Market Segmentation*, 3rd ed., and *Defining Your Market*, as well as more than 70 scholarly articles and papers on customer-focused topics and marketing strategy issues. He was the founder and editor of the *Journal of Segmentation in Marketing*. Dr. Weinstein has consulted for many high-tech and service firms.

CUSTOMER VALUE—THE BUILDING BLOCKS

I

Chapter 1

Customers Want Exceptional Value!

If you do build a great experience, customers tell each other about that.

Jeff Bezos

A lot of companies have chosen to downsize, and maybe that was the right thing for them. We chose a different path. Our belief was that if we kept putting great products in front of customers, they would continue to open their wallets.

Steve Jobs

According to *Fortune* magazine, Apple, Google, Berkshire Hathaway, Southwest Airlines, Procter & Gamble, Coca-Cola, Amazon.com, FedEx, Microsoft, and McDonald's are the ten most admired companies in the world. Stellar corporate reputations are based on nine criteria: innovation, people management, use of assets, social responsibility, management quality, financial soundness, long-term investment, product quality, and global competitiveness.[1] Such criteria are evidenced by companies that practice customer-value (CV) thinking. Designing and delivering superior customer value propels organizations to market leadership positions in today's highly competitive global markets.

By examining relevant CV concepts and marketing applications, this opening chapter accomplishes three objectives. First, it explains why customer value must be the overall basis for business strategy. Second, a review of the macroeconomic environment and its impact on corporate America is discussed. Third, the attributes of value-creating organizations are identified and CV implications for forward-thinking managers are offered for reflection and consideration of implementation.

Importance of Customer Value

Great companies do not just satisfy customers; they strive to amaze, astound, delight, or wow them (at least some of the time). Superior customer value means to continually create business experiences that exceed customer expectations. Value is the strategic driver that global companies, as well as community mom-and-pop small businesses, utilize to differentiate themselves from their competitors in the minds of customers.

How is it that Tesla can sell Model S electric cars for $60,000 and Subway can offer foot-long sandwiches for $5.00 and both are considered good values? Why have Netflix and Redbox thrived in the DVD rental business while Blockbuster was forced to enter bankruptcy protection? Value is the answer—and value is defined by your customers. Companies that offer outstanding value turn buyers ("try-ers") into lifetime customers. Case in point: Apple's recent string of success with iPods, iTunes, iPhones, and iPads has built market share for their Mac line of computers. Apple's creative imagination, spearheaded by the late Steve Jobs, is all about giving customers extraordinary experiences.

So, What Does Value Really Mean?

Value is an amorphous business term, like *quality, service,* and *excellence.* It has many meanings to many people. In fact, the concept of customer value is as old as ancient trade practices. In early barter transactions, buyers carefully evaluated sellers' offerings; they agreed to do business only if the benefits (received products) relative to the cost (traded items) was perceived as a fair (or better) value. Hence, value is "the satisfaction of customer requirements at the lowest total cost of acquisition, ownership, and use."[2]

Value means relative worth or importance. Furthermore, it implies excellence based on desirability or usefulness and is represented as a magnitude or quantity. On the other hand, *values* are the abstract concepts of what is right, worthwhile, or desirable.[3] Management's values impact how an organization creates value and, ultimately, its success. The legends about the Frito-Lay sales rep stocking a small grocery store's potato chip rack in a blizzard and Art Fry's entrepreneurial initiative that brought Post-It to 3M reinforce organizational cultures.

Value may be best defined from the customer's perspective as a tradeoff between the benefits received from the offer versus the sacrifices to obtain it (e.g., costs, stress, time, etc.). Value is created when product and user come together within a particular use situation. Thus, each consumer transaction is evaluated as to a dissatisfaction, satisfaction, or high-satisfaction experience, in terms of the value received. These service encounters influence customer decisions to form long-term relationships with organizations.

According to Woodruff and Gardial,[4] a three-stage value hierarchy exists that consists of attributes, consequences, and desired end states. These levels of abstraction describe the product/service, the user/product interaction, and the goals of the buyer (person or organization), respectively. For example, a new car buyer may seek attributes such as comfortable seating, an easy-to-read instrumental panel, smooth shifting, a *Consumer Reports* endorsement, no pressure sales tactics, and a good service/warranty program. At higher levels of abstraction, buyers may want driving ease, no hassles, and reliability (consequences), and ultimately peace of mind (desired end state).

As an area of formal marketing study, value-based thinking has evolved in its approximately seven-decade life, which originated at General Electric after World War II. Value-driven marketing strategies help organizations in ten areas:[5]

1. Understanding customer choices
2. Identifying customer segments
3. Increasing their competitive options (for example, offering more products)
4. Avoiding price wars
5. Improving service quality
6. Strengthening communications
7. Focusing on what is meaningful to customers
8. Building customer loyalty
9. Improving brand success
10. Developing strong customer relationships

The growth of customer-value thinking has impacted successful marketing practice. Kotler and colleagues[6] explain that we have entered Marketing 3.0—the values-driven era. (Note: Marketing 1.0 was productcentric, and Marketing 2.0 was customercentric and largely tied to the information technology.) The main characteristics of Marketing 3.0 are collaboration, globalization, and creativity.

Collaboration is participative marketing by channel members and/or customers, leading to the cocreation of value (such as Apple's App Store), strong supply-chain relationships and partnerships, and the operationalization of social media communities such as Facebook and Harley Ownership Group (HOG). Globalization is evident in all product categories today. For example, major league baseballs are manufactured in Costa Rica, NBA basketballs are made in China, and NFL footballs are produced in the United States. Creativity and innovation allow the smartest (not necessarily the biggest) companies to win in the marketplace. This third point is discussed in more detail in Chapter 3.

Service, Quality, Image, and Price: The Essence of Customer Value

Providing outstanding customer value has become a mandate for management. In choice-filled arenas, the balance of power has shifted from companies to value-seeking customers. CV can be expressed in many ways. The S-Q-I-P approach states that value is primarily a combination of Service, product Quality, Image, and Price. Top-notch companies often differentiate themselves and create legendary reputations largely due to singular attributes. While a focus on a key attribute is advisable, firms must meet acceptable threshold levels with respect to all of the dimensions—formidable global competition provides little room for weakness in any area.

The service factor must reign supreme in value-creating organizations. Nordstrom, Ritz-Carlton, and Lexus are renowned for unparalleled customer service. The American Express Global Customer Satisfaction Barometer found that excellent service is rewarded; U.S. consumers will spend 13% more with companies that demonstrate that they value their business.[7] (Other results from the American Express study are discussed in Chapter 5.)

Research by CustomerRespect.com found that only 58% of the top 100 U.S. companies responded to e-mails within a day; 27% responded after one day, and amazingly, 15% never responded! Only 35 of these large companies received an excellent or good score based on online customer service. The customer-respect score is a measure of how well companies cater to their online visitors based on ease of use of the Web site, responsiveness, and trust. Some recent leaders in CustomerRespect surveys include Overstock.com, Ralph Lauren, Amazon, Target, Hewlett-Packard, Medco Health Solutions, Intel, American Express, and UPS. Customer respect is a key part of online service that impacts ongoing relationships.[8] And, as we will see in Chapter 10, customers defect to another provider for service reasons about 70% of the time.

LEGO, Motorola, and Rubbermaid are obsessed with product quality and innovation. Ben & Jerry's and Harley-Davidson's cultlike following are attracted to the ice cream and motorcycles, respectively, as well as what the organization stands for (image). And Brands-Mart and Walmart are committed to offering great prices. Successful retailers such as Home Depot, IKEA, and Walgreens realize that price is only part of the value equation: Value is the total shopping experience. In fact, the pharmacy giant CVS initially was called Consumer Value Stores.

Since tradeoffs exist among the S-Q-I-P elements, companies cannot expect to be market leaders in all areas. The cost and resource commitment of developing and sustaining a four-dimensional leadership position would be overwhelming. Clearly, we can see that customer value is a much richer concept than just a fair price: Superb service, top quality, and a unique image are also highly valued by target markets. Realize that CV is a multidimensional construct. Varying emphases on S-Q-I-P explicate a company's value proposition (see Chapter 4).

Business Climate for Value Creation

Former president Bill Clinton said it best: "It's the economy, stupid." This somewhat painful lesson is one that President Barack Obama has learned on a daily basis since his 2008 election victory, as he has been challenged to build a successful formula for jump-starting the nation's economy while maintaining combat operations in Afghanistan and Iraq.

To begin our analysis, let's go back in time to the 1980s. During this period, the battle for customers was won or lost based on quality alone. As TQM (Total Quality Management) became the rage in business, quality gaps diminished and companies began to focus on customer service. Enhanced customer value synthesizes and extends the quality and customer service movements and has emerged as the dominant theme for business success for 21st-century companies.[9]

While this philosophy is commendable, not all companies have embraced a customercentric mindset. Accounting scandals, ethical gaffes, greedy top executives, misreading market needs, and shoddy management practices were all examples of not placing customers first.

Rise and Fall of the New Economy

According to Michael Dell, there are only two types of companies: the quick and the dead. The Internet has been the major change agent of the new economy during the past two decades. In the late 1990s, the Net experienced astronomical growth on several fronts—online users and usage, promotion, public awareness, billions of dollars in venture capital infusion, and Web business startups. During this period of explosive growth (1995–2000), business was typified by excesses that greatly affected profitability: New dot.coms were running $2-million Super Bowl commercials; companies were overinvesting in CRM (customer relationship management) systems, computer technology, and office furniture/furnishings; executives were regularly flying first class; and stock options were liberally dispensed.

The Internet explosion of the middle-to-late 1990s was characterized by a frenzy of entrepreneurial activity and new business concepts, with billions of dollars raised in (often misdirected) venture capital, a soaring stock market, and a marketing mindset advocating e-commerce. Exciting businesses such as Amazon.com, Blue Nile, Citrix Systems, eBay, Google, Netflix, PriceLine.com, and others have achieved remarkable success by pioneering innovative and better ways to create value for customers with changing needs and wants. These businesses survived the dot.com meltdown of 2000 by creating winning strategies based on superior value for their customers.

From the latter part of the year 2000 through 2002 (rapid descent), it became evident that the much-hyped virtual marketspace (dubbed by some the dot.bomb, dot.con, or dot.gone economy) failed to achieve many of its lofty ambitions. Thousands of online businesses and supporting companies failed, hundreds of thousands of highly educated technology managers were laid off, inflated Internet stocks crashed, and local economies in tech-friendly cities like San Francisco were negatively impacted. Unfortunately, most of the start-up Web-based companies lacked a solid business model, strong value proposition, and a long-term focus—and, ultimately they failed.

Newer Economy

By 2003, the dot.com shakeout led to a reenergization—a stabilized and growing Web sector that was a part of, but not the basis of, the new economy. It took online retailers only six years to match the sales level of what the catalog industry obtained in 100 years.[10] By the end of 2009, online retail sales in the United States reached $130 billion.[11] Led largely by upper-income consumers, online sales for the first quarter in 2010 were up 10% from the same period in 2009. Yet, surprisingly, online retail sales still represent less than 4% of total retail sales.[12]

Today's new hybrid economy consists of three major components: (1) the traditional economy (agriculture, construction, manufacturing, wholesale and retail trade, etc.), (2) a dominant services sector, and (3) a technology-based economy (high-tech firms, information-based businesses, and Web-based companies). The newer economy for the second decade of the 21st century is a business evolution and transformation to an entrepreneurial, global, and knowledge-based economy.

The service sector is projected to account for nearly all (96%) of the U.S. job growth between 2008 and 2018. Eight million new jobs are expected to be created, fairly evenly split in two major broad sectors: professional and business services, and health care and social assistance. On a percentage growth basis, the fastest growing occupations will include biomedical engineers, network-systems and data communications analysts, and financial examiners.[13] Tables 1.1 and 1.2 show U.S. employment projections in our service-driven economy for the year 2018.

The Information Technology and Innovation Foundation (ITIF), in conjunction with the Kauffman Foundation, recently completed a major research study that measured the new economy on a statewide basis (previous studies were conducted in 1999, 2002, 2007, and 2008). The project used 26 weighted indicators in five categories to capture the essence of the economic structure of the United States. Table 1.3 summarizes these key factors.

Based on composite scores of greater than 70 (the national average was 62), 11 states—Massachusetts, Washington, Maryland, New Jersey, Connecticut, Delaware, California, Virginia, Colorado, New York, and New Hampshire—can now be considered as active participants or progressives in the new economy. Sixteen other states have aggregate scores of less than 50; these laggards are still firmly rooted in the old economy. The remaining 23 states (which include Florida and Texas) score between 50 and 70; these states are taking definite strides toward entering the new economy. From a regional perspective, 13 of the top 20 new-economy states are found in the mid-Atlantic, Northeast, Mountain West, and

Table 1.1 U.S. Employment Winners and Losers, 2018 Projections

Expected Job Gains			Expected Job Losses		
Job	New Jobs (thousands), 2008–2018	Total Jobs (thousands), 2018	Job	Jobs Losses (thousands), 2008–2018	Total Jobs (thousands), 2008–2018
Registered nurses	581	3,200	Farmers and ranchers	–79	986
Home health aides	461	1,383	Order clerks	–71	141
Customer service representatives	400	2,652	Sewing machine operators	–64	182
Food preparation, serving workers, fast food	394	3,096	File clerks	–55	125
Personal and home-care aides	376	1,193	Postal service employees	–50	701
Retail salespeople	375	4,864	Telemarketers	–49	163
Office clerks, general	359	3,383	Shipping, receiving, traffic clerks	–38	304
Accountants and auditors	279	1,570	First-line supervisors, managers of production/operations workers	–35	646
Nursing aides, orderlies, and attendants	276	1,746	Office, administrative support	–36	271
Postsecondary teachers	257	1,956	Packers and packagers, by hand	–34	725

Source: Adapted from Fort Lauderdale Sun-Sentinel, 10 up and 10 down, September 6, 2010, 6D.

Table 1.2 U.S. Employment Data, 2008–2018

Industrial Sector	Employment (thousands), 2008	Employment (thousands), 2018 Projected	Change (thousands), 2008–2018	Percent Distribution, 2008	Percent Distribution, 2018 Projected
Goods-producing	21,363	21,390	27	14.2	12.9
Mining	717	613	–104	0.5	0.4
Construction	7,215	8,552	1,337	4.8	5.1
Manufacturing	13,431	12, 225	–1,206	8.9	7.4
Services-producing	116,452	131,053	14,601	77.2	78.8
Retail trade	15,356	16,010	654	10.2	9.6
Wholesale trade	5,964	6,220	256	4.0	3.7
Transportation and utilities	5,065	5,450	386	3.4	3.3
Information and finance	11,143	11,818	675	7.4	7.1

Professional and business services	17,778	21,968	4,190	11.8	13.2
Education	3,037	3,842	805	2.0	2.3
Health care and social assistance	15,819	19,816	3,997	10.5	11.9
Leisure and hospitality	13,459	14,601	1,142	8.9	8.8
Other services	6,332	7,142	810	4.2	4.3
Government	22,499	24,186	1,686	14.9	14.6
Agriculture	2,280	2,212	–68	1.5	1.3
Self-employed/other	10,837	11,550	713	6.9	6.9
Total U.S. employment	150,932	166,205	15,273	100.0	100.0

Source: Adapted from U.S. Department of Labor, Bureau of Labor Statistics, Economic News Release (Table 2, Employment by Major Sector), December 11, 2009, www.bls.gov/EMP.

Table 1.3 New-Economy Indicators

Knowledge Jobs	Globalization	Economic Dynamism	Digital Economy	Innovation Capacity
IT professionals	Export orientation	Job churning	Online population	High-tech employment
Professional and managerial jobs	(FDI) foreign direct investment	Fastest-growing firms	Digital government	Scientists and engineers
Workforce education		IPOs	Farms and technology	Patents
Immigration of knowledge workers		Entrepreneurial activity	Broadband	Industry R&D
U.S. migration of knowledge workers		Inventor patents	Health information technology	Nonindustry R&D
Manufacturing value-added				Green economy
Traded-services employment				Venture capital

Source: Robert D. Atkinson and Scott Andes, *The 2010 State New Economy Index* (Washington, DC: Information Technology & Innovation Foundation, November 2010), 54.

Pacific regions. In contrast, the Great Plains, Midwest, and South account for 18 of the 20 lowest ranking states.[14]

Overcoming the Great Recession

Victimized by the subprime mortgage crisis, credit crunch, and dismal economic conditions in the United States and globally, homes and retirement packages have plummeted in value. Large sunbelt states such as California and Florida have been particularly hard hit by the economic meltdown, leading to record numbers of foreclosures, underwater mortgages, and employee layoffs.

Huge government debt due to the automotive industry and financial services (e.g., AIG) bailouts and bank shutdowns have done little to boost consumer confidence that economic conditions will improve anytime soon. The stock market, generally a safe haven when real estate declines in value, has slowly recovered, but most investors face disappointing portfolios. Near-double-digit unemployment and limited job creation has created a bleak economic climate in the United States as well as in most other industrialized nations.

The recession, which began in 2007 and "officially" ended in 2009 (although, many Americans are skeptical of that claim), has dramatically altered Americans' spending habits. How have customers responded to the economic turmoil? Surprisingly, a large segment of the market has participated with an unprecedented buying spree. Apple iPods and iPads, smartphones, large-screen HD TVs, and organic foods have all been gobbled up in record numbers. It's all about perceived value. Products that are real winners are "must-haves." As the late comedian George Carlin might say, pay for the really good "stuff" (even if this means brown-bagging it on a regular basis, buying a lot more store brands, and cutting back on expensive dinners). CV Insight 1 explains how Subaru has thrived in a very challenging economy by creating exceptional value for its customers.

Customer Value Insight 1:
They Love Their Subarus!

The automotive industry was "running on empty" in 2009 as sales plummeted. General Motors and Chrysler needed U.S. government bailouts to survive; Toyota was plagued with product recalls; the recession was in full swing, necessitating "cash for clunkers" programs and federal sales tax incentives to stimulate the purchase of new vehicles. One notable exception in this dismal marketplace was Subaru of America.

Subaru has emotionally connected with its highly educated, environmentally conscious, and outdoor-enthusiast target market by providing well-built, reliable vehicles that consistently win "Car of the Year" awards by R.L. Polk & Company, *Motor Trend*, Edmunds.com, Cars.com, *Kiplinger's Personal Finance*, *Parents* magazine, National Highway Traffic Safety Administration, Japan's New Car Assessment Program, and other organizations.

"Subaru will consistently build customer loyalty, create customer advocates, and strengthen brand value by providing superior purchase and ownership experiences" (Subaru customer philosophy). Consider this interesting anecdote about Subaru quality. A customer with nearly 300,000 miles on his vehicle (200,000 + is not uncommon for Subarus) was unable to start his car. He contacted the service department and was asked if he had a spare key. He did, and was told to try starting the engine. It worked – apparently, the car was fine but the original key was worn out!

Subaru's recent promotional theme "Love, It's What Makes a Subaru a Subaru" has reinforced brand loyalty to meet the company objective of creating lifetime customers. Subaru, a niche marketer that sells about 200,000 units annually in the United States, has one of the highest repurchase rates in the industry.

Questions to Think About

1. What is unique about the Subaru customer focus that competitors are unable to match?
2. Comment on how Subaru loyalty differs from typical customer loyalty in the automotive industry.
3. How can companies in other business sectors emulate the Subaru experience and create brand advocates?

Some marketing implications of doing business in today's economy follow. Realize that tradeoffs are no longer necessary. Customers want fair prices and good quality, *solid value*, and their business to *be valued*, innovativeness and image status, physical goods and value-added services, and retail shopping malls as well as online merchants. As Barnes and Noble learned, customers want bricks-and-clicks or the ability to buy books in the *marketplace* (store) or the *marketspace* (www.bn.com). While their Nook electronic book reader is a hot product, it may be too little, too late. (The company has been on the trading block.)

Managing customer value is even more critical to organizations in the new service and information-based economy. The digital era has truly arrived. Case in point: Amazon's e-books for its Kindle and other platforms have recently outsold hardcover and paperback books (perhaps, you are reading this book in electronic form). Progressive companies that create maximum value for their customers will survive and thrive; they are able to carve sustainable competitive advantages in the marketplace.

Other firms not providing adequate value to customers will struggle or disappear—remember Saturn automobiles? In sum, competitive advantage is now gained through flexible production, innovative business models and strategies, hiring the best people, speed-to-market, and collaboration with the right business partners.

Value-Creating Organization

Organizations should be viewed as value-creating entities. Customercentric companies create value by solving customer problems. Delighted customers perceive a superior value when received benefits exceed costs (price, time, hassle, and/or stress). As Figure 1.1 shows, *value-creating* firms, such as Amazon and Apple, score

	Low	PURPOSE	High
High PURPOSE	WELL-INTENTIONED		VALUE-CREATING
Low	ADVERSARIAL		BUREAUCRATIC

Figure 1.1   The value matrix. (Adapted from G. Capowski, 1995, The force of value. Reprinted from *Management Review*, May, 34. © 1995. American Management Association. Reprinted from the American Management Association, New York, NY. With permission. All rights reserved. http://www.amacombooks.org.)

high in purpose (they understand their business and customers' desires) and high in process (they know how to utilize internal procedures to respond to customers effectively and efficiently).

Unfortunately, many organizations do not master both purpose (customer focus) and process (customer support) activities. Typical of many government agencies, the Internal Revenue Service (IRS) represents a *bureaucratic* organization. While the IRS does a reasonably good job processing tens of millions of tax packages annually, they rank relatively poorly on the purpose dimension. Most Americans perceive the tax system as overly complex, imprecise, time consuming, and at times, unfair or even unnecessary.

Segmentation, targeting, and positioning (STP marketing) and product, price, promotion, and place (the 4Ps) are focal points for value creation actions in the firm. These strategic controllables have major implications for attracting customers (conquest marketing) and keeping them (retention marketing). Sometimes, companies may go too far in one direction at the expense of the latter. For example, in the 1990s, America Online's solitary focus on the former cost the company millions of dollars in bad press, forcing it to deal with customer complaints, dissatisfaction, and defections as well as legal fees. During this time, the company was clearly viewed by its existing clients and the market as adversarial. The AOL–Time Warner marriage failed to get the organization on the right track. While America Online tried to improve on both its purpose and process dimensions, the company never recovered and continues to fight for survival.

Other companies, while well-intentioned, may try real hard, but just cannot seem to get it quite right. A foreign-car repair specialist may do an excellent job of scheduling appointments with busy professionals, only to find that the service technicians generally take longer than promised to fix cars or they routinely run out of stock on key automotive parts.

The value matrix in Figure 1.1 is a most useful tool for marketing management. Where would you place your company and your major competitors in the four quadrants? If your answer is anything other than value-creating, clearly you have some homework to do. Since markets are dynamic, the status quo is not acceptable; even value-creating organizations must constantly work at getting better every day to stay on top.

Customer Value—Marketing Management Implications

Maximizing customer value is an evolving challenge for service marketers. Visionary companies are responding to the new breed of smarter, more demanding customers by: (1) stressing customer retention strategies, (2) using customer value-based decision making, and (3) rethinking some traditional job functions.

The adoption of customer value in management's mission and vision statements means that customer retention (relationship management and collaboration) becomes the primary vehicle for market success. Amazon's Associates Program links more than 1.9 million members and pays these third-party sellers 4% to 15% of any revenues they generate. This clever cyber-based marketing strategy represented 30% of Amazon's unit sales in 2009, and active seller accounts increased 24% annually.[15]

Enhanced customer value goes beyond isolated transactions and builds long-term bonds and partnerships in the marketplace. Strong customer–corporate ties change buyers to advocates. Increased customer loyalty results in increased usage frequency and variety. Perhaps more important, however, is the fact that delighted customers play an important word-of-mouth, public relations role that creates new business opportunities via referrals.

And conversely, bad-mouthing by dissatisfied customers cannot only be harmful, but a death knell to a company. Consider a case in point: One unhappy buyer at a computer superstore estimated that this company lost $50,000 of his business (direct lifetime value) and another $350,000 (indirect lifetime value via referral business) due to negative word-of-mouth comments to his family and friends!

The Customer Value Funnel (CVF) provides a systematic and in-depth approach to understanding markets and improving business decisions. The CVF consists of five levels for management analysis: macroenvironment, microenvironment, organization, customers, and business performance. (This tool is discussed in detail in the Appendix following the 11 chapters.) In addition, the CVF provides the recommended framework to analyze the case studies that follow in Section V of the book.

To adapt more effectively and efficiently to customers, new types of value providers (value adders) are often needed. While some changes may seem to be cosmetic (e.g., renaming the front desk receptionist as the director of first impressions), in reality, they are often sound strategic responses to the changing business environment and the need to deliver superior value to customers. Consider these four examples:

- Merck, Xerox, and other *Fortune* 500 companies have created Market Segmentation Managers.
- Micro Motion's (a Colorado-based division of Emerson Electric that specializes in the production of mass flowmeters) Differentiation Strategist is charged with the responsibility of enhancing the company's customer service activities.
- Procter and Gamble, the quintessential consumer marketer, recently renamed its sales force the Customer Business Development Group. Selling is now only a small part of the CBD rep's job function. More important marketing activities include assisting customers in reducing inventory, tailoring product and price offerings in each market, and creating suitable comarketing promotional plans.[16]
- Sharing the executive suite with CEOs (chief executive officers) and CMOs (chief marketing officers) is a relatively new C-level position: chief customer officers (CCOs). In 2010, more than 300 companies (a tenfold increase from 2003), including Chrysler, Oracle, Samsung, Sears, Sun Microsystems, United Airlines, and Wachovia, have created CCOs, thereby transforming marketing departments into customer departments.[17]

A list of 11 customer-value imperatives for managers to address is summarized in Customer Value Checklist 1. These are the critical marketing-success factors for 21st-century organizations that are emphasized in this book. Taken in combination, these business initiatives represent the strategic building blocks for developing and implementing an effective, efficient, and adaptable program for customer value management.

Customer Value Checklist 1: Guidelines for Creating Exceptional Customer Value

1. Does your company continually exceed customer expectations?
2. Is your management team obsessed with researching and improving customer experiences?
3. Does your organization excel in process management?
4. Do you have an innovative business model and offer winning value propositions?
5. Do your people truly deliver world-class customer service?
6. Are your pricing policies and practices value creating for customers?
7. How successfully do you compete in the marketspace (online environment)?

8. Does your integrated marketing communication (IMC) program engage customers via traditional and social media?
9. Do you nurture and forge enduring relationships with customers and collaborators?
10. Is your marketing emphasis on customer retention (keeping and growing customers)?
11. Do you use marketing dashboards to track and improve customer experiences?

Summary

To succeed in today's challenging business environment, service organizations must do an outstanding job of creating—and maintaining—customer value. Each firm must find the right mix of ingredients (value proposition) to satisfy and delight its target markets. Developing emotional bonds with customers creates loyalty, which leads to high customer retention rates and increased market performance. First, this chapter explained why designing and managing customer value is critical for business success in highly changing and competitive global markets. Second, a revised profile of the new economy identified key sectors and growth prospects. Third, the characteristics and marketing implications of value-creating organizations were examined. Looking ahead, the two dimensions introduced in the value matrix—purpose (customer orientation) and process (customer operations)—are addressed in Chapters 2 and 3, respectively.

Customer Value Action Items

1. What is meant by CV? In general, what do customers truly value in: (a) the marketplace and (b) the marketspace? Provide an example of how a specific retailer and an e-tailer create value for their customers.
2. How does Hewlett-Packard design and deliver value for customers? How can Dell compete successfully against HP in the PC market? As a market nicher, what can Apple do to offer superior value to customers in the computer market?
3. Based on the S-Q-I-P approach, analyze three airlines (your choice) based on the following CV dimensions: service, product quality, image, and pricing. Rate the airlines on a 5-point scale (5 is exceptional and 1 is very poor) on each component, and then compute overall CV scores for each airline (maximum 20 points). What are your conclusions?

4. Identify some "best practices" from service industries/firms that a cable television or cellular phone provider can adapt to deliver better value to its customers.

5. Identify two companies that stress conquest marketing and two others that emphasize customer retention? Are these the appropriate strategies for these organizations? Why or why not?

6. How can your organization improve with respect to purpose (customer focus) and process (customer support) activities?

7. Identify a decliner, adapter, and star in the restaurant industry. What value-based strategies should these restaurants use for repositioning and future growth?

8. How important is an MBA degree in the new economy? What are some specialty areas that today's/tomorrow's executives will need to master?

9. Based on the trends discussed in this chapter, how would you envision the U.S. and world economy of 2020? (Assume you had to prepare a talk to executives in the global pharmaceutical industry.)

10. Write an executive summary of a business plan (one or two pages) sketching out your thoughts on a viable online marketing niche opportunity that would create or maximize value for young, technology-oriented consumers.

Chapter 2

Be Customer Driven and Market Driving

You can drive your business or be driven out of business.

B. C. Forbes

Companies must turn from a make-and-sell philosophy to a sense-and-respond philosophy.

Philip Kotler

"We must be more customer focused, we need to create new market opportunities!" Undoubtedly, you have heard this management mantra or a variant of this theme recently. Executives use terms such as customer (or market) centric/driven/focused/oriented and so forth[1] to motivate their people to do a better job relating and responding to customers. While the idea is sound, too often it's just lip service rather than a major investment to improve all facets of the organization. A true customer orientation changes the business culture and creates and maximizes customer value, which in turn leads to increased business performance.

This chapter explores how a CV-based organization can clarify its purpose and implement a customer-focused foundation to build long-term profitability. First, some examples of service companies that excel in this area are provided. Next, market orientation is examined from a strategic and business performance perspective. The chapter concludes with a practical managerial discussion of what it means to go beyond market driven and become market driving. The ideas of corporate entrepreneurship and cocreation of value are introduced in this context.

Customer Commitment: Follow the Market Leaders

Great companies are truly obsessed about their customers. They are masterful at creating and delivering value to their highly satisfied, loyal client base. Consider these examples: Federal Express changed its name and repainted its trucks to read FedEx, as that is what customers called them ("Let's FedEx this package to Omaha"). Nordstrom's sales associates have been known to buy products from a major competitor, Macy's, to satisfy an unfulfilled customer's request. Zappos.com, an online shoe and accessories retailer, gives its customers a full year to return its product (learn more about Zappos in Chapter 5).

As Customer Value Insight 2 demonstrates, the fun-loving spirit of Southwest Airlines flies high. Southwest's corporate culture creates superior customer value and goodwill. On one pleasant flight from Baltimore to Fort Lauderdale, Southwest flight attendants played games with the passengers (for example, the passengers with the most credit cards, oldest penny, and best memory won cases of peanuts), joked about the captain's age, and encouraged passengers to smile and wave to passengers on the nearby American plane upon landing. Southwest is the only major U.S. airline that does not charge service fees for passengers' baggage or flight itinerary changes.

Customer Value Insight 2:
How Southwest Airlines Makes Fun a Part
of the Customer Experience

Southwest Airlines is a company that is all business but yet doesn't take itself too seriously. For the past four decades, Southwest has been the most profitable U.S. carrier. A large part of their success is due to their customercentric philosophy. Flying out of their Dallas headquarters at the "other airport, Love Field," Southwest's New York Stock Exchange symbol is LUV. Their cofounder and chairman, Herb Kelleher, was renowned as a prankster and partyer and used to serve snacks on planes, occasionally dressed as Elvis Presley. He also engaged a major rival in an arm-wrestling match to settle an advertising slogan dispute. In response to another competitor's claim that Southwest was just a no-frills airline, they renamed their peanuts "Frills" for a while.

As part of their unique business culture, Southwest flight attendants and pilots are known for their entertaining in-flight "safety" messages, which offer a clear differentiator in an industry dealing with stress-filled and weary business and consumer travelers. Five of their classic in-flight announcements are listed below[2]:

- Heard after a very hard landing in Salt Lake City: The flight attendant came on the intercom and said, "That was quite a bump, and I know what y'all are thinking. I'm here to tell you it wasn't the airline's fault, it wasn't the pilot's fault, it wasn't the flight attendant's fault…it was the asphalt!"
- "Weather at our destination is 50 degrees with some broken clouds, but they'll try to have them fixed before we arrive. Thank you, and remember, nobody loves you or your money more than Southwest Airlines."
- Passengers were apparently having a hard time choosing seats when a flight attendant announced, "People, people, we're not picking out furniture here; find a seat and get in it!"
- "There may be 50 ways to leave your lover, but there are only 4 ways out of this airplane."
- "Welcome aboard Southwest Flight 245 to Tampa. To operate your seat belt, insert the metal tab into the buckle and pull tight. It works just like every other seat belt; and, if you don't know how to operate one, you probably shouldn't be out in public unsupervised. In the event of a sudden loss in cabin pressure, oxygen masks will descend from the ceiling. Stop screaming, grab the mask, and pull it over your face. If you have a small child traveling with you, secure your mask before assisting with theirs. If you are traveling with two small children, decide now which one you love more."

Another huge differentiator these days is Southwest's customer-friendly policy that allows bags to still fly for free. While all of the other major airlines charge for checked luggage (and in Spirit's case, carry-ons, too), Southwest is forgoing potentially hundreds of millions of dollars in "lost" revenues to keep customers happy and loyal. You have probably seen their humorous television commercials, the "Bags Fly Free" campaign. More than 250,000 viewers watched the "free bags" video on YouTube. Southwest has 800,000 Facebook followers and more than 1 million followers on Twitter.[3]

Questions to Think About
1. How effective is fun and humor in relating to customers and being market oriented?
2. How can your company inject fun into your business culture to be more successful?
3. How can Southwest continue to differentiate itself from its competitors?
4. Can Southwest afford to fly bags for free when all of its competitors charge fees for this service?

Greatness in marketing and customer service is a function of attitude, not resources. Consider the entrepreneurial tale of Hal and Sal. Hal, the owner of a small diner, not only greets his regulars warmly by name (often with hugs and occasionally kisses) but he frequently sits with them at the table for a couple of minutes to show his genuine concern for how they are doing. Sal, a sidewalk newspaper vendor (yes, a few people still read newspapers), gives his customers upbeat morning cheer and opinion, sports and news updates, and even credit when they do not have the 75 cents in change that day.

Other companies do not do a very good job in customer service: You probably can identify several of these firms. We have all been put on hold endlessly when calling for technical support, been ignored or treated indifferently when visiting a retail site, and sold inferior goods or services upon occasion. While second-rate firms may survive short term, they will not last in business unless they become value creating for customers.

Revisiting and Extending the Marketing Concept

The marketing concept dictates that the guiding business doctrine advocating a company-wide effort (interfunctional coordination) is to satisfy both customers (customer orientation) and organizational objectives (in particular, profitability). The traditional marketing concept—summarized as *customer satisfaction at a profit*—has been the cornerstone of the marketing discipline for more than half a century. This philosophy worked well through the early 1990s, since most companies stressed conquest marketing (getting new business) over retention marketing (keeping customers).

Realize that customer value can be created at three trigger points. These are: company/customers (marketing mix/program), employees/customers (service providers), and technology/customers (e-marketing mix). Each of these areas will be briefly reviewed.

Traditionally, external marketing (the marketing mix or program) was the focus for the majority of customer-directed activities. Here, the four Ps—product, price, promotion, and place—take center stage. In today's services-dominated economy, this view is limiting, and a fifth P—people—becomes paramount. Consider the importance of a manager's social network of business relationships, whether it is via LinkedIn or the old-fashioned Rolodex. In business-to-business markets, who you know is especially valuable for implementing projects.

Customer-oriented service organizations employ personnel that are value adders. Internal marketing is used to develop customer-focused employees. Basic human resource management activities such as recruitment, training, motivating, compensating, and evaluation come into play in this area. Don Schultz, a leading thinker on integrated marketing, believes that if chief marketing officers would shift just 5% of their external customer research budgets to study internal customers (those within the organization who are supposed to deliver the corporate promises), dramatic increases in marketing productivity of 50% or more would result.[4]

Once the people are adequately prepared for their respective business challenges, interactive marketing (face-to-face and other customer contacts) takes over. Exceptional customer service differentiates market leaders from average companies. Home Depot is known for its careful screening and selection process to find job applicants with a high social orientation (strong people skills). While Home Depot is renowned for their low prices and vast product selection, service is a new priority due to formidable competition from Lowes. Although it is a home-improvement superstore, Home Depot's associates are directed to spend "face" time helping customers with their home repair/remodeling projects and to find their needed merchandise (services provided by neighborhood hardware stores).

Two key dimensions for good service providers are the ability to satisfy customer needs and the degree to which interacting with customers is an enjoyable experience. In addition, three personality traits—agreeability, emotional stability, and the need for activity—were found to explain about 40% of the variance in the customer orientation of food service employees.[5]

Best Buy gauges sales applicants on their people skills as well as their technological savvy. Robert Stephens, chief technology officer and founder of the Geek Squad, envisions "blue shirts" (associates) as potential human search engines/problem solvers to take customer service to a higher level.[6]

E-marketing is a powerful 21st-century marketing weapon that should be added to an organization's arsenal. For the most part, these Internet-based marketing techniques originated from e-tailers during the five-year dot.com boom of the late 1990s. According to Kalyanam and McIntyre, the e-marketing mix consists of 11 e-marketing functions (community, customer service, personalization, privacy, security, etc.) and more than 30 e-marketing tools (chats, dynamic pricing, e-coupons, FAQs, remote hosting, reputation scoring, sponsored links, user ratings and reviews, etc.).[7] To be competitive, value-creating organizations must incorporate the latest relevant marketing techniques and technologies into their business plans.

The Web must be an integral part of every organization's business strategy in the 21st century. The Internet can be used as a sales channel, promotional vehicle, customer service center, market research tool, and community builder. In addition, business marketers can use the Net to connect with remote customers and suppliers, reduce sales and travel expenses, minimize inventory levels, be more productive, and add value. Customers want to do business with organizations when and how it is convenient for them to do so. This means any day, any time. While the Web naturally lends itself to a 24/7/365 (24 hours a day/7 days a week/365 days a year) model, many traditional retailers such as Walmart, McDonald's, and supermarkets are now extending their hours to satisfy changing lifestyles.

Service firms are also operating on nights and weekends to better meet customer needs. Bank Atlantic, dubbed "Florida's Most Convenient Bank," is an innovative regional bank based in Fort Lauderdale, Florida, that, besides seven-day branch banking, offers extended weekday branch hours and 24/7 live customer service. Responsiveness is also evaluated by customers or potential customers as to promptness in returning phone calls, e-mail messages, and scheduling appointments, as well as user-friendly Web sites, personalization, time savings, and product mix. These initiatives offer a major source of competitive advantage (or disadvantage) for organizations.

In today's highly competitive global markets, a changing twofold objective exists:

1. Focus primarily on maintaining and upgrading customer relationships—this includes generating referral business
2. Secondarily grow the business by finding new customers

In many cases, this means allocating 80% or more of the marketing budget to customer loyalty and retention programs targeted to existing customers; this is where profits may be reaped. An ever-increasing amount of promotional resources will be invested in online and mobile media, including social networking. The balance (less than 20 percent) should be directed to activities designed to attract prospects; however, realize that many companies have this ratio reversed and emphasize new business development.

Given our 21st-century market environment and the services economy, a revised marketing concept is called for. This philosophy states that all organizations must provide socially responsible business experiences that meet and preferably exceed customer expectations while creating long-term value for all stakeholders (owners, employees, customers, collaborators, communities, etc.). Customer-oriented organizations build on the marketing concept (market orientation is the firm's implementation of the marketing concept), design customer-driven processes and programs, establish a strong marketing information system, segment and target markets, hire the best talent, stress operational efficiency, and continually measure and fine-tune their customer focus (see the accompanying sidebar, Customer Value Checklist 2: Customer Orientation Guidelines).

Customer Value Checklist 2: Customer Orientation Guidelines

1. Do you know your customers' (and their customers') objectives?
2. Is your service offer designed with the customer in mind?
3. Are your internal systems (i.e., e-business, ordering, billing, shipping, computers, financial, etc.) geared toward how the customers prefer doing business with you?
4. Do you constantly measure customer satisfaction, loyalty, and retention?
5. Do you continually meet with your customers to determine their needs today and tomorrow?
6. How is value created, delivered, monitored, and maximized in your organization?

Building a Market Orientation

Why do many companies fail to understand their customers' needs and wants? A major reason is that many organizations are not market oriented.

Business Orientations

Companies have different degrees of commitment to marketing. A five-stage continuum from production driven to market driving exists.

Production → Product → Sales → Market driven → Market driving

Henry Ford pioneered the idea of mass production, which led to mass marketing: Remember, "Give them any car they want as long as it's a black Model-T"? Nearly a century later, many medical clinics still practice the production orientation. Other companies become enamored with their products (for example, many computer software firms) and employ a product orientation without carefully discerning customer problems.

The selling orientation is widely used by automobile dealers, insurance firms, media companies, and network/multilevel marketers. America Online used a sales orientation to build a customer base exceeding 25 million subscribers in about a decade. However, in the late 1990s, when AOL permitted unlimited access for a flat $19.95 monthly fee, it entered a logistical nightmare as the increased customer base took advantage of unprecedented levels of online service usage. Many existing customers became dissatisfied with the provider when they experienced log-on failure rates that at times were as high as 50%. In the bleakest period, the company had customer turnover rates exceeding 20% a month!

Finally, in a late attempt to become market oriented, AOL added tens of thousands of new lines to deal effectively with the increased customer traffic generated. The AOL–Time Warner marriage never lived up to the dot.com-era hype, and this dissolution will be marked in the annals of business history as a colossal failure. Today, AOL is a shell of its former self and continues to fight for survival with its You've Got Video and Web-based advertising and community-oriented and localized initiatives.

Let's review how a sales-oriented company differs from a market-oriented firm. As Table 2.1 shows, a sales-oriented firm bases market decisions on what the top executives think customers want. It often has a strong core product or an established, deep product line and spends heavily on advertising and selling to win new business. Attracting customers (conquest marketing) is the major objective of the firm. A recent study by the CMO Council of Palo Alto, California, found that

Table 2.1 Becoming Marketing Oriented

Marketing Variables	Sales Oriented	Market Oriented
Starting point	Organization	Target markets
Marketing focus	Product/service	Customer needs
Customer focus	New business (attraction)	Existing customer base (growth and retention)
Competitive edge	Lowest delivered cost	Superior quality or service
Product strategy	Generic product	Augmented product
Promotional strategy	Selling/advertising	Integrated marketing communications (IMC), including social media
Pricing strategy	Maximizing profit margins	Profitable use of resources
Marketing objective	Sales volume	Customer satisfaction
Planning approach	Reactive	Proactive
Time perspective	Short term (tactical)	Medium and long term (strategic)

56% of respondents said their companies lacked formal programs to unify sales and marketing functions. The two departments also diverged on time frames, metrics, and vocabulary.[8] Clearly, getting both units to work together harmoniously can pay huge dividends for the organization.

In contrast, market-oriented firms such as Google carefully research and evaluate market opportunities to build high-value products (Ad Words, G-Mail, Google Earth, Google Scholar, Instant Search, etc.) that meet or exceed customer desires. They invest in an integrated marketing communication program that allows them to grow, but its principal marketing objective is customer satisfaction and retention. Customer retention is so critical because it directly impacts the bottom line. A 5% decrease in customer defections can lead to a 25%–50% (or more) increase in profitability. While 15%–30% or higher customer defection rates are common in many industries, Leo Burnett achieved a remarkable 98% customer retention rate in one of the most hotly contested market sectors—advertising.[9]

Citrix Systems, General Electric, Hewlett-Packard, Johnson & Johnson, and Procter & Gamble are renowned for their marketing prowess (market orientation), which has been perfected over the years. Marketing is a relatively newer phenomena for many service organizations (banks, hospitals), professional service firms (accounting firms, attorneys, consulting organizations), information-based companies (high-tech companies, telecommunications firms, mailing list houses), and nonprofit organizations (museums, park and recreation departments, universities).

Regardless of the type of company, a market orientation provides the impetus for building an organizational culture that puts customers first, creates superior value for your customers, and leads to increased, overall business performance. Employees of market-oriented companies such as Ritz-Carlton, Disney, and Princess Cruises become value adders; they know the importance of listening to, responding to, and anticipating the needs of their guests.

Becoming Customer Oriented

As the Southwest Airlines example illustrated, it begins with the business culture—consider values, vision, objectives, people, interdepartmental dynamics, knowledge, organizational systems, and potential strategic responses to the environment. A dual customer (satisfy/delight the buyer) and competitive (marketing likened to war) emphasis is needed, as well as a long-term view. The Japanese are known for long-term marketing plans (some last 25–100 years), which often will outlive the executives in the company sculpting the strategy.

Customer orientation ascribes to Regis McKenna's philosophy that marketing is too important to be left to the marketing department. It is the responsibility of everyone in the organization.[10] A customer orientation is a service organization practicing Japanese-style marketing—putting the customer first. In fact, the Japanese word *okyaku-sama* literally means "honored customer" or "the customer is

God."[11] Is the customer really king in the United States? When leaving an American restaurant, sometimes one is barely acknowledged; in contrast, it is not uncommon at a Japanese dining establishment to have several parties graciously bow farewell in thanks for the customer's patronage.

At times, excellent companies such as General Motors, IBM, Microsoft, Kodak, and Sears have become complacent. Management and employees lose their competitive edge and enthusiasm and become satisfied with the status quo. Fortunately for the market, strong rivals emerge, such as Toyota, Dell, Apple, Fuji, and Walmart; these companies provide a loud wake-up call to action and force once-invincible giants to change or fade away.

For the first time in 20 years, Apple's quarterly profits exceeded Microsoft's. While Apple seems to make all the right decisions (iPod, iPhone, iPad), Microsoft has struggled to keep pace with the market shift toward smartphones and tablets (PC shipments dropped 8% and netbook sales plunged 40%—the major areas of Microsoft's emphasis).[12] Microsoft is trying to save its old business rather than embracing new opportunities in the computer and telecommunications sectors.

To overcome complacency and stay relevant in the market, organizations must avoid marketing myopia, be creative in programs and processes, adapt and be flexible with respect to changing market conditions and tastes, and use a *kaizen* (continuous improvement) philosophy.

Recognize that today's customers are quite smart and sophisticated, and that they are looking for companies that (1) create maximum value for them based on their needs and wants and (2) demonstrate that they value their business. Road Runner Sports, which bills itself as the world's largest running and walking store, is a San Diego–based distributor of running shoes, sports fashion accessories, and related exercise-oriented products. As part of their multichannel strategy (retail, phone, and Web—www.roadrunnersports.com), Road Runner sells a complete line of specialized products to highly loyal customers (many of whom are members of their Road Runners Sports VIP Club) at very competitive prices.

Value-seeking customers are choice seeking, demanding, and knowledgeable. They believe that loyalty must be earned, are price conscious, are concerned about the environment, and are convenience oriented (often time impoverished). Astute marketers recognize and respond to these issues when designing value propositions and marketing strategies. Furthermore, customer-oriented firms know how to use mass-customization techniques, databases/marketing information systems, research, integrated marketing communications (IMC), and the human touch (getting close to customers) to develop personalized marketing relationships that build long-term loyalty and ensure customer retention. A major driver in the transformation of today's marketing practices is technology—customer relationship management (CRM) systems and online and mobile contact through e-mail; blogs; webinars; and LinkedIn, Facebook, and Twitter initiatives.

Market Orientation and Business Performance: Research Findings

Managers intuitively know that becoming market oriented favorably impacts business success. Although there has been much academic research conducted on this subject in the past two decades, the empirical evidence of the consequences of a market orientation (MO) on business performance (BP) is still evolving. In a research study conducted in cooperation with the Tennessee Association of Business, Barrett and Weinstein found a highly significant correlation between MO and BP.[13]

According to Narver and Slater, market orientation consists of three major components: customer orientation, competitor orientation, and interfunctional coordination. Their research showed a strong link between MO and BP.[14] Kohli and Jaworski argued that the market orientation construct comprises intelligence generation, intelligence dissemination, and responsiveness.[15] Hence, market orientation involves learning about customers and competitors. A meta-analysis is an analysis of analyses and is one of the best sources for reliable research in business. Three meta-analyses of market orientation provide important insights for marketing management: Dawes found that 14 studies used subjective measures of performance, and 12 of those were significant. In contrast, only three of the six studies that used objective measures (e.g., ROI, sales growth, profit margins, market share, etc.) found a significant or marginally significant relationship between MO and BP.[16]

Cano and colleagues examined market orientation research in 23 countries spanning five continents. They concluded that the relationship between MO and BP is stronger for service firms (r = .45) than manufacturing companies (.33) due to person-to-person interactions. In addition, they found that, overall, market orientation explains 12% of the variance in business performance.[17]

Liao and his research team examined more than 500 scholarly articles on market orientation from 1995 through 2008. Based on their mega-analysis, they presented an integrated three-level (strategy, capability, and survival/growth), eight-variable conceptual model incorporating environment, learning, market orientation, quality, culture, innovation, marketing, and performance.[18]

Firms operating in competitive industries are most likely to benefit from a market orientation. In a multistate study of hospital executives, "responsiveness to competition" was the only MO issue that correlated with three hospital performance dimensions—financial performance, market/product development, and internal quality.[19]

Market orientation inputs are also valuable for formulating an initial definition of your market as well as staying in touch with your customer base. A reliable two-part scale for market orientation of global sellers in business markets (responsive and proactive customer orientation) was recently developed and is provided in Table 2.2. Marketing managers can use this valuable tool to assess their current level of market focus as well as think about how their organization can improve in this critical area.[20]

Table 2.2 Responsive versus Proactive Customer Orientation

Responsive Customer Orientation[a]	Proactive Customer Orientation[a]
"Compared to what we expect from our company's best providers, this service provider…"	
Always responds effectively when we ask them to make changes.	Excels at anticipating changes in what we need from them before we even ask.
Takes immediate action when we tell them we've changed what we want from this relationship.	Seems to spend time studying changes in our business environment so they can exercise better foresight about our future needs.
Reacts quickly to our requests for changes.	Successfully anticipates changes in our needs.
Is always flexible to adapt to changes we ask for.	Presents new solutions to us that we actually need but did not think to ask about.
Never stops short of fully accommodating our requests for changes.	Is always looking for clues that might reveal changes in what we value beyond what we currently ask of them.
Is always willing to accommodate our requests for changes.	Presents new ideas to us that help us keep pace with our changing environment.

Source: Adapted from C. P. Blocker et al., "Proactive Customer Orientation and Its Role for Creating Customer Value in Global Markets," *Journal of Academy of Marketing Science* 39 (2011), 231.

[a] 1 (strongly disagree) to 7 (strongly agree).

Market-Driving Practices

While market-driven strategy is a great way to stay on top of current customer needs (emphasis on existing business practices, including what is observed and what is articulated), often companies must go beyond the established market and create new market opportunities. Perhaps, a small CPA firm specializing in audit and tax services for businesses expands into financial planning and counseling or management consulting.

Market-driving companies go beyond accepting given market structures and behaviors. Rather than working in the status quo (existing customer preferences and direct competitive sets), truly innovative firms try to shape or change markets by eliminating, adding, or modifying the players in a market and their functions.[21]

As an example, Expedia redefined the travel agent paradigm and nullified the need for travel retailers. Companies such as Amazon, Apple, CNN, FedEx, IKEA,

JetBlue Airways, Lexmark International, Netflix, Starbucks, and Virgin Group rewrite industry rules and compete in new market arenas. Their unique business ideas and systems deliver large leaps in customer value.[22]

Let's discuss three of these companies in a little more detail: Apple, Amazon, and Lexmark. Apple, Inc., (the company dropped the term *computer* from its name) dramatically altered the landscape of personal entertainment and communication devices worldwide. Its innovative, cool, and customer-friendly products struck a responsive chord in the marketplace. Under Steve Jobs's high-profile leadership, Apple has sold millions of iPads, tens of millions of iPhones, hundreds of millions of iPods/iTouches, and billions of iTunes to its adoring customer base in the past decade. The Apple product mix catapulted its Mac line of computers into double-digit market share.

Amazon's vision is to be the Earth's most customercentric company. As the trailblazer in online retailing, it revolutionized the book-buying experience. Today, online purchases are the preferred marketing channel for many readers, and Amazon continues to innovate with its best-seller, the Kindle electronic book reader. Amazon e-book sales have now surpassed hardcover and paperback book editions.

Lexmark International became a global leader in printing solutions (printers, supplies, and services) by competing in new market space. As part of Lexmark's multipronged blue ocean strategy, they tapped high-end laser printing, service, and training; served underserved international markets in Latin America, the Middle East, and Africa; redefined buyer groups via market intelligence; entered joint ventures (Dell); and focused on creating lifelong customers.

Market-driving companies lead customers from the established to the emerging and even the imagined—this is similar to Steve Wozniak and Steve Jobs's original vision (circa 1979) of putting a personal computer on the desk of every man, woman, and child in America. Market-driving companies go beyond traditional target marketing and customer satisfaction to segment-of-1 marketing and customer delight. According to Sheth et al., "customer-centric marketing emphasizes understanding and satisfying the needs, wants, and resources of individual consumers and customers rather than those of mass markets or market segments."[23] The new customerization framework is contrasted with the "old" marketing model in Table 2.3.

Creating a Bias for Action

Great companies go beyond satisfying customers: They are able to predict customer needs and wants and practice anticipatory marketing. These organizations invest in research, get close to the customer, innovate, and accept reasonable business risks. According to Barrett, there is a five-stage bias-for-action continuum.[24]

Nonresponsive → *Reactive* → *Responsive* → *Proactive* → *Anticipatory*

Table 2.3   Traditional Marketing versus the Customer-Centric Approach

Marketing Function	Traditional Marketing Model	Customerization Model
Customer relationship	Customer is a passive participant	Customer is an active coproducer
Customer needs	Articulated	Articulated and unarticulated
Segmentation	Mass market and target markets	Customized segments and "segments of one"
Product innovation driver	Marketing and R&D	Customer interactions
Product offerings	Product modifications	Customized products and services
Pricing	Fixed prices, discounting	Value-based pricing
Promotion	Advertising, personal selling, sales promotion, public relations	Databases, Internet, integrated marketing communications (IMC)
Distribution	Retailing, direct marketing	Augmented by online distribution and third-party logistics services
Competitive advantage	Marketing power	Customers as partners

Source: Adapted from J. Wind and A. Rangaswamy, "Customerization: The Next Revolution in Mass Customization," *Journal of Interactive Marketing* 15 (Winter 2001), 20.

At the nonresponsive level, there is limited awareness of external stimuli (for example, IBM initially ignored the PC market). At the reactive level, the firm is aware of the stimuli, but only after repeated prodding does it reply (e.g., Xerox was slow in developing competitive strategies to win back the low-end sector of the copier market from Canon in the 1980s).

Most companies are at the responsive level. Customers may force the firm to enter new product markets, sometimes reluctantly. Many companies will then take appropriate action, assuming that the opportunity fits the present business mission and adequate resources are available.

Proactiveness is the fourth stage and implies that corporate entrepreneurism has surfaced in the organization. This means that larger companies simulate the innovation, flexibility, creativity, and speed-to-market of their smaller counterparts. Anticipatory marketing is the aspirational level and is attained by relatively few firms (and then only infrequently). At this point, companies understand virtually all of the market nuances and treat their customers as business allies and partners. FedEx Office (formerly known as Kinko's Copy Centers) have done a good job in this area by offering round-the-clock service and anticipating the desires of its customer base in its new product offerings. An effective market definition and strong customer orientation can guide organizations through the continuum to, ultimately, the proactive and anticipatory stage.

Corporate Entrepreneurship

Medium and large organizations can "act small" and reap great benefits from a corporate entrepreneurship (CE) strategy. Smaller companies make decisions quicker, are able to get close to the customer, and are willing to innovate. In contrast, many larger companies are bureaucratic, resistant to change, and have short-term thinking—they want to maximize current quarterly earnings rather than invest for the long term.

Corporate entrepreneurship (CE) is based on three key tenets: product innovation (launch new products and concepts that have not been done before), risk-taking propensity (go out on a limb, since that's where the fruit is), and proactiveness (know your customers' desires even better than they do themselves).[25] Ten CE market leaders include AT&T, General Electric, Gillette, Google, Hewlett-Packard, IBM, Procter and Gamble, Texas Instruments, Yamaha, and 3M.

3M is the classic practitioner of corporate entrepreneurship in action. The company allows employees to spend 15% of their time on entrepreneurial projects. Seven percent of sales is invested in research and development, and 30% of strategic business unit (SBU) revenue is derived from new products. Individuals and departments are financially rewarded for success. Seed capital is provided for promising projects, and failed projects do not affect performance evaluations. (Remember, the Beatles failed their first audition for a recording contract, and Dr. Seuss was rejected by more than two dozen book publishers!)

Google's success is built on new business opportunities, and the company evaluates employees' annual performance in this area. Google is an ecosystem of entrepreneurs devoting 20% of their time to creating the profit centers of tomorrow. At any given time, Google is likely to support more than 100 new business concepts in varying stages of development. It is estimated that 70% of these initiatives support the company's core business, 20% represent emerging business ideas, and 10% are speculative experiments.[26] This is analogous to the idea of established, emerging, and imagined market opportunities.

How does a company effectively manage both new and mature businesses? IBM evaluates emerging business opportunities (EBOs) in three areas: developing a clear strategy, defining an executable business model, and winning in the marketplace. Based on an evaluation of 25 business "bets" ($100 million was invested to grow

Table 2.4 Value Creation and Marketing Opportunities

Value-Creation Emphasis	Marketing Strategy	Market Focus
Customer	Market driven	Established market
Company	Market driving	Emerging or imagined markets
Customer and company (simultaneous)	Cocreation of value	Established, emerging, and imagined markets

emerging businesses) over a five-year period ending in 2004, IBM reported only three failures, with the rest being evolving or successful businesses. This resulted in $31 billion in additional revenues! Fourteen of the most successful launches were then moved into IBM's existing business groups.[27]

Chances are that you do not work for 3M, Google, or IBM. Nonetheless, corporate entrepreneurship is still an important part of market-driving behavior that can pay huge dividends to your organization. Realize that all global giants were once fledgling start-ups. A CE philosophy can help established companies (of any size) regain their entrepreneurial spark and enthusiasm and provide a springboard for new strategic directions.

Cocreation of Value: An Overview

Customer focus no longer means just researching current and future needs to design expected or desired products and services. A new trend in business is cocreating value with customers. Some examples include retailers getting the customer involved in the shopping experience to save time (Home Depot's self-checkout) or costs (IKEA's assembly and transporting products by customers), personalizing smartphones through app selection or online buying (Dell Direct), and management consultants collaborating with clients to add value in research projects. Cocreation of value can lower costs and improve the overall service experience (this concept is discussed in more detail in Chapter 5). As Table 2.4 explains, cocreation of value has a dual emphasis on the customer and company as value creators and is an applicable business strategy in a wide variety of market contexts.

Summary

A firm that has a strong customer orientation fares well on the purpose dimension of the value matrix (introduced in Chapter 1). A market orientation builds the necessary business culture and customer-focused framework to enable service providers to deliver superior value to their target markets. This is accomplished by being market driven and market driving. As applicable, a cocreation of value perspective can yield positive results to the organization. In the next chapter, we will discuss how innovation and business processes can be used effectively by service organizations to create enhanced value for customers.

Customer Value Action Items

1. How market oriented is your neighborhood shopping center? What changes should be made to become more customer driven?
2. How market oriented is e-Bay? How does their market orientation assist them in delivering superior customer value? What role does their business model, culture (business philosophy), electronic community, and marketing strategies play in getting, keeping, and growing customers?
3. How customer oriented is Marriott? Comment on each of the following attributes:
    a. Customer focus: Who are their customers? What do they value?
    b. Competitive focus: Who are their competitors? What are their strengths and weaknesses?
    c. Interfunctional coordination: How is the company organized? How do the various departments interact?
    d. Market-driven objectives
    e. Market-intelligence utilization
    f. Target marketing
    g. Performance measures
4. Cite an example of a high-tech company and a service firm that practices market-driving behavior. How can a solar power company or an online matchmaking service utilize the market-driving philosophy?
5. Within the global automobile industry, identify manufacturers or products that are or were: nonresponsive, reactive, responsive, proactive, or anticipatory? Consider marketing programs and processes and provide anecdotal support for your view.
6. How good a job does your organization do in creating value for your customers based on the marketing mix, service providers, and the e-marketing mix? Explain how these areas can be improved. What role should internal marketing play in this process? How can your company cocreate value with customers?
7. Based on *Fortune* 500 rankings, the U.S. Postal Service, an independent government agency, is the 29th largest organization in America, with revenues of more than $67 billion. As the nation's second-largest employer (more than 580,000 employees), the USPS delivers more than 170 billion pieces of mail annually. (Visit www.usps.gov for further details on this organization.)

a. How does the U.S. Postal Service create value for its customers in a digital world?

b. Analyze the components of market orientation—customer orientation, competitive advantage, and interfunctional coordination—and their impact on this organization.

c. What changes should this organization implement to improve its market orientation?

d. Propose a market-driving initiative and a way to cocreate value with customers.

Chapter 3

Process Management— Best Practices

Our business is about technology, yes. But it's also about operations and customer relationships.

Michael Dell

Corporations will be defined not so much by their industry or products, but by the nature of their processes.

Ralph P. Mroz

As Chapter 2 explained, practicing a market orientation is fundamental to creating sustainable customer value. Exceeding customer expectations, knowing the competition—their strengths, weaknesses, and strategies—and encouraging cross-functional sharing and decision making leads to superior business performance.

This chapter focuses on designing excellent business processes that lead to continued customer satisfaction and, in turn, increased market share. The overwhelming success of Hyundai Motor America can be traced to building very good cars (with lots of standard equipment) at very good prices. Their ten-year, 100,000-mile power-train warranty made a loud statement to the market that they manufacture quality vehicles—these are no Yugos.

Process design needs to follow a simple litmus test: Does the process create superior customer value? Moreover, value should drive process design. Note that the goal of the organization is to maintain a fit between value and processes.

Successful organizations recognize that value and process are "seamless" in the eyes of their customers.

Economic pressures such as the increased costs of materials, higher fuel prices, paying competitive wages, and investment in new technology must be carefully managed to maintain and upgrade business processes. Consider the experience of successful companies that have recognized the link between process and value.

- Responding to the needs of their large global clients, IBM developed standardized worldwide processes for order fulfillment and product development that reduced speed-to-market, improved on-time delivery, increased customer satisfaction, and saved the company billions of dollars.
- As a market-oriented company, General Electric asked how it could improve the customers' service experience? The response to that question became the GE Answer Center, a fully-staffed customer call center that operates 24 hours a day offering repair tips and helping owners of GE appliances with their problems.
- Giant retail brokerage firms like Merrill Lynch and PaineWebber have for years excelled at four business processes crucial to overall business success: client management, information delivery, portfolio modeling, and operational statistics. With the Web becoming the preferred investor channel, on-line trading has emerged as a fifth critical process; albeit reluctantly, they shifted much of their business to the Internet.

Organizations that view themselves as a collection of processes that must be understood, managed, and improved are most likely to succeed. A process is a specific group of activities and subordinate tasks that results in the performance of a service that is of value. Thus, the focus needs to shift from managing departments to managing processes. Business process design involves the identification and sequencing of work activities, tasks, resources, decisions, and responsibilities across time and place, with a beginning and an end, along with clearly identified inputs and outputs. Processes must be able to be tracked as well, using cost, time, output quality, and satisfaction measurements. Businesses need to continually monitor, review, alter, and streamline processes to remain competitive.

Processes are not simply obscure, backroom operations of the service concern, but instead are an integral part of delivering the value proposition. Realize that processes and service are inseparable, i.e., *the process is the service* (and customers expect outstanding service). An effective process is results driven, deriving its form from customer requirements—how and when customers want to do business with you.

Processes create value in the make, design, and market stages.[1] While there are many different processes employed by organizations (e.g., business process reengineering, lean six sigma and total quality management, outsourcing, scenario and contingency planning, etc.), we will focus on three key processes dealing with creating (innovation), connecting (customer experience management, or CEM), and checking (benchmarking). First, let's examine Deming's wisdom in process planning.

Deming's (PDCA) Cycle

Dr. W. Edwards Deming pioneered the use of statistical tools and sampling methods for use in both product and process quality control. His hands-on consulting and guidance helped rebuild Japan after the devastation from World War II and transformed the country into a global industrial powerhouse. In the mid-1980s, his work resonated with corporate America as the market-perceived quality of U.S. products and services began to diminish from an international competitiveness perspective.

While Deming's PDCA (plan, do, check, act) cycle appears to be deceptively simple, the framework is a powerful tool to assist organizations in identifying opportunities for process improvement, control, and organizational change.[2] Each of these four activities are held in equal balance—yet are linked—and are equally important for process mastery and business planning. That is, if you plan but never do, you won't improve. Moreover, the cycle indicates that the task of process improvement is never done, as past results drive future action.

Plan

The first step in the process is *planning*, which involves examining how the type of value firms offer their customers affects their processes. Planning must consider required capital, labor, and technology resources. The alignment between the value that customers want and the value the company is capable of delivering or delivers is an overall effectiveness measure of strategic fit.

To ensure that an excellent fit exists between value and process, a value statement (proposition) should be developed that answers the questions: "What do we do for our customers and why should they use us instead of our competition?" The value proposition should carry a strong, differentiated appeal to its customers about how its offer differs from its competitors relative to price/performance characteristics. For example, Southwest Airlines's value statement communicates fun, fast, and economy. Starbucks' value message implies the following: reinventing a commodity product as a high-quality, high-price beverage for image-conscious, upscale buyers. Finally, Charles Schwab's value offering consists of delivering low-price and convenient investment trading through highly automated systems. Other examples of value propositions are examined in Chapter 4.

Do

The second step in the Deming Cycle is the *do* phase, dealing with process design and congruency issues. Once a value proposition is created or refined, processes need to be assessed according to their efficacy and congruence with the firm's value statement. A series of questions such as those listed in Customer Value Checklist 3 can help determine where to direct process improvement efforts.

Customer Value Checklist 3: Key Success Factors for Improving Business Processes

The following questions represent some key issues in developing processes that are truly value-added. Circle the response (yes or no) that most closely fits your company's situation.

1. Does your company organize around value-added processes, not tasks?	Y or N
2. Do those who use the output of the process perform the task (that is, are the people closest to the process the ones who actually perform the activity)?	Y or N
3. Does your company forge links between functions and coordinate them while their activities are in process rather than after they have been completed?	Y or N
4. Does your company put the decision point where the work is performed, and build control into the process?	Y or N
5. Does your company capture information once and at the source where it was created?	Y or N
6. Does your company design processes in cooperation with customers?	Y or N
7. Does your company "blueprint" the process cycle, defining not only the steps performed in the process, but also the timing and sequencing of relationships of those steps?	Y or N
8. Is process simplification practiced regularly, removing unnecessary and bureaucratic procedures?	Y or N
9. Does your company utilize appropriate process measurements (i.e., cycle response time, customer satisfaction, etc.)?	Y or N
10. Does your company reward process improvement efforts?	Y or N

Table 3.1 Tools of Process Improvement

Process Tool	Purpose
Benchmarking	Measuring and comparing process results to a standard of excellence
Data collection tools (surveys, sampling, check sheets)	Document internal and external customer assumptions and perceptions about appropriateness and effectiveness of a process and reveal unstable processes
Control chart	Identifies stability, capability, and central tendency of a process
Scatter diagram	Show graphically the relationship between process performance data and some overall performance measure such as customer satisfaction or service quality
Pareto chart	Separates the "vital few" causes of process failures
Fishbone diagram	Show possible causes of process shortcomings or weaknesses

Check

The third step in the Deming Cycle is *check*. Once processes are evaluated for their value-creating effectiveness and measures are developed, then data-driven tools can be used to routinely monitor, inspect, and improve them. Table 3.1 lists some common tools for measuring, monitoring, controlling, and improving process quality.

Act

The final step in the Deming Cycle is *act*. Based on data collected using the process-improvement tools described, corrective actions should be taken to improve processes that fail to add value. For example, Savin Corporation found that callbacks were related to deficiencies in the training process (necessitating a service recovery and training program). Listed below are five ways to improve business processes:

- ▪ Eliminate tasks altogether if it has been determined that they are unnecessary.
- ▪ Simplify the work by eliminating all nonproductive elements of a task.
- ▪ Combine tasks, where appropriate.
- ▪ Change the sequencing to improve the speed and execution.
- ▪ Perform activities simultaneously.[3]

Once a process improvement has been made, the change must be measured and evaluated for effectiveness. Comparing before and after indicators would be useful here as well as comparing results with the targeted performance. Also, efforts should be made to celebrate and reward those participating in the process-improvement activity.

Creating Value—Process Innovation

Many companies trace their success to process innovations. FedEx was a pioneer in installing computers in delivery vehicles, designing sophisticated automation for corporate shipping services, and developing package tracking capabilities. Southwest Airlines is known for its 15-minute turnaround, and Walmart is renowned for its innovative supply chain management practices. Realize that creativity spawns innovation, leading to the creation of customer value and enhanced market performance.

IBM's 2010 white paper, "Capitalizing on Complexity," provided research findings based on interviews of 1,541 CEOs, general managers, and senior public sector leaders who represent different sizes of organizations in 60 countries and 33 industries. According to these senior executives, creativity is now the most important leadership quality.

> Today's CEOs know that creativity is an essential asset and that it must permeate the enterprise…. Instill the pursuit of creativity into your organizational mission through informal and formal training. Challenge every team to prioritize creativity, and support and reward employees who step outside their comfort zones to innovate.[4]

Whirlpool is another example of a company that believes in innovation. It invested $45 million to embed creativity into its business culture and commit to new offerings. The results were most impressive—going from $10 million in new product revenue the first year to $760 million by the end of the fifth year of this innovation process.[5]

A study of 70 technology firms in California, Florida, and nationwide explored market segmentation strategies and innovative business practices. For the most part, companies were successful in innovation, as evidenced by success rates of 82% for product technology, 70% for management know-how, 66% for innovative culture, and 60% for R&D expertise; process technology (ideas embodied in the manufacturing/operations) was the one weak link, practiced successfully by only half (49%) of the companies surveyed.[6]

Perhaps one of the reasons that process innovation suffers in business is because creative processes plummet dramatically as people age. A study on originality shows these incredible numbers: age 4 (90%), age 7 (70%), and adult (2%).[7] With this little original thinking, in combination with a groupthink mentality further stifling creativity and a play-it-safe business culture, is it really surprising that great ideas are often limited in many organizations?

So, how can organizations successfully innovate? A five-step process can be quite insightful and is summarized as follows:

1. *Identify the problem or business challenge*: For example, how might we improve Product X or improve our customer satisfaction scores and retention rate?
2. *Generate ideas*: Brainstorm, offer lots of possible ideas, think out of the box.
3. *Find a tentative solution*: Develop appropriate decision criteria: As a starting point, consider cost savings (efficiency), effectiveness, and flexibility (adaptability); select the best available option.
4. *Pretest*: Try out the proposed solution on real customers and get their feedback for possible improvements.
5. *Go to market/adjust*: Roll it out, make necessary changes, and profit from it.

Creativity should be viewed as a core business activity within an organization that leads directly to entrepreneurial opportunities. One of 3M's seven pillars of innovation success is to have a broad base of technology. 3M has this expertise in more than 40 diverse areas. As an example of this company's multidimensional thinking, the science behind layered plastic lenses was used to make more durable abrasives, more reflective highway signs, and better-gripping golf gloves.[8]

Brands's 5D approach to innovation contends that it begins with the "wild idea" or *dream* stage and progresses through a *discovery* phase, to *design*, then *development*, and finally, *delivery*.[9] Hence, innovation management needs to be studied as a process-improvement technique across a spectrum of activities (R&D, new-product management, cycle time reduction, creative personality types, etc.) and over the short-term and longer planning horizons.

Here are a few tips for successful product innovation.

1. Commit to innovate: Whether your organization is a mom-and-pop small business or a global giant, the establishment of a creative climate is the necessary starting point to generate successful ideas that turn into profitable marketing opportunities. Encourage risk-taking, tolerate failure, reward success, and promote open and collaborative business relationships.
2. Get the customer actively involved in the innovation process through cocreation of value or customer tool kits such as Web-based tools (the Web is a great value adder).
3. Always be innovating: Service firms are often stretched to capacity servicing existing client needs, or manufacturers may be pressured putting out daily fires (crises). These organizations may have little or no time for innovation. Yet, such situations make innovation even more important. Crisis situations can lead to process improvements. Consider these examples:
   a. The Tylenol poisonings in the 1980s led to the introduction of tamper-proof medicine bottles, which ultimately resulted in increased customer confidence and loyalty to Johnson & Johnson.

b. Staff layoffs can stimulate the development of more efficient procedures, minimizing the need to work 60-hour weeks to pick up the tasks of those no longer employed.

4. Plan for innovation: Break out of the routine through occasional "creativity" retreats to reenergize and motivate your people on business strategy and new market opportunities. Such activities could include quarterly brainstorming sessions, occasional dinner work-meetings, or a weekend out-of-the-office experience (get done by noon on Saturday). And, supplement face-to-face briefings with technology initiatives to stay on track.

Connecting Value—Customer Experience Management

The Aberdeen Group says, "Customer Experience Management (CEM) programs examine the people, processes, organization, key performance indicators (KPIs), and supporting technology to ensure that the company is focused on providing the right touch to the right customer at the right time, every time."[10]

Simply stated, CEM evaluates individual service encounters (transactions) or a series of service experiences (relationships). It examines the difference between customer expectations and the experience delivered. Does the product or service match expectations (customer satisfaction), exceed expectations (highly satisfied), or fail to meet expectations (dissatisfaction)?

Customers set the value agenda and have varying requirements as to what matters most to them. For some customers, it's about the shopping experience or Web site navigation. Others may value ease of use, customer or technical service, connecting with online communities, personalization, or rewards for loyal behavior.[11]

Solid data for analysis and decision making is a key to effective customer experience management. Gaylord Hotels, a network of upscale, meetings-focused resorts is changing the way it communicates with guests based on market research. The hotel chain learned that the first 20 minutes of the hotel experience drives overall guest satisfaction. For example, having an associate walk the guests to their destination rather than just point directions and say "over there" was one of five key ways to improve the service experience. Previously, Gaylord believed there were 80 things it had to do well to get a recommendation.[12] Customer Value Insight 3 explores this issue in an online context.

Customer Value Insight 3: Customer Feedback

Good strategic business decisions are built on customer feedback. The Web provides a great forum for dialoging with customers: Consider customercentric companies such as Amazon, Zappos, and Kashi (health food brand) as positive examples.

Also, PlanetFeedback.com provides a site for customers to voice their opinions.

QUESTIONS TO THINK ABOUT

1. When was the last time you provided feedback about a brand or organization? Did that company value your opinion?
2. Why do many companies act like they don't want customer feedback?
3. What role should customer feedback have in guiding marketing strategy?

To improve the customer experience, several sequential frameworks have been proposed by service researchers. Integrating and extending three previous models, Johnston and Kong recommend an eight-stage road map for service improvement consisting of instigation and objective setting, coordination, customer research, define the experience, prioritization, action research, develop and pilot the changes, and change support systems.[13]

CEM—Research Findings

A survey by Bain & Company found that 80% of senior executives said their company provided a superior customer experience, but only 8% of their customers agreed.[14] Clearly, there is a huge reality gap between management and customers' perceptions of the service experience. This issue, called *gap analysis*, is discussed in Chapter 5. Aberdeen's study of 190 companies provided a comprehensive review of CEM processes and best practices. Some of their key findings are summarized in Table 3.2.

According to Forrester Research, 90% of executives say that customer experience is very important to strategy, and 80% want to use this as a form of differentiation. Currently, 62% of companies have some form of voice-of-customer (VOC) program in place, and nearly half (49%) have a senior executive in charge of customer experience initiatives. Despite these encouraging findings, only one in ten companies (11%) have a "very disciplined" approach to CEM.[15] The implications of these results are readily apparent: Industry is buying into the idea of CEM but can benefit from processes for improvement in this area.

The 2011 Temkin Experience Ratings (headed by Bruce Temkin, formerly of Forrester) ranks 143 companies in 12 industries based on feedback from 6,000 U.S. consumers. Three dimensions of customer experience were evaluated:

1. Functional: meeting consumers' needs
2. Accessible: being easy to work with
3. Emotional: how consumers feel about the experience

Table 3.2 Customer Experience Management—Organizational Performance

Category	Selected Measure[a]	Best-in-Class (% usage)	Average (% usage)	Laggard (% usage)
Process	Review all customer processes	53	46	22
Organization	Formalized employee training	61	38	24
Knowledge	Centralized repository of customer information	66	51	48
Technology	Multimode CRM system	47	38	34
Performance	Metrics over a multiyear timeline	38	22	15

Source: Adapted from D. Boulanger, *Customer Experience Management: Is Your Entire Really Focused on the Customer?* (Boston, MA: Aberdeen Group, 2008), 11–12.

[a] Only 5 of the overall 17 measures are listed in this table. Interested readers should consult the source document.

The top five companies were Amazon.com, Kohls, Costco, Lowes, and Sam's Club. Retailers were the highest rated industry (good), and TV service providers and health plans were the lowest rated industries (very poor/poor). Only 24 companies (17%) earned a "good" or "excellent rating."[16]

Checking Value—Benchmarking and Related Process Tools

A recent study by Bain & Company ("Management Tools and Trends," 2009) confirmed that benchmarking is the most important tool for evaluating and improving processes. Of the 25 management tools studied, benchmarking was used by 76% of the organizations; strategic planning was next most popular, at a 67% usage rate.[17]

Benchmarking compares a company's own practices (processes or tasks) against similar practices of firms recognized as superior in these areas. By comparing itself against the best possible practices, the benchmarking firm seeks to identify gaps between its current processes and the processes it should implement. Sound benchmarking programs ensure that a company, division, or business unit will become market competitive by adapting to the best and latest industry practices in their sector.

According to Camp, benchmarking is a process of consistently researching new ideas for methods, practices, and processes, and either adopting the practices or adapting the good features, and implementing them to obtain the "best of the best."[18] When done persistently for each company process, management can determine where improvements are possible and realistically assess how much improvement is possible. Benchmarking does not set hard goals for how much progress is possible, but it does provide a source of rich ideas for improvement that goes beyond internal experience. The upshot is that benchmarking facilitates the search for the practices that will lead to superior industry performance.

Besides uncovering industry-best practices, benchmarking offers others advantages as well. For example, benchmarking may help identify technological breakthroughs that might otherwise have gone unrecognized. While benchmarking traditionally focuses within an industry, many firms look outside the industry for breakthroughs in process redesign. For example, Xerox gained knowledge of warehousing and materials-handling operations technology by studying L.L. Bean.

Benchmarking also enables companies to more adequately meet customer requirements, leading to higher customer satisfaction. In addition, benchmarking helps firms determine true measures of productivity. Isolating the factors leading to higher productivity can facilitate process simplification and redesign. Finally, benchmarking helps firms attain a competitive position. While some organizations view benchmarking as a fad (28%), most companies clearly endorse the benchmarking concept. The great majority of companies (79%) believe they must benchmark to survive, and 95% feel that they do not know how to benchmark effectively.[19]

Which companies are worthy of being benchmarked? Of course, that depends on the particular core process. Table 3.3 reveals a list of companies that excel in applying quality practices in selected core processes, and thus represent ideal candidates for process benchmarking. Companies considered ideal candidates for benchmarking should also be of similar size or attracting similar customers. For example, Northern Telecom, the Canadian telecommunications giant, benchmarked other high-tech companies, not just other telecommunication companies.

How is benchmarking conducted? In his book *Benchmarking: The Search for Industry Best Practices That Lead to Superior Performance*, Camp describes a benchmarking process, looking at a range of business processes across a range of different industries (see Figure 3.1).

It should be noted that the generic benchmarking process is divided into two parts: benchmark metrics and benchmark practices. Metrics represent the best practices in quantified form. Practices are the methods used to perform a process. Benchmarking should begin by investigating industry practices first. Once industry practices are understood, they can then be quantified to show their numeric effect. Benchmarking must also be understood by the organization in order to obtain the commitment necessary to take action. Management commits to benchmarking by

Table 3.3   Exemplar Companies in Selected Service Marketing Areas

Core Processes to be Benchmarked	Companies
Customer loyalty management	Apple, Netflix
Sales and service support	IBM, Cisco Systems
Order fulfillment	L.L. Bean, Dell Computers
Logistics	FedEx, Ryder Systems
Transaction processing	Amazon.com, eBay
New service development	Charles Schwab, Google
Customer database management	Harrah's Entertainment, American Express
Procurement	Walmart, General Electric
Customer service	Lands' End, Ritz-Carlton

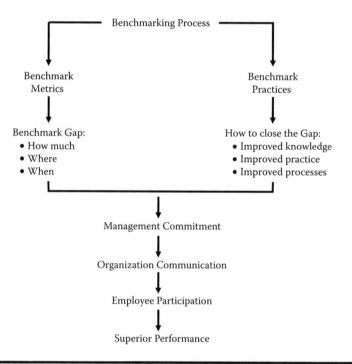

Figure 3.1 Generic benchmarking process. (Adapted from R. Camp, *Benchmarking: The Search for Industry Best Practices That Lead to Superior Performance,* **Milwaukee, WI: ASQC Press, 1989.)**

communicating its importance to employees and securing their participation, leading to the ultimate goal of benchmarking: superior business performance.

Perhaps the most difficult part of benchmarking is identifying what variables/ issues are to be benchmarked. The key to determining what is to be benchmarked is to identify the *result* of the business process. For example, the marketing cycle function of logistics consists of several strategic "deliverables," such as the level of customer satisfaction expected, the inventory level to be maintained, and the desired cost level to be achieved. These deliverables serve as a starting point for benchmarking, where each of these would need to be broken down further into specific activities to be benchmarked. Customer satisfaction may be benchmarked by investigating the factors that are responsible for customer satisfaction, such as service response time and reliability, as well as professionalism, competence, and empathy of the service worker.

Finally, there are several common denominators in using the benchmarking process. First, you need to thoroughly know your operations, assessing the strengths and weaknesses of your internal processes. Where are the opportunities or gaps in the marketplace where your organization can gain a competitive advantage? Secondly, you should know the leaders and key competitors in your industry as well as the strategies of the up-and-comers in the market. In what ways are they better and how much better are they? What do they do that can be adopted by your firm? Thirdly, learn from industry leaders in related industries and emulate their strengths. For example, Southwest Airlines looked to Formula One racing when it wanted to improve its refueling process. Adopting Formula One turnaround processes used during pit stops, Southwest can now refuel an airplane in 12 minutes. Fourthly, use benchmarking as a proactive tool by looking not just at competitors, but at their customers. What do those customers value and how are other processes/practices meeting those needs? Lastly, benchmarking needs to be continuous and institutionalized as part of your company culture.

Other Process-Checking Tools

While benchmarking is an important technique for improving business processes, other tools should also be employed (review Table 3.1). For example, data collection tools such as surveys or checklists can be extremely helpful in assessing customers' view of your business processes, especially the importance and relevance of specific activities and tasks. Typical information obtained from surveys or checklists include: (1) What happened? (2) How does it happen? (3) How often does it happen? (4) How long does it take? (5) How important is this?

Control charts are useful for monitoring the performance of a process by reporting measurements that are predictable within a given process and those that are random in nature. Control charts usually show fluctuations within a process that occur within control limits. Points that fall outside the control-limit range should be reported or investigated. A scatter diagram examines two variables at one time to determine the relationship that exists between them. The graphic display can help determine possible process "fail points" or measure the results of recently changed processes. For example, a direct mail company might want to use a scatter diagram to better understand how order fulfillment time is related to customer retention.

Pareto charts are used when there is a need to determine the relative importance of certain variables in process variation. They help isolate the "vital few" (as opposed to the trivial many) causes of process variation. For example, by analyzing their online banking customers' deposit activity, a bank can determine which customers represent the greatest potential for new services.

The fishbone (or cause-and-effect) diagram is useful in process analysis and redesign by stimulating thinking about a process under investigation, helping to organize thoughts into a rationale of the whole process. The fishbone diagram documents the level of understanding about a process and provides a framework for expanding an understanding of the "root cause" of the problem. A hospital experiencing delays in lab results could begin by first defining the *effect* (i.e., lab result delays) and then brainstorming the *causes* by diagramming the "bones" of the fish (i.e., equipment, policies, procedures, and people). It is a graphic representation between a problem and its potential causes.

Summary

Dramatic shifts have occurred in information technologies that are transforming how firms connect with their internal and external customers. The effective use of process integration is enabling firms to organize in new ways and to better manage supply chains and business relationships. Winners in the new economy will be those companies that can clearly define their processes, organize around those key processes, and work closely with their business partners. Strategic planning via the PDCA cycle, process innovation, customer experience management, and benchmarking are best-practice tools that leading organizations (large and small) use effectively to create maximum value for customers. Building on this knowledge base, our next chapter explains how to build a successful business model and value proposition.

Customer Value Action Items

1. Describe the relationship among process, service, and value.
2. Explain the purpose of the Deming Cycle for assessing process effectiveness.
3. Your company plans on undergoing an in-depth analysis of its processes within the next 10 days. How should you proceed in this review? What customer-focused process questions would you ask? (Note, management's goal is to become a "best-in-class" player in its industry.)

4. Suppose you were the manager of a quick-serve restaurant and you begin to notice that your lunch business is steadily declining. Moreover, you notice that customers are "queuing up" longer at the drive-thru window. Which of the process-improvement tools would you consider using and why?

5. You are brought in to consult for a medium-sized electronics company. The chief marketing officer (CMO) is concerned that revenues from new products introduced within the past two years has declined from 36% to 27% over the past 18 months. What would you advise the CMO to do to jump-start the company's innovation process?

6. You work for a small Internet firm in the business intelligence sector. Describe a process for introducing CEM into your organization. How can you employ social media to improve service experiences?

7. You were recently hired as a market research manager for a regional health food manufacturer. Your boss, a cofounder, feels that the firm needs to develop a benchmarking program to compete effectively with larger national companies. What companies and industries should be benchmarked? What are some key metrics that should be evaluated?

DESIGNING A SUCCESSFUL CUSTOMER STRATEGY

II

Chapter 4

Building a Winning Business Model and Value Proposition

It ain't that hard to be different.

Tom Peters

We believe that we know where the world should go. But unless we're in touch with our customers, our model of the world can diverge from reality. There's no substitute for innovation, of course, but innovation is no substitute, for being in touch, either.

Steve Ballmer

One of the most critical challenges for service firms is to differentiate themselves from competitors. It is relatively easy to be like everyone else; great companies have their own unique identities and carefully conceived value propositions. Realize that different isn't always better, but *better is always different*! In this chapter, we explore how a business model provides the basis for a customer-centric marketing strategy, how to design and refine successful value propositions (VP), and creative ways to add value for customers.

Business Models

A business model describes the rationale of how an organization, creates, delivers, and captures value.[1] The business model provides all stakeholders (owners, shareholders/investors, employees, suppliers, partners, customers, communities, and media) with a shared understanding of how the business operates. A strong business model provides a competitive edge in the marketplace/marketspace by demonstrating that a company's goods, services, or ideas are different, more innovative, and better than its rivals.

Howard Schultz, founder and CEO of Starbucks, commented on his company's phenomenal success:

> Customers don't always know what they want. The decline in coffee-drinking was due to the fact that most of the coffee people bought was stale and they weren't enjoying it. Once they tasted ours and experienced what we call the "third place"—a gathering place between home and work where they were treated with respect—they found we were filling a need they didn't know they had.

Herbert Kelleher and Rollin King sketched out the Southwest Airlines business model on a cocktail napkin at breakfast in 1967. Recognizing a need for a service-oriented low-cost airline, the "Texas triangle" meant that Southwest would fly dozens of daily flights between Dallas, Houston, and San Antonio. When the company faced a cash crunch during its challenging first year, the company sold one of its four airplanes but kept the existing flight schedule, launching the start of the company's renowned 15-minute turnaround.

Osterwalder and Pignon explain that, to design winning business models, entrepreneurs or managers should explicate nine building blocks: customer segments, value proposition, channels, customer relationships, revenue streams, key resources, key activities, key partners, and cost structure. They recommend preparing a business model canvas to get participation and buy-in from all key decision makers. (See LEGO Factory example in Figure 4.1; this is a customized LEGO toy set created online by customers.) In fact, these authors employed this research process in writing their book *Business Model Generation* (www.businessmodelgeneration.com). This project represented a true cocreation of value, as 470 participants from 45 countries provided input to their guidebook.[2]

Internet commerce is well suited to many new types of business models. Rappa reported nine major types (categories) and more than 40 subcategories of online models. These basic categories include brokerage (Orbitz), advertising (Yahoo), infomediary (DoubleClick), merchant (Lands' End), direct manufacturer (Dell), affiliate (Commission Junction), community (Flickr), subscription (NetFlix), and utility (Slashdot).[3] An alternative view by Wirtz and colleagues looked at a 4C Internet business model consisting of content (*Wall Street Journal*), commerce (Amazon), context (Google), and connection (Earthlink).[4]

KP	KA	VP	CR	CS
Customers who build new LEGO designs and post them online become key partners generating content and value	LEGO has to provide and manage the platform and logistics that allow packaging and delivery of custom-made LEGO sets	LEGO Factory substantially expands the scope of the off-the-shelf kit offering by giving LEGO fans the tools to build, showcase, and sell their own custom-designed kits	LEGO Factory builds a Long Tail community around customers who are truly interested in niche content and want to go beyond off-the-shelf retail kits	Thousands of new, customer-designed kits perfectly complement LEGO's standard sets of blocks. LEGO Factory connects customers who create customized designs with other customers, thus becoming a customer match-making platform and increasing sales
	KR		**CH**	
	LEGO has not yet fully adapted its resources and activities, which are optimized primarily for the mass market		LEGO Factory's existence depends heavily on the Web channel	

C$	R$
LEGO Factory leverages production and logistics costs already incurred by its traditional retail model	LEGO Factory aims to generate small revenues from a large number of customer-designed items. This represents a variable addition to traditional high-volume retail revenues

Figure 4.1 LEGO Factory: customer-designed kits. KP = Key Partners, KA = Key Activities, KR = Key Resources, VP = Value Proposition, CR = Customer Relationships, CH = Channels, CS = Customer Segments, C$ = Cost Structure, R$ = Revenue Streams. (Reprinted from A. Osterwalder and Y. Pigneur, *Business Model Generation* [New York: John Wiley and Sons, 2010], 73. With permission.)

The digital era has been the primary driver of many recent business transformations. Apple's iTunes (www.Apple.com/iTunes) is a great example of the changing music industry. Record companies, distributors, and music retailers once controlled the marketing channels and profits; today, artists and the platform (iTunes) have the market power. While in the past it was not uncommon for a band to earn only $1 from a $16 CD sale, today they often generate $7 from a $10 downloaded album on iTunes.

Newspaper publishers have struggled to stay relevant; they are attempting to morph into information providers as their readership base ages and defects to other media. The *Wall Street Journal, New York Times*, and *USA Today* have stellar reputations, translating into large and loyal customer bases, and they can charge fees for their online content. In contrast, most major metropolitan newspapers are a less viable option, as free alternatives (Web sites, smartphones, community magazines, television) abound.

Business models can be viewed from the perspective of shapers versus participants (types include influencers, hedgers, and disciples). Google, Microsoft, Facebook, Apple, and Salesforce.com are examples of shapers, since they open up platforms for third parties. These proactive organizations are market drivers and open up new market space. Companies that adopt, embrace, and enhance shapers' platforms are participants and may include applications (apps) developers, service firms, or online e-tailers. These companies include influencers (Bank of America for Visa), hedgers (advertisers that support Google and Microsoft platforms), or disciples (Dell's exclusive commitment to the Wintel platform).[5]

Zynga, a Silicon Valley social-gaming company, has generated hundreds of millions of dollars in revenues, largely through Farmville, its hugely popular game. Millions of Internet users manage virtual plots of land, grow crops, raise animals, and use online tools such as tractors. It has been estimated that there are 20 times more people today playing Farmville than there are actual farms in the United States.[6] Some other examples of commonly used business models are listed in Table 4.1.

Value Proposition

A value proposition (VP) is a "statement that matches up the firm's distinctive competencies with the needs and preferences of a carefully designed set of potential customers."[7] It helps firms as a communications device and is a basis for creating a shared understanding. A well-designed VP is a strategic business tool that includes, but goes beyond, the product mix, pricing, and promotion (marketing communications) to define the organization's competitive advantage through offerings, people, processes, and technology.

For example, the "Passionate Pursuit of Perfection" is the Lexus value proposition. This value statement encapsulates the essence of this upscale Japanese automobile manufacturer's worldwide marketing commitment to customer delight and

Table 4.1 Business Models

Type of Business Model	Description	Corporate Examples
Bricks and mortar	Traditional retail stores	Blockbuster Video, Whole Foods
Bricks and clicks	Retail and e-tail	Best Buy, Target
Internet pure-play	Online presence only	Blue Nile, Overstock.com
Software as a Service (SaaS)	Delivering applications over the Internet as a service	ADP, Salesforce.com
Community of users	Users generate knowledge, solve problems, and offer place for exchange	eBay, Wikipedia
Shaper	Open up new market space/ platforms	Apple, Facebook
Platform participant	Enhance platforms by creating user applications	Zynga, Foursquare
Multisided markets	Company serves multiple customer segments, e.g., readers and advertisers	USA Today, Visa
Bundling	Sell two or more products for a discount	Comcast, Microsoft Office
Unbundling	Sell a single product even though company offers related products	AT&T DSL service, Windows Live Essentials
Long tail	A vast product selection is available, yet most products sell infrequently	Amazon, Netflix
Free as a business model	Product is provided to users at no cost; revenues are generated from other sources	Skype, YouTube
Open business model	Companies share products for a very low cost (way below branded options)	Linux (Red Hat), Qualcomm
Pay what customer thinks it's worth	Customers have the option to pay what they perceive a product is worth/what they can afford	Radiohead CDs, neighborhood café

retention with respect to product-line quality, sales philosophy, dealership atmospherics, customer service, image, distribution, and logistics. A positioning strategy that supports the VP is how the organization delivers and differentiates value to its customers (this is discussed later in the chapter).

Since all organizations are separate entities, ideally they should each have their own identities. This requires a careful analysis of all potential value-proposition ingredients: service, quality, image, and price. The more unique the articulation of the core and augmented VP elements, the more memorable the message and more likely the success.

A good value proposition is difficult to imitate. While there are many online companies or Internet pure-plays, there is only one eBay—known for making inefficient markets efficient. The eBay marketplace has over 94 million global users accounting for $62 billion in trade in 2010, or $2,000 every second. Overall, the company generated $9.2 billion in revenues, earning $2.3 billion in profit with an impressive 23.7% operating margin.[8] In this virtual global marketplace where innovation and community collide, devotees can "win" (buy) or sell almost anything such as art, books, cars, electronics, fashion, home products, movies, etc. Trading on eBay is characterized by low transaction costs, vast selection, motivation to engage in repeated transactions, and technological empowerment.

A value proposition can be defined as benefits less costs. Here's a value equation from a health-care provider. This example clarifies how consumers measure value:

$$VP = (Quality + Service + Intangibles) - (Price + Nonmonetary Costs)$$

- *Quality* or outcomes is the correct diagnosis and treatment, prevention of illness, etc.
- *Service* includes accessibility, compassion, dependability, employee knowledge, etc.
- *Intangibles* include the reputation of the provider, special services, long-term outcomes and the relationship, use of latest technology, etc.
- *Price* is the consumer's expenditure for the service.
- *Nonmonetary costs* include time, energy, and psychological stress.[9]

Value propositions should be clear, concise, credible, and consistent over time. For example, the "Intel inside" personal computer campaign demonstrated that an industrial part (computer chips) could be differentiated in a similar manner to consumer products (potato chips). The overwhelming success of this program demonstrated that users valued Intel as a trusted component, the heart of the PC. In fact, the so-called Wintel standard (Microsoft Windows software, Intel microprocessors) has become more valued than the hardware manufacturer/assembler to many computer buyers.

IBM's "service, software and solutions for a small planet" is another highly effective VP. This strategic thrust illustrated that this business giant was fully prepared to deliver e-business solutions to companies, large and small, across the globe. It reflected the new reality that IBM was no longer just a hardware company and was now generating a majority of its revenues from services such as consulting, software, maintenance contracts, etc. Realize that a good value proposition is more than just a catchy slogan or a short-term positioning effort; it is a corporate commitment to pursue a specific strategic direction. The following list presents 10 additional examples of effective value propositions (note that these are simple yet powerful messages):

Amazon: "Amazon.com and you're done"
Expedia: "Puts travelers first in every thinkable way"
FedEx: "When it absolutely, positively has to get there overnight"
Jet Blue Airways: "You above all else"
Motorola University: "Right knowledge, right now"
Office Depot: "Taking care of business"
Publix Super Markets: "Where shopping is a pleasure"
Snapple: "Natural beverages, made from the best stuff on earth"
SunTrust Bank: "Live solid, bank solid"
Visa: "It is everywhere you want to be"

Since customers rather than management set the true value agenda, organizations must carefully assess customers' interpretation of value. How do we know if our value proposition or value statement is effective? Customer Value Checklist 4 lists several questions for management to address.

Customer Value Checklist 4: Critiquing Your Value Proposition

1. Does it take the customer's perspective?
2. Is it easy to understand?
3. Does it encapsulate the value you offer to: your people, the sales channel, the press, and your customers?
4. Is it strategically compatible with your business?
5. Is it acceptable given your organizational culture?
6. Is it honest?
7. Is it promotable? That is, is it logical, easily communicated, and solutions oriented? Does it have a headline or graphic with stopping power? Does it have different benefits for different buying influences? And is it original?

Source: G. P. Dovel, "Stake It Out: Positioning Success, Step by Step, *Business Marketing*, July 1990, 43–51.

Table 4.2   Value Disciplines

Value Disciplines	Value Focus	Image Driver	Image
Product leadership	Quality	Unique attribute	Best product/service
Operational excellence	Cost	Low cost	Best deal
Customer intimacy	Service	Relationship	Best friend

Source: Adapted from C. Scholey, *CMA Manage.* (October 2002), 1.

A starting point for creating a value proposition is the selection of an appropriate value discipline to emphasize. Treacy and Wiersema argue that companies can excel by practicing one of three principal business strategies: product leadership, operational excellence, or customer intimacy. The core capabilities required to successfully implement these strategies are innovation (product leadership), process efficiency and low cost (operational excellence), and relationship building (customer intimacy).[10]

Let's examine some examples of how firms successfully execute the value-discipline idea as the basis of their VP and business model. Product leaders such as Apple, Johnson & Johnson, and Nike strive for the best-quality goods and services. Operational excellence is delivered by Ameritrade, Southwest Airlines, and Target Stores. The best total solution (customer intimacy/service) is provided by Harrah's Casino, Publix Super Markets, and Nordstrom. A summary of the three core-value approaches is presented in Table 4.2.

Service, Quality, Image, and Price— The Crux of Customer Value

As noted in Chapter 1, customer value consists of four major components: service, quality, image, and price (see Figure 4.2). Extracting key differentiators from one or more of these core elements provides the basis of an organization's value proposition. The vertical axis on the diamond (service and quality) represents the backbone of the firm's offerings, while the horizontal axis (image and price) provide signaling cues to the target market. The S-Q-I-P elements create value for customers, establish a solid business philosophy for the organization, guide all strategic decisions, and ultimately affect business performance.

Since trade-offs exist among the S-Q-I-P elements, companies cannot expect to be market leaders in all areas. The cost of developing and sustaining a four-dimensional leadership position would be overwhelming. Clearly, we can see that customer value is a much richer concept than just a fair price; superb service, top quality, and a unique image are also highly valued by target markets. Since CV is a multidimensional construct, varying emphases on S-Q-I-P explicate a company's

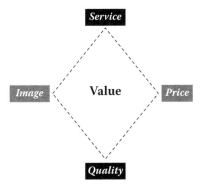

Figure 4.2   The S-Q-I-P diamond.

value proposition. Realize that top-notch companies often differentiate themselves and create legendary reputations largely due to singular attributes. While a focus on a key attribute is advisable, firms must meet acceptable threshold levels with respect to each dimension—formidable global competition provides little room for weakness in any area.

The service factor must reign supreme in value-creating markets because customers defect primarily for service reasons (poor service, service failures, lack of service recovery, etc.), and these issues are largely controllable by management. Many companies compete successfully on service dimensions. For example, service can be operationalized based on speed or time. Today, 24-hour dry cleaners, ExxonMobil's Speedpass, and drive-through wedding chapels all respond to the customer need for convenience or immediate gratification.

Air Around the Clock's (a South Florida–based air conditioning and appliance service contractor) differentiation is based on outstanding service, which includes emergency night and weekend repairs, a preferred-customer program, a fleet of more than 90 trucks, and a "fix it right the first time" philosophy executed by knowledgeable technicians. Guardian Swimming Pool's trucks advertise the fact that they "show up" and that they provide next-day service. (This sends a clear signal to their target market that their competitors are likely to be weak in customer service; hence, Guardian gains an important competitive advantage.)

FedEx built its reputation based on a strong value proposition that guarantees package delivery by 10:30 a.m. the next morning. In contrast, the U.S. Post Office's priority mail service suffers some because of a much weaker value statement. While the flat-rate, 1-pound envelope seems like a good deal, its relatively slow two- or three-day delivery is a serious drawback. Many customers often send items via priority mail because of image rather than speed: The red, white, and blue package looks more important than regular mail when it arrives on a client's desk.

Broderbund Software knows that quality products are essential to its business success. It has used innovative offerings and niche marketing to compete effectively in the educational and gaming software markets. Value innovation can be fostered in companies by reducing investment in business units that are settlers (offer me-too products and services), increasing investment in migrators (businesses with value improvements), and using corporate entrepreneurship initiatives to create pioneers (businesses that represent value innovations). Research on the source of high growth in diverse organizations found that only 14% of new business initiatives were true value innovations; yet, these breakthrough concepts yielded 38% of total revenues and an impressive 61% of total profits.[11] Companies such as 3M and Microsoft have lost some of their innovative spark in the past few years, and this has impacted their bottom line and dampened their corporate reputation.

The American Productivity & Quality Center (APQC) has studied more than 100 companies and found that learning how to tap and use knowledge can be an important source for creating customer value and obtaining a competitive advantage in the marketplace. Specifically, five knowledge-based routes to designing successful value propositions have been identified. These are

1. *Knowledge as a product*: selling consulting services, databases, etc.
2. *Knowledge transfer*: adapting best practices from high-performing unit of an organization
3. *Customer-focused knowledge*: data mining, using database information, customized responses to customer concerns, etc.
4. *Personal responsibility for knowledge*: empowering front-line service employees to have the necessary information and ability to act to solve customer problems
5. *Intellectual-asset management*: using patents, licensing, and technology to generate value for the customer and the company[12]

How much does an image matter to an organization? In outstanding companies such as Virgin Enterprises, market perception or image defines their essence. While strong leadership and quality products and services are a given, customers often choose to patronize certain businesses because of who they are and what they stand for. Virgin uses a strong brand name and a unique, global image to create value for customers. Richard Branson's business empire now extends into an airline, cell phones/service, music production business, music retail stores, soft drinks, and other youth-oriented products. In business, names matter; the success of the Virgin idea has been demonstrated. Slipped Disc was rejected because it wasn't as catchy and lacked wide appeal for other product lines.[13]

From a brand-equity perspective, each new high-performing Virgin business adds more value to the overall brand. Of course, critics might argue that the brand is overstretched and value is diminished when an occasional venture is not a market success (Virgin Cola). Further discussion on how Virgin competes on image may be found in Customer Value Insight 6 (see Chapter 6).

Organizations may have to proactively change an image that is unfavorable or weak to its target market. This is particularly true in professional sports, where image is elevated to an even higher plane. A sports franchise's image can favorably or unfavorably impact fan support, marketing/merchandising opportunities, and even performance on the playing field. In the Tampa Bay, Florida, market, the Buccaneers and Rays both began winning after they shed inferior inherent characteristics about their teams. In the case of the National Football League Bucs, the "creamsicle" (orange and white) uniforms and the friendly mascot known as Bucco Bruce were replaced with a fiercer pewter and red look with a menacing pirate theme. The American League (baseball) Tampa Bay Rays dropped the "devil" as their middle name and instantly began winning after a decade of total futility. (It should also be noted that in both cases, the teams also greatly benefited from new management and better player selection.)

Price can play a major or support role in the value proposition. Companies such as Budget Car Rental, Costco, Discount Auto Parts, and Priceline.com communicate to the marketplace that they are price leaders. Readers are encouraged to review the pricing chapter (Chapter 6) for an in-depth review of this strategic marketing variable and how it impacts customer value management.

Customer Value Insight 4 examines the S-Q-I-P model as a basis for building a value proposition in the context of Starbucks. Another useful means for understanding and critiquing VPs is the Customer Value Assessment Tool (CVAT). The CVAT is a strategic marketing audit that examines 42 measures of customer value in the four major VP areas: service, quality, image, and price (see appendix to this chapter). CVAT is a diagnostic instrument that is most valuable for capturing information on how CV thinking is being practiced (and can be improved) within the organization.

Customer Value Insight 4: Starbucks

Starbucks is a total sensory experience. It tastes good; smells good; looks good; has relaxing music, comfortable seating, and wireless technology; is everywhere; and for many is their "third place" to hang out (besides home and work). I would probably rate them as a 4-4-5-2 based on the S-Q-I-P model, with atmospherics their big value adder and price as their weakest link. Given this value-proposition evaluation, opportunities for improvement may be to encourage return visits via a preferred-customer program (coffee club) or a Starbucks-for-bucks promotion ($1 espresso shots, $2 cappuccinos).

QUESTIONS TO THINK ABOUT

1. Offer two additional recommendations for management: one product based and one promotional.
2. Can Starbucks win the morning coffee market from Dunkin' Donuts and McDonalds? If so, what do they need to do?
3. Provide another numerical and descriptive S-Q-I-P evaluation of a service company and explain your rationale for your ratings.

Differentiation—Adding Value

A major challenge for firms is to be seen as different by the market; this requires the development of a unique value proposition. While the S-Q-I-P idea discussed in this chapter may be sufficient, many 21st-century companies find that the best path to creating value and setting them apart from the rest of the field is to change the rules of the game (recall the market-driving concept introduced in Chapter 2).

Blue Nile is the largest online retailer of diamonds and fine jewelry, offering customers vast selection, great quality, and personalization at affordable prices. A customercentric company, Blue Nile has won the Circle of Excellence Platinum Award from Bizrate.com every year since 2002. (Note: This award recognizes the best online customer service ranked by actual customers.) A highly productive Internet pure-play, Blue Nile.com generates more than $300 million in annual revenues with fewer than 200 employees.[14]

Smart companies recognize the compromises their business/industry imposes on their customers and seek to break these compromises, thus releasing tremendous value. Customer-focused companies can exploit these unnecessary concessions to find a competitive advantage. Charles Schwab has revolutionized the discount-brokerage industry and prospered by breaking industry trade-offs for more than 30 years—for example, low price and excellent service as well as a bricks-and-clicks presence.

Airlines and hotels are two service industries (among many) that have created artificial resistance barriers for customers. For airlines, it is the Saturday night stay-over requirement, which can double or triple round-trip fares. Southwest Airlines does not force its customers to spend a Saturday evening somewhere they choose not to be so that they can obtain lower fares. Hotel check-in times are often imposed through standard operating procedures that go unquestioned. Inconvenient hotel check-in and check-out policies often mean that a day is not really a day. While the folly (or short-term profitability) of these unnecessary requirements are readily apparent, great companies do not take these industry rules as given; these firms design their own rules for the game. Crowne Plaza and Sheraton are two hotel chains that have experimented with more-equitable day rates for their valued guests. As these travel-industry examples illustrate, companies do not have to succumb to questionable industry trade practices or standard operating procedures: They must constantly search for better ways of doing business in a time-conscious society.

Strategic Implications of Differentiation

As markets change, so must firms' value propositions. Consider the approaches used by two of the office superstores, Staples and Office Depot (note that both sell essentially the same products and have similar service and pricing strategies). Staples uses its extensive database for target marketing, promotional activity, and product enhancements. This office supply store chain learned that as many of their small business customers grew larger, they defected to competitors with delivery services. Staples recently introduced this value-added option to do a better job retaining customers.[15] In contrast, Office Depot emphasizes customer retention via its workplace rewards program and has built its online store into one of the most highly trafficked Web sites. Hence, the competitive situation and potential target market opportunities should guide management's thinking about the appropriate value strategy to employ.

As Figure 4.3 shows, companies may occupy one of five positions—best value, discount value, expensive value, fair value, or poor value—in the mind of the customer. Bradley Gale, a leading thinker on customer value, explains that the fair-value (FV) line is the line of points at which competitors would neither gain nor lose market share with respect to price-quality trade-offs.[16] Discount, fair, and expensive values have benefits consistent with their costs. Best value (above the FV line) represents a strong competitive advantage, while poor value (below the FV line) is a prescription for failure for an organization.

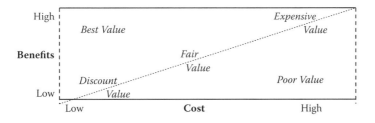

Figure 4.3   Assessing a company's value. (Adapted and expanded from R. E. Reidenbach. Follow the Value Chain to Superior Performance, *Bankers Magazine* [Nov.–Dec. 1996] 51.)

After years of market dominance, Toys "R" Us struggled due to complacency and lack of innovation. Competition from Walmart, Target, and other discounters; membership warehouse chains; online companies; and new/creative competitors in the educational toy market eroded market share. In the case of Toys "R" Us, we can conclude that the company lost ground in the marketplace, moving from the "best value" to "fair value" position. Their Toy Registry initiative is a relatively new strategy aimed at winning back some of the lost market share. The registry acts as a wish list to let family and friends know what toys children want for birthdays, holidays, or special occasions. In addition, store redesign into specialized areas and a stronger electronics/video section has helped the company regain some of its lost stature.

As part of the business renewal process, organizations should use cost/benefit analysis to periodically assess how their value proposition compares to competitive options. Is it superior, on par, or inferior to their direct and indirect rivals?

Summary

The business model and the value proposition (VP) establish the foundation for developing a unique position in the marketplace. Service, quality, image, and value-based pricing are the central elements of the VP. Companies that are value winners also innovate, strengthen their value statements, and are not afraid to occasionally break industry rules. Rather than viewing the value proposition as subparts, good managers try to create synergy among all of the components to achieve differentiation and secure short- and long-term competitive advantage. Furthermore, you should rethink and reshape the value proposition when changing market conditions call for the adoption of a revised business strategy. Service and quality, the core offerings, are considered in more detail in Chapter 5.

Customer Value Action Items

1. You have an interesting idea for a new and potentially profitable entrepreneurial venture. Briefly describe this business concept. Which business model in Table 4.1 would you use and why?
2. The band Radiohead lets fans pay what they think an album is worth. Critique this innovation in the music industry. Cite other examples of where you might apply this approach (pay what customer thinks product is worth) successfully in the marketspace and/or marketplace?
3. Your chief customer officer (CCO) has given you a high-profile, make-or-break assignment at work—develop a customer value plan for your firm. Consider the following seven questions in your 2–3-page executive summary for this report.

a. What core aspect of the value proposition (VP) does your company emphasize—service, quality, image, or price?

b. What value discipline does your organization emphasize (product leadership, operational excellence, or customer intimacy)?

c. Explain your company's business model and value proposition. What is unique about your strategy?

d. How does your company work on a daily basis at being different and better than the competition? Consider purpose and process issues in your response.

e. Has your company broken any industry "rules" lately? If so, explain.

f. Does your firm offer a *best value, discount value, expensive value, fair value*, or *poor value*?

g. What can your organization do to truly deliver superior customer value?

4. You were hired as a management consultant by one of the leading dot. coms in the *USA Today* top 25 consumer firms index (see Chapter 7, Customer Value Insight 7, for further information) and asked to design/ refine the value proposition for this company. How would you proceed in this project? Provide a draft (and rationale) of the working VP for this company to assess.

5. Compare and contrast how two of these companies—Google, Hewlett-Packard, Intel, JetBlue Airways, and Target—create value for their customers.

6. Assume you are thinking about purchasing a new car. Go to the manufacturer's or auto dealer Web site and Kelley Blue Book (www.kbb.com) to obtain product information about your vehicle. Based on this research, discuss the value-based pricing, quality, service, and brand-identification (image) strategies being used to market this automobile.

7. Farm Stores recently introduced the iExpress business model that combines online grocery ordering with drive-through pick-up service. In contrast, the PublixDirect approach failed (see Publix case study in the Appendix in Part V of this book). Do you think the Farm Store approach is a viable business strategy? Why or why not?

8. Hulu is a Web site for watching television shows (most videos are free). The Hulu Plus plan is a subscription for $9.95 a month with a much deeper selection of popular shows. How should Hulu's "freemium" service (both products) compete with Netflix, Comcast, Apple TV, and others in this market?

9. Using a company that you are highly loyal to (e.g., favorite restaurant or small business, bookmarked Web site, etc.), use the CVAT (see Appendix to this chapter) to conduct a mini value audit of this organization. Based on this informal analysis, identify three to five potential problems and possible strategies to overcome these shortcomings.

Appendix: Customer Value Assessment Tool (CVAT™)*

The CVAT has been created as an instrument to help product and service providers evaluate and improve their value delivery to their customers. Supplying outstanding service and value must be a dynamic process; therefore, this tool has been designed to be utilized on a regular basis. This helps to evaluate the extent of any changes and improvements that may need to be initiated. The four S-Q-I-P components used to appraise customer value in this tool are the perceived: service quality, product quality, image, and value-based price. The survey focuses on each component as an individual indicator of customer service and value. Collectively, the four components will help companies achieve excellence in managing customer value.

Guidelines for Using the Customer Value Assessment Tool

The purpose of the CVAT is to rate your current employer based on the four components used to appraise customer value. Rank how well your company matches the statement given.

1 means it happens all of the time.
2 means it happens most of the time.
3 means it happens some of the time.
4 means it never happens.

The results obtained via the CVAT can be organized into a report that will help identify the strengths and opportunities for improving customer value in your organization.

Perceived Service Quality

Service Quality Definition: The service given is viewed to be timely and appropriate by the customer. This service may also anticipate the future needs or wants of the customer.

1. The company conducts focus groups with customers to determine what they view as strengths and weaknesses about the customer service the company provides.

    1   2   3   4

2. The company continually conducts customer satisfaction surveys and utilizes the results in order to improve services provided.

    1   2   3   4

---

* Developed by Brett A. Gordon, MBA, and Pamela Gordon, MBA. © June 1998, Brett A. Gordon and Pamela A. Gordon. All rights reserved.

3. The company provides special training for all employees on customer service, including ways to handle difficult customers.

    1   **2**   **3**   **4**

4. The company has a monthly "Best Practices" newsletter that details innovative ways to provide customer service.

    1   **2**   **3**   **4**

5. The company provides its customers with a range of professional and technical assistance.

    1   **2**   **3**   **4**

6. The company commits to and exhibits empathy when dealing with customers.

    1   **2**   **3**   **4**

7. The company constantly seeks ways to enhance its relationships with customers.

    1   **2**   **3**   **4**

8. The company provides a means for customers who wish to comment or complain.

    1   **2**   **3**   **4**

9. The company provides its customers with complete, easy-to-understand information concerning products or services.

    1   **2**   **3**   **4**

10. The company ensures that complaints and problems are resolved to the complete satisfaction of the customer.

    1   **2**   **3**   **4**

11. The company regularly compares its customer satisfaction levels with those of the competition.

    1   **2**   **3**   **4**

12. The company rewards employees for innovative actions/ideas concerning customer service, irrespective of sales outcome.

    1   **2**   **3**   **4**

13. The company regularly reviews progress on customer service goals and objectives.

    1   **2**   **3**   **4**

14. Policies and procedures for serving customers are consistent across departments.

> 1   2   3   4

Comments on Service Quality:

_____
_____
_____
_____

Perceived Product Quality

Product Quality Definition: The product is viewed as being dependable (zero defects) and meets or exceeds the consumer's expectations.

1. The company conducts focus groups with customers to determine what they view as strengths and weaknesses about the company's products.

> 1   2   3   4

2. The company forms strategic alliances with vendors, suppliers, and distributors.

> 1   2   3   4

3. The company selects vendors on the basis of quality, not just price.

> 1   2   3   4

4. The company uses Quality Function Deployment (i.e., builds customer expectations into the product).

> 1   2   3   4

5. The company is committed to design quality: "do it right the first time."

> 1   2   3   4

6. The company uses external benchmarking to determine the strengths and weaknesses of its own products.

> 1   2   3   4

7. The company has a system for analyzing product performance data (e.g., Quality Control Data) and translating the results into continuous product improvements.

> 1   2   3   4

8. The company monitors supplier/vendor performance to ensure that the company's quality requirements are met.

    1   2   3   4

9. The company views corporate setbacks as an opportunity to develop a new approach to solving the problem.

    1   2   3   4

10. The company's marketing programs, methods, and strategies add value to the firm's offerings.

    1   2   3   4

11. The company demonstrates through thought, word, and deed that low quality is expensive and that high quality has a high return on investment.

    1   2   3   4

12. The company is viewed as having a commitment to continuous improvement: "Kaizen."

    1   2   3   4

Comments on Product Quality:

_____

_____

_____

_____

Perceived Image

Image Definition: The company is viewed as having a commitment to the customer, top management, continuous improvement, and the firm as a whole.

1. The company treats its internal customers with the same care and respect as it treats its external customers.

    1   2   3   4

2. The company conducts focus groups with customers to determine what they view as strengths and weaknesses about the company's image.

    1   2   3   4

3. The management style exhibited by the leaders of the company reflect that of a facilitator, coach, and enabler.

    1   2   3   4

4. Employees are viewed as positive representatives of the company's ideals.

    1   **2**   **3**   **4**

5. The company uses "systems thinking" to solve its internal and external challenges. (For example, the company understands that all events within the corporation are interrelated and each has an influence on the other.)

    1   **2**   **3**   **4**

6. The company encourages its employees to seek a good balance between their work and family lives.

    1   **2**   **3**   **4**

7. The company eliminates obvious examples of excess.

    1   **2**   **3**   **4**

Comments on Image:

_____

_____

_____

_____

Perceived Value-Based Price

Value-Based Price Definition: The price level that a customer is willing to pay to receive a given level of product and/or service performance.

1. When establishing a price for a product or service, the company starts with the customer first, considers the competition, and then determines the appropriate price, as opposed to setting price only according to costs.

    1   **2**   **3**   **4**

2. The company's product or service is viewed by the customer as exceeding the expected benefits of a competitive product.

    1   **2**   **3**   **4**

3. The company meets customer expectations without hindering financial performance.

    1   **2**   **3**   **4**

4. The company offers as many convenient payment methods and terms as possible in order to better satisfy its customers.

    1   2   3   4

5. The company looks for ways to cut back on costs and still deliver products or services that meet customer expectations.

    1   2   3   4

6. The company utilizes new technologies that allow it to lower prices and increase profits.

    1   2   3   4

7. The company creates innovations that allow it to offer more for less than the competition.

    1   2   3   4

8. The company raises both quality and service to new levels.

    1   2   3   4

9. The company is viewed as a value-adding entity with respect to the price it charges for its product or service.

    1   2   3   4

Comments on Price:

_____

_____

_____

_____

Overall S-Q-I-P Evaluation:

_____

_____

_____

_____

Chapter 5

Service and Quality— The Core Offering

Quality in a service or product is not what you put into it. It is what the customer gets out of it.

Peter Drucker

There are no traffic jams along the extra mile.

Roger Staubach

As we learned in Chapter 4, service and quality are the heart of the value proposition. (Price and image, the communicators, compose the other axis and are detailed in Chapter 6.) The search for excellent quality is one of the most important business trends over the past three decades, as demanding buyers have come to expect great products accompanied with service that is fast, reliable, and customer friendly. Consider these three examples:

- Cell phone and Internet users want enhanced product quality and service features at reduced monthly costs. AT&T and Verizon must carefully monitor Comcast's strategic moves to preserve and grow their customer base. Comcast's previous four-hour window for a service call (e.g., 1–5 p.m.) has been reduced to two hours (e.g., 3–5 p.m.) with previsit telephone calls (offering a more exact time) to increase customer satisfaction.

- Ritz-Carlton's employees engage in several weeks of customer service training as they master the inner workings of what it takes to truly "move heaven and earth." All Ritz-Carlton associates from housekeepers to hotel managers are empowered to improve guest stays by making sound business decisions and, if necessary, authorizing and implementing minor room improvements, repairs, or special amenities to delight customers.
- Johnson & Johnson recently introduced a product line of 98% natural baby products (derived from fruits and plants) to environmentally conscious parents, worldwide.[1]

This chapter consists of three parts. First, it explains what is meant by a service, discusses the idea of cocreating services, and reviews the importance of good customer service. Next, quality is examined in a generic fashion. The chapter concludes by tying these two components—service and quality—together to understand *service quality*.

Services Create Value

What Is a Service?

Products can be defined as goods, services, and ideas. Today, there are very few pure goods. Almost all consumer and business products (for example, cars, cell phones, computers, etc.) are packaged with strong service components. This can include a service warranty, monthly rate plan, 24-hour access to technical support, and other service options. In the majority of cases, companies market blended products. A fast-food meal is the classic example; while the burger, fries, and Coke are the goods, the service experience (speed, brand image, atmospherics, etc.) is often more highly valued by consumers.

Pure services such as insurance are highly intangible and present unique challenges to marketers. Management consulting is an example of an idea (selling a client a feasibility study or reengineering plan). As Figure 5.1 illustrates, a continuum exists based on the degree of product tangibility. Effective service marketers must be able to tangibilize the intangible.

To shed further light on business opportunities in the service sector, a 2 × 2 services classification matrix—consisting of four cells and four examples of organizations in each category—is presented in Figure 5.2. Two caveats are called for.

Figure 5.1   Three types of products.

Type of Service	Business	Consumer
Professional	Accounting, legal, marketing research, and management consulting	Attorneys, dentists, financial planners, and physicians
Other	Logistics, janitorial, printers, and security	Fast food, hair stylists, lawn care, and pest control

Figure 5.2   Service classification matrix. (Adapted and expanded from C. Gronroos, An Applied Theory for Marketing Industrial Services, *Industrial Marketing Management* 8 [1979], 45–50.)

First, some companies compete in more than one cell (banks, CPAs, insurance agents, etc.). Second, the term *professional* used in the context of the matrix is to describe firms that have specialized knowledge and advanced education or training.

In contrast, professionalism is a critical success factor for all organizations. The automotive detailer that takes two days to return telephone calls, shows up an hour late for scheduled appointments, or fails to make your car "shine" appropriately will not stay in business for long.

Service marketers must change in response to changing environmental forces (e.g., societal trends, economic conditions, new technologies, etc.) and market forces such as competition, collaboration, and regulation. As an example, global leaders such as American Express, Dow Jones, Lufthansa, Nortel, Royal Caribbean Cruises, and United Parcel Service are obsessed with using information to improve customer service. Eight value-adding practices identified in a recent study were personalization, offering tiered service levels, collecting information to enhance customer experiences, keeping it simple, responding to what customers do not like doing, providing one-stop shopping, balancing customer self-service with support, and getting to know the customer best.[2]

Cocreation of Services

Prahalad and Ramaswamy have pioneered a recent stream of research on cocreating experiences and feel that this is the next wave of value creation activity.[3] They argue that companies should escape the traditional view of value creation where customers are outside the firm. Cocreation of value means an "obsessive focus on personalized interactions between the consumer and the company." They add that "communities of informed, networked, empowered, and active consumers" are driving value creation in a variety of service sectors, including travel, online auctions, medical treatment programs, video gaming, and business services. Hence, value creation occurs where the roles of the company and customer converge.

A great example of the new cocreation of value model is illustrated in the case of Crushpad, a Silicon Valley–based winery. Crushpad's value proposition is "Make Your Own Wine" and has transformed its business through technology. Consumers can participate on a limited- to a full-scale basis depending on their interest in the wine-making process. Some activities that customers engage in include creating a wine-making plan; monitoring the grapes; picking, crushing, and fermenting the grapes; and even packaging the bottles. Support services include party planning, advice on wine creation, and business guidance on how customers can sell their own wine. Web sites, blogs, and community events help spread the word about this unique type of cocreation of value.[4]

Airlines, supermarkets, supply chains, theaters, theme parks, and retailers have all embraced cocreation of service opportunities through self-serve initiatives such as check-in, check-out, price checks, information/purchase kiosks, and other technology enhancements. For the most part, the net result of these activities has been increased benefits and reduced costs for both customer and company, and this trend is expected to escalate in coming years.

Customer Service—Research Findings and Managerial Implications

Ritz-Carlton works hard at learning its customers' preferences to better serve them in the future. From the moment guests book a room for the first time at a Ritz-Carlton hotel, their guest-history profile begins. Every preference they have is recorded, and all Ritz-Carlton hotels and resorts have access to the information. Ritz-Carlton employees take every opportunity to note guest preferences, which are later recorded in the guest-history files. For example, if a guest likes an iron in the room, or prefers not to have turndown service, or requests a Cadillac instead of a Lincoln when needing car service to the airport, the information will be recorded, and will follow the guest to every subsequent stay.

While quality customer service is more important to customers in today's economic environment (61% of customers said this in the American Express Global Customer Satisfaction Barometer), 55% of them feel that companies have not increased their focus on delivering quality service. Remember that "extra mile" that NFL great Roger Staubach referred to in this chapter's opening quote? Only one-quarter (24%) of respondents believe that companies value their business and will go that extra mile to keep it. Other interesting and powerful findings from the AMEX study include

- Three out of four (75%) customers will speak positively about a company following a good service experience.
- The three most important factors when deciding which companies to do business with are personal experience, a company's reputation, and recommendations from friends and family.

- A majority (59%) of customers are very likely to speak negatively about a company after poor service (and they are not shy about telling others about these experiences through Web postings and social media, as is discussed further in Chapter 8).
- Nearly half (48%) of consumers always or often use online posts or blogs to get others' opinions about a company's customer service reputation and put greater credence in negative reviews than positive ones.
- Customers will spend an additional 9% in the United States for excellent customer service. This is comparable to numbers found in India (11%), Japan (10%), and Italy (9%) and more than Canada, the United Kingdom, Germany, and Netherlands (all at 7%).[5]

Some additional recent research on how customer service impacts business performance found that nearly one in five (17%) customers will defect after a single poor service experience and another two in five (40%) after two service blunders. Only 28% of respondents feel that telephone support is an effective response to inadequate or failed service. Nontelephone channels such as Web self-service, social media, e-mail, etc., are preferred (45%).[6]

Many top executives fail to acknowledge their corporate shortcomings in customer service. A study by Accenture reported that 75% of managers believed that their customer service was above average; yet, 59% of their customers said that their experience with these companies' service was dissatisfying![7] The good news is that a distorted view of reality can be readily detected through gap analysis, a service quality tool that is discussed later in the chapter.

Former Disney chairman Michael Eisner established the "Disney Vision of Excellence—Quality, Service and Smiles," a value proposition that inspires service personnel to deliver a memorable customer experience. Good customer service is all about the service experience. Does your organization meet or (preferably) exceed customer expectations? Managers of service organizations should pay close attention to the cardinal principles of service quality and use these insights to make service quality a winning value-added strategy.

Cardinal Principles of Service Quality

- *Listening precedes action*: Integrating the voice of the customer in designing processes and establishing service standards. Chat rooms and e-mail are excellent listening posts for responding to customer concerns and complaints.
- *Reliability is key*: A huge factor in service quality. Without reliability, customers lose confidence in the service provider's ability to deliver on its promises.

- *Flawless execution of the basics*: Mastering those competencies that you as a service provider are expected to perform well at, e.g., Dominos delivering food that is hot and what the customer ordered.
- *Pay attention to service design*: Service design, not people, is often responsible for inconsistent and unreliable service delivery. Service systems that are not properly designed or maintained hinder service personnel from performing their jobs and in satisfying customer needs. Further, without process consistency, quality is impossible.
- *Perform service recovery well*: Service failures are almost inevitable; however, a well-managed recovery from a service failure can create levels of loyalty from a customer that are greater than before the failure occurred—assuming the problem is handled promptly and is favorably resolved.
- *Surprise customers*: Discover the "wow" factor by seeking excellence in both the service process and outcome. Meeting customer expectations is simply the admission price to compete; customers will shift their loyalty to service providers that can perform the unexpected.
- *Practice fair play*: Customers expect equitable treatment, and become distrustful when they perceive otherwise. Customers expect two types of justice: *Distributive justice* refers to the perceived fairness of the actual outcome, or consequence of a decision, e.g., the level of refund or exchange offered; *procedural justice* refers to whether the procedures, or criteria, used in making the decision are perceived as fair, e.g., how quickly a problem was resolved and when information that is presented is given due attention and consideration.
- *Promote teamwork*: When service workers help one another and are invested in one another's success, service tends to improve. Smooth handoffs among service workers are also critical for a satisfying customer experience.
- *Internal service begets external service*: Employees themselves are customers of internal service; internal service quality is improved to the extent to which tools, policies and procedures, teamwork, management support, goal alignment, effective training, communication, and rewards and recognition are properly introduced.

Adapted from R. Zemke, "The Customer Service Revolution," *Training* 39 (2002), 46.

One online company that excels in customer service is Zappo.com, as demonstrated in Customer Value Insight 5.

Customer Value Insight 5: Zappos and Customer Service Is a Very Good Fit

Shoes are not the most exciting product category, right? Try telling that to Tony Hsieh (pronounced Shay), CEO of Zappos. com. In less than a decade, Hsieh has built Zappos into a billion-dollar business through delivering a vast selection of shoes, clothing, handbags, and other products (over 3 million items available) and unsurpassed customer service. The company was acquired by Amazon in 2009 and operates as an independent entity.

Mr. Hsieh is a self-professed scholar of "happiness" and, as part of his vision to create the world's most customercentric online company, aims to deliver "happiness in a box." This three-part formula is to

1. *Meet expectations* by delivering the right items.
2. *Meet desires* through free shipping, free return shipping when necessary and a 365 day return policy.
3. Often *delight customers* via surprise upgrades to overnight shipping (5-day shipping is standard).

The Zappos customer experience (obsession) is all about developing relationships, emotional connections, and high-touch "WOW" customer service. The Zappos 10-point program for customer service is summarized as follows:

■ Make customer service a priority for the whole company, not just a department.
■ Make WOW a verb that is part of your company's everyday vocabulary.
■ Empower and trust your customer service reps.
■ Realize that it's okay to fire problem customers.
■ Don't measure call times, up-sell, or use scripts.
■ Don't hide your 1-800 number.
■ View each call as an investment in building a brand.
■ Celebrate (companywide) great service.
■ Find people passionate about customer service.
■ Give great service to everyone: customers, employees, and vendors.[8]

Questions to Think About

1. What prevents other companies from adopting customer service best practices (review the 10 Zappos guidelines)?
2. How can the Zappos philosophy of creating exceptional value be adopted by your company?
3. Critique the Amazon–Zappos marketing marriage.
4. How do you view the long-term prospects for Zappos?

Quality Matters

Today, quality has become one of the most powerful competitive forces facing U.S. companies. Many of the products and services we use have become standardized, where even private-label brands meet or exceed minimum standards. Modern communications permit, and in some cases encourage, customers to shift their patronage from one producer to another. Global competition has resulted in increased choice and has raised customer expectations of what constitutes acceptable quality. Consider this example of high product quality courtesy of Lands' End for their Zipper Gripper.

> What good is a zipper if you can't zip it? You'll notice we've sewn on a little tab at the end of this zipper. It's there to help you guide that tiny zipper pin into the zipper box on the other side. To operate the zipper, fully and securely seat the pin into the slider and box, and zip up. Makes for a perfect zip every time. And speaking of perfection, this is a coil zipper—chosen for its superior strength and performance. It has no teeth to break and the ability to self-correct. If the zipper ever separates, simply unzip and begin again.

Realize that marketing is a contest for the consumer's attention, and the Internet is now competing for that attention as the number of Internet users worldwide continues to soar. The Internet has shifted power away from businesses to consumers, who can quickly compare products and prices from a range of suppliers like never before. Now competition is "just a click away." All these developments point to the need for companies to offer customer-defined quality that differentiates them in the global and digital marketplace. Companies like Cisco Systems and Blue Nile.com have established superior positions with respect to product quality in the marketspace.

A research study using employees in two automobile parts manufacturing facilities found that quality improvement practices significantly increased productivity and were a key to competitive success in global markets.[9] Kenneth Case, president of the American Society for Quality (ASQ), identified the following seven key forces that will influence quality in the future:

1. Quality must deliver bottom-line results.
2. Management systems will increasingly absorb the quality function.
3. Quality will be everyone's job.
4. The economic case for a broader application of quality will need to be proved.
5. Global demand for products and services will create a global work force.
6. Trust and confidence in business leaders and organizations will decline.
7. Customer expectations will rise.[10]

What Is Quality?

Quality is one of those elusive concepts that are easy to visualize but difficult to define. Quality has many definitions ranging from specific to general and varies by functional area. According to the American Society of Quality,

> Quality is a subjective term for which each person or sector has its own definition. In technical usage, quality can have two meanings: 1) the characteristics of a product or service that bear on its ability to satisfy stated or implied needs; 2) a product or service free of deficiencies. According to Joseph Juran, quality means "fitness for use"; according to Philip Crosby, it means "conformance to requirements."[11]

To expand on this definition, quality must provide goods and services that completely satisfy the needs of both *internal* and *external* customers. Moreover, quality serves as the "bridge" between the producer of goods or services and its customer. Quality gurus such as Deming viewed quality as reducing variation. Table 5.1 presents Deming's quality philosophy summarized in his 14 points, aimed at changing both cultural and organizational systems of a company.

Garvin takes a more aggressive and strategic approach to defining quality. He views quality as a means of pleasing customers, not just preventing annoyances. He eschews the defensive quality posture practiced by many U.S. companies in favor of a more strategic approach based on a combination of eight quality dimensions, including a product's performance, features, reliability, conformity, durability, serviceability, aesthetics, and perceived quality. Implied in Garvin's eight quality dimensions are five overall categories of quality, including

1. *Transcendent*: some form of innate excellence
2. *Product-based*: measurable based on attributes of the product itself
3. *Manufacturing-based*: conformance to requirements
4. *User-based*: quality is "in the eyes of the beholder"
5. *Value-based*: defined in terms of price/cost tradeoffs[12]

Table 5.1   Deming's 14 Points on Quality

Principle	Explanation
1. Institute constancy of purpose	Continuation of business requires a core set of values and a purpose that is stable over time
2. Adopt the new philosophy	Learn new responsibilities and take on leadership of change
3. Cease dependence on mass inspection	Quality does not come from inspection, but rather than from improvements in the process
4. End the practice of awarding business on the basis of price alone	Price has no meaning apart from perceived quality; work on minimizing total costs
5. Improve constantly and forever the system of production and service	Build quality into the product in the first place; systems should be redesigned continually for improved quality
6. Institute training	Equip managers and workers with the tools they need to evaluate and improve systems, including basic statistical methods
7. Institute leadership	Leaders should know the work they supervise; the aim of leadership should be to help workers do their jobs better
8. Drive out fear	Deming claimed that workers perform best when they feel secure. Fear breeds hidden agendas, padded numbers and may cause workers to satisfy a rule or quota at the expense of the company
9. Break down barriers among staff	Workers in various functional areas need to work together as a team
10. Eliminate slogans, exhortations and targets	Such exhortations only create adversarial relationships; the real cause of low quality is in the system
11. Eliminate work quotas	Emphasis on extrinsic motivators, such as quotas or other numerical goals, work against quality and productivity improvements
12. Remove barriers to pride of workmanship	Remove any bureaucratic hindrances that rob workers' pride of workmanship. Listen and follow-up on worker suggestions and requests

Table 5.1 (continued)   Deming's 14 Points on Quality

Principle	Explanation
13. Institute a vigorous program of education and self-improvement	Deming advocated life-long learning-formal or informal
14. Put everyone to work on the transformation	Everyone needs to be involved if business systems are to be improved

Source: E. Deming, *Out of Crisis* (Cambridge, MA: MIT Center for Advanced Engineering, 1986).

There are four stages of quality: conforming to engineering standards, customer satisfaction, market-perceived (competitive) quality, and customer value management. Most construction equipment dealers are still at stage 1 (some did not even achieve this level of performance quality). Their goal is to get beyond establishing and measuring quality benchmarks (stage 1) and create happy customers by evaluating customer satisfaction levels (stage 2). Some progressive dealerships have mastered performance quality and customer-satisfaction tracking and are now focusing on beating the competition (stage 3). The ultimate goal is to understand customer value management as a long-term strategy and enter stage 4. Few companies in this industry have attained this stage of quality.[13]

To implement a customer value management strategy, firms must understand all drivers that contribute to value creation. A model from the box-manufacturing market regarding print equipment suppliers found that eight quality factors (product and service indicators such as product support, maintenance, installation, special features, etc.) predicted 54% of total value, and the communicators—image (20%) and price (26%)—accounted for the balance of value creation. Overall, this model explained an impressive 82% of variance.[14]

Integrating the voice of the customer ensures a practice known as quality function deployment (QFD). This process needs to precede new product or service introductions in order to ensure design quality. QFD enables companies to identify and prioritize customer needs and respond to them effectively. Toyota improved its rust-prevention record from being one of the worst to one of the best in the world by coordinating design and production decisions to focus on this key customer concern. The importance of each design dimension varies by product (or service). For example, aesthetics would be less important for Dell Computers, which sells direct via the phone or Internet. The goal of QFD is to determine not only *what* customers want, but which product or service attributes are most important to them.

Along the same lines, customers prefer to conduct business with companies whose quality levels are consistent, i.e., with little or no variation. Six Sigma is a methodology consisting of analytically based practices and procedures aimed at eliminating variation in any process. A six sigma process—producing only 3.4

defects per million opportunities—was introduced in manufacturing: It was pioneered by Motorola and made famous by GE. According to Gregory Watson, a consultant and past president of the American Society for Quality, "Six Sigma might be the maturation of everything we learned over the last 100 years about quality." Six Sigma involves a five-step approach:

1. *Define* the process.
2. *Measure* it to obtain a performance baseline.
3. *Analyze* the data to determine where errors are occurring.
4. *Improve* the process.
5. *Control* it to ensure the errors do not recur.

Many Six Sigma efforts are too internally focused, where such internal improvements will never positively affect the customer.[15]

The importance of the concept of the Six Sigma process in quality improvement is not limited to manufacturing, however. Services and transactions can also benefit from Six Sigma principles. For example, Starwood Hotels & Resorts introduced a comprehensive six sigma program for all of their hotel properties. The focus of the program is to deliver consistent and exemplary service to their guests worldwide. From the reservation and check-in process, to room standards and cleanliness, Starwood's goal in implementing Six Sigma is to provide each guest with a flawless experience during each and every visit.

Wellmark Inc., a Des Moines managed-care company, significantly reduced the time it took to add a new doctor to Blue Cross & Blue Shield medical plans, slashing the time to 30 days from 65 days or more. When Wellmark applied the Six Sigma analytical tools, they found that half the processes they performed were redundant.

Managing Service Quality

For many years, most managers associated quality with manufactured goods. However, during the 1980s, a broadened definition of quality emerged to include services as well as goods. Defining quality for services is more difficult than for products due to the intangible, variable nature of service characteristics.

Furthermore, unlike product quality, consumers frequently lack the necessary information to evaluate service quality. For example, consumers of durable goods such as cars or major appliances often conduct research before making a purchase, allowing them to use *search quality* prior to the purchase. Moreover, consumers can also use *experience quality*, based on postpurchase evaluation of the product, to determine whether their expectations were met.

With services, however, consumers are usually limited to using *credence quality* to evaluate the experience, relying solely on the overall credibility of the service provider. A consumer receiving legal services or medical treatments has little basis from which to judge the quality, other than the reputation of the law firm or medical facility. Here consumers are not always sure what to expect and may not know for some time, if ever, whether the outcome was performed satisfactorily. These factors make it more difficult for consumers to evaluate services in advance while at the same time creating greater risk. Managers can help reduce this risk by providing information that helps customers evaluate alternatives before the purchase as well as provide documentation of the firm's service reputation.

Service Delivery Stages—From Pre- to Postsale

Another challenge presented in assessing service quality arises when viewing services along a continuum ranging from presale to postsale activities. Figure 5.3 shows the progression of these activities and where the potential for service failures may occur in the process.

Presale services: Provide valuable information that prospects can later use to choose a product or service (i.e., brokerage house putting portfolio planning software online to help prospects or customers chart their financial future; hotel that calls guests prior to arriving).

Transaction services: How effectively and efficiently service was delivered—speed and convenience of completing the transaction. (Amazon.Com utilizes "collaborative filtering" software to identify past customers and allow for "one-click" shopping; Microsoft has introduced an electronic purchasing service called PASSPORT ["wallet technology"] allowing customers to enter credit card and shipping information only once.)

Postsale transactions: Service after the sale.

For example, a brokerage house might offer free seminars on estate planning as part of presale services, providing valuable information that participants can later use when choosing a particular investment plan. Lincoln Suites Hotel proactively manages presale services by calling its guests several days before their scheduled arrival date, confirming their arrival and departure dates, the number of people in

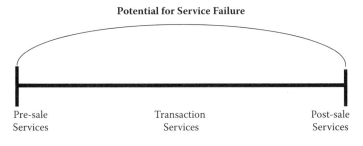

Figure 5.3   Continuum of services.

the party, smoking/nonsmoking preferences, directions to the hotel, etc. This attention to detail prior to check-in minimizes hassles later and eases travel anxiety by addressing last-minute concerns. By the same token, firms risk alienating prospects by poorly handling presale services. Most of us have experienced the frustration of calling a firm's toll-free line only to be placed on "endless hold" or to get trapped in the "voice-mail maze."

Customers also form perceptions of quality during the *service transaction*— how effectively and efficiently the service was delivered and the speed and convenience of completing the transaction. Anyone who has purchased a product over the phone has experienced the frustration when the "computers go down" and processing the order and payment grinds to halt. Amazon.com has revolutionized online buying and flawlessly handles customer purchase transactions. For starters, it builds customer profiles by preference with each visit, recommending products within categories and sending e-mails to prompt browsing. Most importantly, it gives the customer a sense of power over the entire retail transaction, from initial entry to random search to final selection and ordering. There is no need to supply your name, address, and credit card number each time you shop, either, as Amazon creates a user profile from your initial visit.

Finally, customers evaluate support activities that occur after the transaction, that is *postsale services.* Joe Girard, who holds the Guinness Book of World Records for most retail automobile sales, believes that when a customer returns with a complaint or needs service, the service provider should drop everything and make sure that the customer gets the best service available. He maintains that "the sale begins after the sale." He is also known for sending out birthday cards to his customers every year. Sales follow-up in the form of phone calls, letters, or cards show a genuine concern for the customer and lead to repeat business and business loyalty. Phil Breslin, a Domino's Pizza franchisee in Baltimore, required his store managers to make customer calls at the end of each business day, even if that means letting close-outs wait until the next business day. These examples demonstrate a commitment to build repeat business through effective postsale follow-up.

In most cases, a well-run organization should have few service problems, since service delivery is a controllable variable. Nonetheless, occasional service failures will occur even in the best-managed companies. The effective handling of service complaints can strengthen customer bonds with the firm. Customers form perceptions of fairness when assessing service-recovery initiatives. Outcome, procedural, and interactional fairness explain 85% of the variation in satisfaction with complaint handling. A General Motors vice president of sales, service, and marketing said it best: "The goal is to fix both the car and the customer."[16]

SERVQUAL and Gap Analysis

Generally, a user of services has a set of attributes or characteristics in mind when judging service quality. Via an extensive research program, Parasuraman, Zeithaml, and Berry found that customers assessed service quality using the following five major dimensions[17] (note that this is a reduced set from their original list of 10 SERVQUAL factors):

- *Reliability*: Ability to perform the promised service dependably and accurately
- *Responsiveness*: Willingness to help customers and provide prompt service
- *Assurance*: Knowledge and courtesy of employees and ability to inspire trust and confidence
- *Tangibles*: Physical facilities, equipment, and appearance of personnel
- *Empathy*: Caring, individualized attention that the firm provides to customers

Research on the relative importance of these dimensions found that reliability was consistently the most critical dimension, followed next by responsiveness, with empathy being the least important.[18]

Parasuraman and his colleagues found that service quality is a measure between *service perceptions* as well as *expectations*. Service quality stems from a comparison of what a consumer feels a service firm *should* offer (desires or wants) versus the perception of what the service firm actually *does* offer. Thus, ensuring good service quality involves meeting or exceeding consumers' expectations. Hence, *service quality is a measure of the difference between service expectations and the experience*. This research team further determined that customer perceptions are influenced by a series of "gaps," which are presented in Table 5.2. The task of managers is to "close the gaps" using the following recommended strategies:

- GAP 1 (Research): Learn what the customer values, and values most, using such tools as benchmarking, quality function deployment, and competitive analysis.
- GAP 2 (Planning): Design a proper system using blueprinting and other quality tools such as fishbone diagrams.
- GAP 3 (Implementation): Ensure good employee-job fit, foster teamwork, provide employees with the appropriate tools or technology to form the job, create a work environment where employees feel "in control," and introduce good supervisory control systems (i.e., appraisal and formal/informal feedback procedures are in place).
- GAP 4 (Communications): Provide accurate information by informing customers of true level of service they can expect and holding to those pledges.

Parasuraman, Zeithaml, and Berry later operationalized these gaps in the form of SERVQUAL, a 21-item instrument that evaluates both expectations and customer perceptions of the service encounter. Their measurement scales also reflected the respondent's "zone of tolerance" or the range of the company's performance between "acceptable" and "desired" service levels.[19]

SERVQUAL can serve as an effective diagnostic tool for uncovering broad areas of a company's service quality shortfalls and strengths.[20] For example, a

Table 5.2 Service Quality Gaps

Service Quality Gap	Definition
1. Research gap	Managers have difficulty in translating customer requirements into service quality specifications or precise performance standards.
2. Planning and design gap	Performance standards and specifications (as well as systems) don't always measure up to what the customer expects.
3. Implementation gap	Discrepancy between service quality specifications and the *delivery* of service performance in accordance with those specifications. Affected by job design, employee selection/development, perceived control by the employee, and low role ambiguity and role conflict.
4. External communications gap	Discrepancy between the level of service quality delivered and the communication of that delivery to the customer (i.e., overpromising and underdelivering).

Source: A. Parasuraman, V. Zeithaml, and L. Berry, "A Conceptual Model of Service Quality and Its Implications for Future Research," *Journal of Marketing* 49 (Fall 1985), 41–50.

study of Indonesian hotel guests found that the managerial perceptions of value delivered had no relationship with the actual customer value received as experienced by the customers. Hotel management may be investing in capabilities that they believe customers want but do not value and fail to provide the benefits sought by guests.[21]

The SERVQUAL scale also offers the potential to determine the relative importance of the five major service quality dimensions and to track service quality performance over time. The scale serves as a suitable generic measure of service quality, transcending specific functions, companies, and industries. Service quality ratings are obtained from the scale when consumers compare their service expectations with actual service performance on distinct service dimensions—reliability, responsiveness, assurance, empathy, and tangibles. Poor service quality results when perceived performance ratings are lower than expectations, where as the reverse indicates good service quality.

Explicating Service Quality

Service quality can also be defined according to both the *what* and the *how* a product or service is delivered. Grönroos distinguishes between "technical quality" and "functional quality."[22] Technical quality is concerned with the outcome of the delivered product or service, such as a restaurant meal that is well prepared or an acceptable haircut or styling. Customers use service quality attributes such as reliability, competence, performance, durability, etc., to evaluate technical quality. For example, when bringing a laptop computer in for repair, the customer would expect the computer to be properly serviced, eliminating the problem and preventing it from occurring again.

Functional quality has more to do with how the technical quality is transferred to the consumer. Back to our computer example, the customer would expect not only competence and accuracy in the repair, but also that the service personnel were helpful and courteous. Service quality attributes such as responsiveness and access would be important in helping the customer judge the functional quality of the service encounter.

Service quality can also be judged by considering the various "spheres" or thresholds of the service offering, as presented in Figure 5.4.

The *core benefit* is the most fundamental level for which the service offering stands, that is, it is what the consumer is actually seeking. The core benefit represents basic reasons why people buy, such as hunger, safety, convenience, confidence, status, self-esteem, and so on. Grönroos uses the term *service concept* to indicate the core of a service offering, such as offering a car rental as a solution to a short-term transportation need.[23]

The *hygiene factors* constitute the minimally acceptable level of service attributes that customers would expect to be present in the service offering. For example,

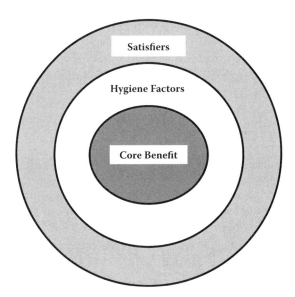

Figure 5.4   Levels of service.

a midpriced hotel catering to business travelers would be expected to offer such services as express checkout, fitness room, high-speed Internet connections, a restaurant, and a lounge. Failure to offer these services or to perform or deliver them poorly will likely lead to dissatisfaction. In contrast, simply offering these services and performing them adequately will not delight the customer—the customer expects them as part of doing business.

Truly delighting customers requires service providers to carefully consider *satisfiers*. Satisfiers are those service attributes that both differentiate the service firm from its competitors, while at the same time exceeding customer expectations in one or more areas of service, by delivering above what is expected. According to Naumann, hygiene factors need to be delivered at an acceptable level before satisfiers become important.[24] Satisfiers have the potential to create high customer satisfaction levels once expectations on hygiene factors have been met. Firms that would offer satisfiers need to consider the value-added services that would both delight and surprise the customer.

Consider some of the following examples in the effective use of satisfiers. Before a guest ever sets foot in Le Parker Meridian Hotel in New York, he or she can use the hotel's QuickTime Virtual Reality (QTVR) enabling potential guests to "walk" through the lobby and rooms. In addition to virtual-reality tours, the site offers in-depth, timely information about room rates, events, and points of interest for the business and pleasure traveler. The hotel also welcomes repeat guests with amenity baskets accompanied by handwritten notes.

Finally, it should be emphasized that quality is more than simply meeting specifications and that the customer's point of view on quality is key. That is, *quality is what the customer says it is*. Remember, it is the customer, not the company, that sets the quality and value agenda. The losers in the quality battle will be those who attempt to "do things right," while the winners will be the organizations that learn to do the "right things."[25]

Improving Service Quality

Enhancing quality is a lot like taking vitamins, eating healthy, and exercising regularly. Although the results may not be immediate, the long-term benefits are significant. Quality is not a "quick fix" nor the "program of the month," but rather a *way of life* for companies who are serious about improvement (see Customer Value Checklist 5 for help in diagnosing service quality problems).

Quality, as we have already seen, is fundamental to creating value, yet it is a moving target and must meet customers' current definition of quality. Thus, the following set of 10 recommendations as ways for improving service quality and ultimately delivering superior customer value are offered:

- Design services in cooperation with customers. Learn what customers truly value by incorporating the "voice of the customer" earlier in the service development process. Also, it is important to not only determine customers' service attributes, but their *relative importance* as well.
- Focus your improvement programs outward, on market "break points." Only by defining these episodes where the customer comes in contact with the organization and focusing on the ones most critical can you see things as the customer sees them. Also, visualize the complete sequence of moments-of-truth a customer experiences in getting some need met. Remember, the customer sees service in terms of a total experience, not an isolated set of activities. Mapping the service cycle helps companies see these activities as the customer sees them.
- Create a tangible representation of service quality. Hotels and restaurants often advertise and display on their properties ratings by one of the major motor clubs, such as AAA or Mobil Oil. Hertz #1 Club Gold service communicates a premium, value-added bundle of services to business travelers seeking a hassle-free car rental experience.
- Use teamwork to promote service excellence. Service workers who support one another and achieve together can avoid service burnout.
- Create a "service-bias" based on each of the following service quality determinants: professionalism, attitudes/behaviors, accessibility and flexibility, reliability/trustworthiness, service recovery, and reputation/credibility. These criteria can be used as guidelines for influencing positive service quality perceptions.
- Develop proper measurements. Use metrics that are specific in nature, such as a 95% on-time delivery, customer wait time, or order processing time. Benchmark the "best practices" for each service area being measured, such as wait time or order delivery.
- Employee selection, job design, and training are absolutely crucial to building customer satisfaction and service quality. Structure the job of service workers that maximizes their ability to respond quickly and competently to customer needs. Also, train service personnel in areas of service delivery and attitude. Role-play different service scenarios, showing various service-recovery strategies. Provide service workers with some basic tools, such as those discussed in Chapter 3, to help control service quality variation and uncover service problems.
- Reward total quality efforts in marketing. Look for opportunities to reinforce quality behaviors when they occur. Employees should be rewarded on the basis of these behaviors (commitment, effort) rather than strictly on outcomes, such as sales quotas. Rewarding a salesperson for meeting or exceeding quota with a bonus while giving a nominal award such as a pin or plaque to the person who fixes the product or process sends a clear message about the company's true concept of quality.

■ Think of service as a process, not a series of functions. Service quality occurs when the entire service experience is managed and the organization is aligned to respond accordingly.

■ Integrate customer information across sales channels. Regardless of which channel a customer uses to contact the firm, the information made available to online and offline customer service representatives should be consistent.

Customer Value Checklist 5: Probing for Service Quality Improvement

1. Does your company do a good job of *listening* to its customers? Give a specific example of how listening resulted in improved service quality to your customers.

2. *Reliability* is the ability of the company to perform the promised services dependably and accurately. On a 10-point scale, where 1 is unreliable and 10 is perfectly reliable, where along this scale would you place your company and why?

3. How well does your company perform the *service basics*, that is, knowing and responding to the fundamental service expectations in your industry (e.g., an automobile service department that "fixes the car right the first time")?

4. How effectively does your company manage the *service design* elements-systems, people, and the physical environment? Provide an example of how lack of planning in one of these areas resulted in a "fail point" during a customer encounter.

5. *Service recovery* refers to how effectively companies respond to service failures. Cite an example of when a service failure occurred in your company and how it was handled.

6. *Teamwork* is an important dynamic in sustaining service workers' motivation to serve and in minimizing service-performance shortfalls. Rate your company on its ability to foster teamwork on a scale of 1 to 10, where 1 indicates the absence of teamwork and 10 indicates maximum teamwork. How would you improve teamwork if you rated your company low on this attribute?

7. *Internal service* is crucial to service improvement, as customer satisfaction often mirrors employee satisfaction. To what extent does your company assess internal service quality (i.e., asking employees about the adequacy

of systems to support the service, how they interact and serve one another, and where service failures are occurring)? Give examples of how internal service might be measured in your company.

Summary

The modern quality revolution, which began in Japan in the early 1950s and was exported to the United States during the 1980s, has forever changed how corporations and institutions are managed. The sheer size of the service economy, competing demands on scarce resources, and more-demanding customers force management to place greater emphasis on creating high-quality customer experiences. Competing in a global economy requires firms to understand what "world-class" service really means. The challenge facing firms today is to know their customer's definition of service quality and how to deliver that at a reasonable cost—in short, how to create superior customer value. In this chapter, we have discussed various types of services, the idea of cocreation of value, customer service research, quality concepts, building a service-centered organization, how to assess service quality, and practical strategies for improving service quality.

Customer Value Action Items

1. Why has quality become such a priority today? What are some of the "common denominators" in the definition of quality?
2. What is meant by cocreating value in service markets? Using a cafe, explain how service quality can be managed effectively via input from customers and companies. Then, provide another example of cocreation in practice.
3. How does your company's current service mix create value for customers? What new service products should be introduced that your firm does not offer? Are there new types of value providers (adders) that your organization should employ to do a better job of serving customers?
4. Determine the extent of *search quality*, *experience quality*, and *credence quality* for each of the following situations:
   a. Buying a personal computer
   b. Applying to graduate school
   c. Setting up a retirement program
   d. Dining at a local restaurant
   e. Visiting a theme park
5. Suppose you were interested in purchasing personal tax preparation software. Give examples of how service failures could occur during presale, transaction, and postsale phases of the buying process.

6. Suppose you were managing a midpriced hotel catering to business travelers. Determine the key factors for assessing service quality; also, suppose you were a customer of that same hotel. What factors would you use to judge service quality? Rank your choices for each situation and then compare the two lists.

7. Provide examples of how service quality and customer service training is important to a business's success in the following situations:
   a. Professional service
   b. Business service
   c. Consumer service
   d. Online service

8. Service encounters are the means that customers use to assess the functional quality of a firm's value offering. Every service encounter consists of a repeatable sequence of events in which the firm's service personnel attempt to meet the customer's needs and expectations at every potential point of contact. The *cycle of service* begins with the very first point of contact between the customer and the firm. Further, each point of contact between the customer and the company has the potential to leave an impression, either positive or negative. When these *moments of truth* go unmanaged, according to Albrecht and Zemke, "The quality of service regresses to mediocrity."[26] The metaphor of the *moment of truth* is a very powerful idea for helping service businesses shift their points of view and think like a customer. These *moments of truth* represent the times and places where service firms evidence their service competency or lack of it. Consider the cycle of service for a drugstore visit, which might include the following episodes: (a) parking the car, (b) entering the store, (c) getting a shopping basket, (d) selecting a few over-the-counter remedies, (e) requesting help from a clerk, (f) waiting in line at the pharmacy, (g) talking to the pharmacist about a medication, (h) paying for the items selected. Think about a typical service experience (e.g., dry cleaner, movies, fast-food meal, haircut, airline) and diagram the cycle of service. Also, give examples of potential moments of truth and the potential effect on service quality perceptions. Finally, recommend strategies to effectively manage those moments of truth.

Chapter 6

Price and Image— The Communicators

Price is what you pay. Value is what you get.

Warren Buffett

I want Virgin to be as well known around the world as Coca-Cola.

Sir Richard Branson

Price and image express value to potential customers. Just as a traffic light indicates go, slow, or stop, price and image communicates higher quality or economy class. Marketers use these two components of the value proposition to signal value for their products or services, differentiate their offerings from competitors, or shift customer demand.

Priceline has revolutionized the pricing of airline tickets and hotel rooms by allowing prospective customers to announce what they are willing to pay and then alerting them whether or not their bid was accepted. In the marketspace, especially in reverse auctions, price functions as part of a demand-collection system. Customers bid on a unit of demand, and sellers then decide whether or not to fill that demand. A key part of Priceline's success has been built on entertaining television commercials featuring its celebrity spokesperson, William Shatner (formerly Captain Kirk of *Star Trek* fame), who is known as the Negotiator.

Product and service quality greatly influence buyers' perceptions of value. Customercentric companies recognize that value is not just providing the best price.

This chapter examines how customers view and evaluate price—the "give" component of the value equation. Price is considered in the context of a company's overall marketing strategy. Six different approaches to pricing are discussed as well as principles that lead to better pricing decisions. The chapter then explores the image dimension: specifically, defining corporate image, factors that impact image and how to manage it effectively, image-based differentiation and positioning, and what it means to be a "cool" company.

How Price Relates to Value

Customers consider price as a cue of how much they have to give up to acquire the possession or use of the service. Competitors view price as a signal to match, beat, or use as a weapon to block another company's entry. A pricing strategy can help penetrate an existing market, such as the approach AT&T took to enter the credit card market, initially offering its card at no annual fee for life.

Prices are often determined based on the type of purchase. Big-ticket items such as automobiles, furniture, and high-end electronics are often subject to some price flexibility. Negotiated prices are even more common in business-to-business settings: case in point, advertising media, telecommunications, and consulting services. Today, managers set prices for goods and services before consumers and businesses ever meet. Marketers often consider costs, customer demand, and competition (the 3Cs)—the hallmarks of value pricing—before arriving at a final price. This does not imply that pricing has become an exact science. Price is often set based on convention or rules of thumb, or even intuition about what the customer will (or should) pay. Regardless of whether price is viewed as an art or science, the price set is only as good as the value delivered to the customer.

In today's competitive markets, companies cannot afford to neglect sound pricing practices. In a study of 10 product categories for engineering raw materials, industrial buyers ranked price as the second most-important factor (behind quality and ahead of reliable and speedy delivery and service) when selecting a new supplier. A large majority (71%) of the respondents stated that a lower price may prompt a change in a supplier for a finishing service.[1]

Setting the right price can often make or break the bottom line, especially for new products and services. Although most companies view price decisions as important, prices are often set on purely tactical grounds or in response to a competitor's move. Instead of simply a knee-jerk response to market conditions, pricing decisions should be made based on segmentation research, cost-benefit analyses, demand elasticities, and the firm's overall value proposition (see Chapter 4).

Value is often misunderstood to mean low price or bundled price. Yet, the essence of customer value revolves around the trade-off between the benefits buyers receive from a product or service and the price that they pay for the offering.

From a customer's standpoint, price only has meaning when paired with the benefits delivered, both tangible and psychic. For a given price, value increases when product or service benefits increase. For example, Men's Warehouse, a retailer of men's suits based in Fremont, California, offers low prices on brand-name men's suits, but also offers free pressing for as long as their customers own their suit, sport coat, or trousers.

By the same token, value decreases when the perceived benefits package goes down relative to price. Many companies were initially attracted to managed health care because of its ability to control skyrocketing health-care costs. Yet, despite the cost savings, employees of these companies became frustrated by the loss of control over their medical destiny, i.e., reduced choice of physicians and reductions in certain types of care normally available under traditional fee-for-service coverage. These managed-care companies were shortsighted by equating price to value.

Moreover, consumer value assessments are often comparative. Value judgments by consumers as to the worth and desirability of the product or service are made relative to competitive substitutes that satisfy the same need. Hewlett-Packard, one of world's largest high-tech companies, successfully introduced a line of Photosmart digital photography gear that pitted them against Kodak, Canon, Fuji, and other industry leaders. HP has been a pioneer in the digital imaging technology market, turning its gear into a "home digital darkroom" comprising printers, scanners, cameras, and papers that enable users to produce true-to-life prints to rival anything from a photo lab.

The price of perceived product or service substitutes also go into consumers' evaluation of value. A great measure of success in cell phone retailing by T-Mobile and Metro PSC is due to their value-pricing strategy. In contrast, Verizon is the market leader due to service, and AT&T's product dominance was largely due to its once exclusive iPhone affiliation. Thus, consumers determine a product or service's value based on a company's perceived benefits and price as well as those from a competitor's offer.

About Reference Prices

Buyers often use price as a perceptual cue to indicate the product or service quality. That is, all things being equal, the higher price, the higher the perceived quality. Historically, product quality has been treated as the mirror image of price. This is still particularly the case when the brand is relatively unfamiliar to the buyer, such as with medical-related products. The quality-price link also tends to be stronger for durable goods than for nondurable goods, such as major appliances or furniture.[2]

Buyers also use "frames of reference" to evaluate prices. Reference prices are any price set against which other observed prices are evaluated.[3] Reference prices may be internal, stored in the consumer's memory to serve as a basis for judging or comparing actual prices. Consumers store, retrieve, and use a rich array of price information in making price judgments. These internal benchmark prices are influenced by the product's perceived quality and by previously acquired information based either on prior purchasing situations or on advertising cues. Consumers approach purchase situations with a target price (usually a range) in mind and react positively or negatively when price deviations fall within or outside the zone of acceptance. Thus, the challenge for marketing managers is to determine what that acceptable range is and set prices accordingly. Sellers can enhance buyers' value perceptions by comparing a lower selling price to a higher advertised reference price. Sears does this effectively with their good, better, and best price philosophy.

Reference prices may also be external, determined in the presence of marketing stimuli, such as point-of-purchase shelf tags indicating suggested retail price or the price of another product against which price is compared. For example, it is not uncommon for stores selling private-label brands to encourage shoppers to compare the house brand with the nationally advertised brand. Sellers can also create value for their customers by showing the "suggested retail price" alongside the sale price. Buyers respond favorably to this approach as long as the suggested retail price is not inflated. Furniture retailers have been attacked for misleading and deceptive advertising practices, advertising furniture at bogus discount prices which in actuality were the everyday list price.

Strategic Pricing

Intelligent pricing (or the lack thereof) determines winners and losers in a host of competitive markets such as airlines, fast food, and telecommunications. Price is a critical element of a company's marketing mix and is the only one that directly generates revenue. It seems that most companies react rather than proactively manage their businesses, which would necessarily lead to more profitable pricing. Strategic pricing involves managing customers' expectations in order to encourage them to pay for the value they receive.[4] Yet, price cannot be considered apart from the other marketing mix variables, given their interdependence, and thus must be viewed in the context of the overall marketing strategy. Too often, pricing is treated as a tactical response in the marketplace instead of part of a well-integrated marketing strategy. Pricing initiatives, like all other marketing tools, need to be strategically integrated with all other brand messages in order to send customers and potential customers a coherent, meaningful statement.[5]

Moreover, the price established needs to be consistent with the company's overall value proposition. Target Stores is a good example of pricing that aligns with the company's value proposition (Expect More, Pay Less). Target's typical customers are more upscale than those of Walmart, and its stores offer exclusive products like fashion and housewares by noted designers such as Isaac Mizrahi, Liz Lange, Mossimo, and Rachael Ray. Target now sells midmarket varietals from many of the world's leading wineries, even featuring its own sommelier. These wines, priced between $7 and $12, are in keeping with Target's "cheap chic" image.

Price also tends to be managed by functions within organizations, such as finance or sales, who frequently have their own agendas and conflicting views with marketing. Because of these competing agendas, companies end up with a pricing policy that bears little or no connection to marketing. For example, the sales staff may want authority to cut special deals, while marketing wants to retain a high-price, high-quality image. University recruiters may admit students that do not meet the prescribed academic standards. Surprisingly, most companies do not manage pricing cross-functionally even though pricing can have a much greater bottom-line impact than other marketing initiatives.

Firms can become more strategic in their pricing decisions by considering the following four points:

- *Prepare a value map.* A value map shows the value position of each competitor in a market by comparing relative price to relative quality. A value map represents a powerful tool for comparing value positions with an industry, suggesting strategic shifts in either price or quality, depending on the company's perceived location on the map. The "market wants" line (or fair-value line) represents a trade-off between quality and price that customers are prepared to accept. Note that as long as congruence exists between each competitor's price and relative quality, their position (on the market-wants line) and market share will be unchanged. Price and quality are the leverageable factors depending on the market wants. For example, a competitor can shift its relative position in an innovation-driven market, i.e., moving to the right of the market-wants line, by building a strategy to increase relative quality.[6]
- *Relate pricing to the target market's demand elasticity.* A given industry such as airlines or hotels comprise customer segments with varying degrees of price sensitivity. The challenge for management is to determine the price floor and the price ceiling of the offering along with the price-value segments in the middle. For example, airlines use very sophisticated "yield-management" systems to not only manage seat inventory, but to customize prices to match demand. This use of revenue management ensures that companies will sell the right product to the right consumer at the right time for the right price. The premise here is that no two customers value the product or service in exactly the same way. For example, leisure travelers and business travelers may be buying a ticket on the same flight, but they pay widely different fares. Leisure travelers are willing to book well in advance and are flexible on schedule, but are not willing to pay as much as business travelers, who book on short notice with little flexibility in scheduling, yet are less price sensitive.
- *Make your pricing strategy reflect the perceived value of the service, not simply delivered value.* For example, Bugs Burger Bugs Killer (BBBK), a pest control

company, is able to charge many times that of other firms serving the commercial property industry by focusing on a segment of the market that is not price sensitive, i.e., hotels and restaurants. BBBK meets a critical need of these establishments: pest elimination rather than simply pest control. This segment will assign such a high importance to the guarantee that price becomes almost irrelevant when they assess the value of the offering

■ *Assign price-setting responsibility to a dedicated staff function.* Choose someone with a "blended" background in marketing/sales, finance, and economics to head up the department. Give this person the latitude to coordinate with other departments in aligning price as an overall business strategy. Continental Airlines assigns a high priority to pricing, having a created a position called senior vice-president of pricing and revenue management. Other industries such as telecommunications, services, and pharmaceuticals are already experimenting with this approach.[7]

Pricing Methods

The purpose of this section is not to review all the possible pricing methods, but to discuss those that are truly customer oriented and value creating. Many traditional pricing methods are either cost or profit driven. Cost-driven methods seek to recover a reasonable return over the product's full cost. Profit-driven pricing attempts to maximize profitability by making trade-offs between price changes and changes in sales volume. Value-driven companies may use any of the following six market-based pricing approaches:

■ Price-driven costing
■ Demand-based pricing
■ Value-based pricing
■ Price customization
■ Psychological pricing
■ Price differentiation

Price-driven costing involves setting a price by starting with the estimated price customers are willing to pay and working backwards from this price specification. This requires the firm to "figure out" how to get the costs down to sell the product or service at the price customers are willing to pay for an appropriate package of features while allowing for a reasonable profit. Apple used this strategy when revamping its iPod/iTouch product line.

Demand-based pricing requires that price be set based on an estimate of volume that can be sold at different prices, based on market conditions, purchase situation, and price sensitivity. In certain situations, customers are sensitive to price increases, especially when their purchasing power has eroded. The price for Super

Bowl tickets or a pay-per-view fight will often vary based on the teams and the fighters, respectively. Airline pricing is often subject to the "Southwest effect" or the substantial reduction (20%–50% or more) in fares that occurs when Southwest enters a new market. Each of these examples demonstrates that price is often set based on what the market will bear.

Value-based pricing involves adjusting the value equation either by lowering prices or raising quality, or both. One of the keys to profitable marketing is setting a price that is commensurate with the value the customer actually receives. IKEA sets price to reflect and capture customer value. Its prices are quite affordable for quality home furnishings. Trade-offs such as assembly and delivery by the customer keep prices down, while the perceived image (Scandinavian quality furniture) is relatively high.

Value pricing can be reinforced by using service guarantees. For example, Hampton Inn will refund a guest's money if for any reason they were unhappy with their hotel room. Berry and Yadav also recommend using relationship pricing, such as offering "price bundling" by selling two or more services together at a cost lower than if the individual services were purchased separately.[8] Comcast, AT&T, and other telecommunication firms are now offering bundled offerings consisting of telephone service, Internet access, and cable TV for a set price.

Value pricing is often associated with low prices, such as McDonald's extra-value meals or dollar menu. Managers using value pricing need to educate the customer to redefine value from its current perception of inexpensive. A useful tool for guiding value pricing is the price-value grid, which helps firms determine the efficacy of their value pricing. As Figure 6.1 illustrates, this grid is defined along the price/quality dimensions, the cornerstones of value creation. A firm offering a

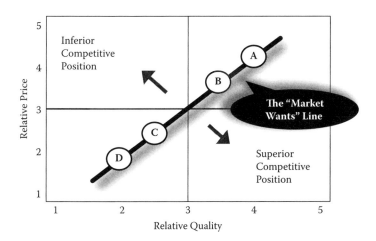

Figure 6.1   Price-value grid.

high-quality offering at low prices would possess a strong value proposition, e.g., Walmart selling well-known brands at everyday low prices or Southwest Airlines offering reliable and enjoyable air travel at extremely affordable prices. Firms whose offerings have low perceived quality at high prices would represent a poor or troubled value proposition. People in many local communities view cable service as a "poor value" due to regular price increases with limited measurable improvement in programming quality. This value proposition puts firms at a major competitive disadvantage if reasonable substitutes are available. The point here is that value pricing will be effective to the extent that both price and quality are considered in tandem. Customer Value Checklist 6 provides guidance to firms considering value pricing by providing managers with a set of six key questions to ask.[9]

Price customization (also known as discriminatory pricing), which may be a form of price discrimination, occurs when the company seeks to modify its price to accommodate differences in customers, locations, and the manner or time in which the product or service is used. As indicated earlier, the airline companies are masters at price customization, using data-driven tools to wring out as much revenue as possible from each flight. A humorous view of airline pricing is captured in Figure 6.2.

Customer Value Checklist 6: A Value Pricing Framework[*]

1. What is the market strategy for the segment?
2. What is the differential advantage that is transparent to the customer?
3. What is the price of the next best offering?
4. What is the cost of the supplier's market offering?
5. What pricing tactics will be used initially or eventually?
6. What is the customer's expectation of a "fair price"?

Price customization—selling the same products to different buyers at different prices—is a legal practice as long as it does not have a negative effect on competition (price is set in "good faith" to meet the competition; price reflects different uses of the product or distribution in different markets or sales at different points in time). Price customization is often based on the type of customer being served. For example, seniors or children frequently receive discounts at restaurants and

---

[*] *Source*: Anderson et al. 2010.

Buying Paint From a Hardware Store

Customer: Hi, how much is your paint?

Clerk: We have regular quality, which is $12 a gallon and premium for $18. How many gallons would you like?

Customer: Five gallons of regular quality, please.

Clerk: Great. That will be $60, plus tax.

Buying Paint From an Airline

Customer: Hi, how much is your paint?

Clerk: Well, sir, that all depends.

Customer: Depends on what?

Clerk: Actually, a lot of things.

Customer: How about giving me an average price?

Clerk: Wow, that's too hard a question. The lowest price is $9 a gallon, and we have 180 different prices up to $200 a gallon.

Customer: What's the difference in the paint?

Clerk: Oh, there isn't any difference; it's all the same paint.

Customer: Well, then, I'd like some of that $9 paint.

Clerk: Well, first I need to ask you a few questions. When do you intend to use it?

Customer: I want to paint tomorrow, on my day off.

Clerk: Sir, the paint for tomorrow is the $200 paint.

Customer: What? When would I have to paint in order to get the $9 version?

Clerk: That would be in three weeks, but you will also have to agree to start painting before Friday of that week and continue painting until at least Sunday.

Customer: You've got to be kidding!

Clerk: Sir, we don't kid around here. Of course, I'll have to check to see if we have any of that paint available before I can sell it to you.

Customer: What do you mean check to see if you can sell it to me? You have shelves full of that stuff; I can see it right there.

Clerk: Just because you can see it doesn't mean that we have it. It may be the same paint, but we sell only a certain number of gallons on any given week. Oh, and by the way, the price just went to $12.

Customer: You mean the price went up while we were talking?

Figure 6.2 If Airlines Sold Paint. (From Hess, A.H. 1998. Bountiful, UT: Hess Travel.)

Clerk: Yes, sir. You see, we change prices and rules thousands of times a day, and since you haven't actually walked out of the store with your paint yet, we just decided to change. Unless you want the same thing to happen again, I would suggest that you get on with your purchase. How many gallons do you want?

Customer: I don't know exactly. Maybe five gallons. Maybe I should buy six gallons just to make sure I have enough.

Clerk: Oh, no, sir, you can't do that. If you buy the paint and then don't use it, you will be liable for penalties and possible confiscation of the paint you already have.

Customer: What?

Clerk: That's right. We can sell you enough paint to do your kitchen, bathroom, hall, and north bedroom, but if you stop painting before you do the bedroom, you will be in violation of our tariffs.

Customer: But what does it matter to your whether I use all the paint? I already paid for it!

Clerk: Sir, there's no point in getting upset; that's just the way it is. We make plans upon the idea that you will use all the paint, and when you don't, it just causes us all sorts of problems.

Customer: This is crazy! I suppose something terrible will happen if I don't keep painting until after Saturday night!

Clerk: Yes, sir, it will.

Customer: Well, that does it! I'm going somewhere else to buy my paint.

Clerk: That won't do you any good, sir. We all have the same rules. Thanks for flying—I mean painting—with our airline.

Figure 6.2 (continued).

entertainment activities. Business travelers pay higher airfares than leisure travelers when taking the same flight. Prices may also be customized based on the channel of delivery. For example, staples such as soft drinks or milk are often priced higher in convenience stores than in supermarkets. Customers sometimes pay higher prices depending on the "urgency" of the purchase, such as when placing rush or custom orders with the seller. Finally, a seller's price may also be determined by time and place. For example, rates for hotel rooms, car rentals, and long-distance telephone calls may all vary depending on the time the service is used. By customizing price, marketers can recognize the convenience that customers incorporate into the perceived value ratio.

The Web is now making the practice of price customization and price discrimination much easier. Computers can now collect and analyze highly detailed data on individual customers as they make their purchases over the Internet or at the cash register. New software will distinguish the thrifty from the spendthrifts and price accordingly. Bill Gates predicts that Web sites will soon recognize individual consumers, remember what they paid for items in the past, and charge them a customized price based on that history. "Sellers will use technology to extract the highest price they can from a particular shopper," Gates wrote recently.

Amazon.com discovered, much to its chagrin, that charging different prices for the same item left customers feeling duped. It occurred when some shoppers in the DVD section of Amazon noticed that prices were not always the same, and soon discovered that, indeed, some shoppers were getting "test" prices. When customers discovered the differential pricing, they flooded chat boards with complaints against the company. Amazon quickly dropped its differential pricing and refunded the difference to customers who paid the higher price. Amazon was trying to gauge what impact price variations have on buying habits, a practice CEO Jeff Bezos referred to as "random pricing."

Psychological pricing implies that a price is a clear signal of quality and that customers respond to various price points. As an example, we frequently see prices for consumer products ending in 5 or 9. Gas stations are notorious for this: It is not $3.79 for a gallon of gas but $3.799. And real estate agents may list the price of a home on sale at $299,950 rather than $300,000 to be "seen" in the $200,000 rather than $300,000 price range.

Realize that price is more than economics (there is a key psychological component to pricing) and is often about positioning a product line in the mind of the customer. A fine restaurant may have a deep wine list with some bottles priced hundreds of dollars. While these rare vintages sell infrequently, they round out the product line. More realistic wine choices for patrons may be built around other price points—for example, house wines, bottles under $20, bottles $20–$50, over $50, etc. Other variants of psychological pricing include odd-even pricing (does a consumer prefer the dollar store or the 99 cents store?), price-lining (limited-price-point options such as a men's apparel store offering $25, $50, or $75 ties), loss leaders (paper towels that are two rolls for a dollar), and bundled pricing discounts (buy two, get one free).

Price differentiation is a pricing approach taken in response to competitive forces. There are four strategic options: beat their price, meet their price, do not compete on price, or retreat due to price. Often the competitive strategy chosen to compete in a given market determines how prices will be established. For example, Walmart has chosen a strategy of "beat their price" in competing in the mass-merchandising industry. Often, price leaders tell us by their name—Budget Rent-A-Car, Costco, Dollar General, PayLess Shoes, and Priceline.com.

Companies may also choose to "meet the price" of their competitors. Office Max offers a low-price guarantee boasting in its ads and on its Web site that it will match any legitimate price deal from a competitor. Airlines typically follow a competitor's move to lower fares in selected destinations. For example, several years ago Southwest Airlines offered a round-trip fare from Baltimore to Los Angeles for $209, compared with a ticket on American Airlines priced as $418. American quickly dropped its price to match Southwest's discounted fare.

Some companies opt for the "not to compete (on price) approach," preferring to compete on nonprice factors instead, such as service. Nordstrom and Ritz-Carlton compete primarily based on their high levels of customer care. Customers appreciate and are willing to pay for the "extra" services they enjoy while patronizing these companies.

Sometimes it does not make sense to compete, either because of the lack of resources or because of scale economies and, thus, firms should "retreat on price." Xerox stopped competing in the financial services market when it was no longer profitable by cutting its losses and exiting the market.

Making Good Pricing Decisions

Pricing decisions draw on many areas of marketing expertise. The pricing decision requires a comprehensive understanding of the forces that shape the market, including competitive interactions, technology, and consumer psychology. Sometimes these forces interact. For instance, customers have learned to anticipate the price reductions that often accompany technological innovation. Yet, it seems that few companies conduct serious pricing research to support effective pricing strategy. One study found that 87% of the companies surveyed had changed prices; however, only 13% of the price changes came as a result of a scheduled review of pricing strategy.[10]

A shift is occurring on how price is determined. The trend is that pricing is moving away from the traditional "cost-plus" heuristic (compute costs and add desired markup) and toward "smart" pricing. For example, the Ford Motor Company's effort to better formulate its pricing began in 1995, when the company experimented with using margins and value-added rather than strictly unit sales as metrics in assessing the effectiveness of its pricing. In addition, research was conducted to identify "features that 'the customer was willing to pay for but the industry was slow to deliver.'" This research helped Ford's decision makers to better understand both demand at different price points and consumer perception of value-added features. As a result, the company slightly reduced prices on higher margin cars (e.g., Crown Victorias and Explorers) producing an increase in unit sales of 600,000. Ford also raised prices on lower-end cars (e.g., Escorts and Aspires), increasing margins although selling 420,000 fewer units. Although Ford lost nearly 2% of market share between 1995 and 1999, earnings during 1999 were $7.2 billion, a new auto industry record. The five regions in which its new pricing strategy was tested beat profit targets by a collective $1 billion.[11]

As Figure 6.3 shows, some of these factors are likely to put downward pressure on prices, such as substitutes, technological advances, price-driven competition, customer experience, and changes in internal forces, such as sales forecasts.

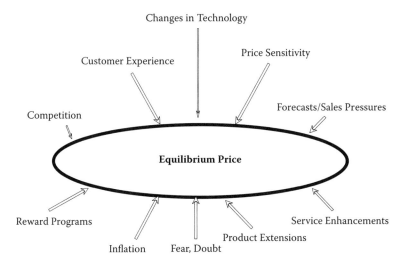

Figure 6.3 Sources of pricing pressures. (Adapted from E. Mitchell [1989], *Marketing News*, November 20, 9.)

Customer experience makes it difficult to raise prices, as repeat customers' ability to perceive incremental value of a company's product/service diminishes over time, especially as substitute or competitive products emerge. Increased internal expectations, in the form of expected sales increases or new budgets, can also send prices on a downward spiral. Customer price sensitivity may also serve to keep prices in check, especially in the presence of available competitive substitutes or among a company's marginal customers.

Even in a deflationary economy, there are opportunities to keep prices from dropping or to even raise prices. For example, product/service enhancements or improvements often warrant maintaining, if not increasing, price due to higher customer perceived value. A case in point: A hotel that offers a new business services center may be able to maintain above-market rates. However, customers must perceive that these enhancements deliver a genuine, meaningful benefit, or they will continue to seek lower-cost alternatives.

Price deflectors, such as loyalty or frequency programs, may effectively insulate a company from destructive price competition. Many airline travelers, especially business travelers, will not select an airline based solely on price, but rather on the mileage program in which they are members.

Finally, business customers who are motivated to reduce risk will not be overly concerned with price as they evaluate the value of a product or service. As we saw earlier, hotels feel that high-priced BBBK offers considerable value. The sighting of an undesirable pest can drive away many profitable guests. Risks may be internal as well as external. In the early days of the PC industry, IT managers often reminded us, "No one ever got fired for buying an IBM," which suggests the importance of FUD (fear, uncertainty, doubt) in buying decisions.

Why Price Cuts Are Seldom the Answer

Firms should be motivated to avoid price decreases that can erode margins and chip away at brand equity. In contrast, well-conceived price increases can have a dramatic impact on the bottom line. According to research by McKinsey & Co., a price rise of 1% at an average company in the S&P 1500 index would generate an 8% increase in operating profit if sales volume stays steady. By contrast, a price discount of 1% reduces profit by 8%. Typically, to offset the impact of a 5% price cut, volume would have to rise by about 19%.[12]

It is quite easy to become seduced by the quick results produced by price discounting and fail to recognize the long-term consequences. Sometimes a firm will try to gain an advantage from being the lowest-price competitor. This advantage disappears if competitors follow with price reductions of their own. Some marketers view this pattern as a form of the "prisoner's dilemma" game. In the classic prisoner's dilemma, if neither prisoner confesses, both go free; however, if only one confesses, he goes free but the other prisoner faces severe consequences. Therefore, each prisoner has to guess what the other will do.

Similarly, in a market with a small number of competitors, each firm must guess how others will respond to a price reduction: If everybody drops their price, all will lose profits. Consider the example of Phillip Morris. Phillip Morris (PM) discovered this when it dropped the price on its leading Marlboro brand. In a sequence of events begun on Marlboro Friday, other cigarette brands also dropped their prices and some discount brands were introduced. As a result, PM's net operating profits dropped by $2.3 billion despite the increase in the brand's market share by 7%.

Discounting as a regular practice is perilous for other reasons as well. Brand loyalty usually suffers when firms engage in regular discounting. Price-seeking customers are rarely loyal, pitting one seller against another. They will maintain repeat patronage only until such time as the next deal is presented. The company unwittingly "prostitutes" the brand to the point where it eventually assumes a commodity status. Perpetual discounting also produces undesirable effects on the brand's image, often cheapening it. Izod Lacoste all but destroyed the brand's cache in the late 1970s by repeatedly discounting the brand. Low prices ultimately made the crocodile logo become an endangered species. Finally, repeated discounting also conditions customers to seek price rather than the *value* of the firm's offer. For example, owners of finicky cats have been conditioned to watch for sales of premium Fancy Feast cat food, and then stock up on the brand. Firms can avoid the pitfalls that are associated with price discounting by better understanding how their customers value different product/service and company attributes. The objective here is to find segments of customers who have problems for which unique and cost-effective solutions can be developed.

Future Pricing Issues

As Woody Allen once said, "The future isn't what it used to be." Well, neither is pricing in today's marketplace. The electronic marketplace is ushering in an era of wide-sweeping changes that will leave no business untouched. Case in point: Smart-phone price-comparison apps have exploded in usage, resulting in a new era of price transparency. For Black Friday, 2010, 5.6% of e-commerce was transacted via mobile devices. According to IE Market Research, cell-phone merchandise purchases in the United States are projected to surpass $50 billion by 2014. Furthermore, 73% of mobile-powered shoppers prefer checking their phone for getting basic assistance rather than talking to a retail clerk.[13]

One of the major results of the digital era will be fluid pricing as never seen before, as prospective buyers can now easily compare products and prices, putting themselves in a much better bargaining position. The more price information diffused across the Internet, the more skillful customers will become at haggling, and the less sellers can defend posted list prices. Today, online auctions let consumers bid on everything from antiques to treadmills. The Internet has made interaction costs so cheap that competitive bidding for everything is now possible.

So, what does this mean for marketers doing business in the 21st century? Clearly, the balance of market power has shifted from the marketer to the customer. Customers now have access to information that once was the exclusive purview of marketers. Customers using the Internet can now call up intelligent agents or "bots" such as cnet.com, mysimon.com, price-bot.com, pricescan.com, and shopzilla.com to search the Web, ruthlessly seeking the product or service at the best price according to specifications set by the user. Imagine the effect of these intelligent agents that work 24 hours a day constantly searching for the lowest prices on branded products and services. Typical information resulting from a search of tablet computers via cnet.com is shown in Figure 6.4.

However, companies are not powerless when competing in the digital arena. Long's Drugs as well as supermarket chains D'Agostino's, Winn-Dixie, and Safeway are using powerful "price-optimization" software designed to generate an ideal price for each item they sell at the individual store level. These programs are based on sophisticated algorithms that compute individual demand curves for each product in each of their stores. A host of other companies (besides the airlines, who helped pioneer this type of pricing) such as Best Buy, DHL, Ford Motor Company, Home Depot, JC Penney, Saks, Staples, UPS, and General Electric are adopting scientific or "smart pricing," using sophisticated computer programs to set prices. Systems produced by SAP and startups DemandTec and ProfitLogic sift

CNET Home Tablets and Tablet PC Reviews

Read reviews of new tablets and slates, including the Apple iPad and its competitors, and learn what you need to know to shop for tablets. **Also try:** Tablet buying advice, Popular tablets **Related searches**: tablet reviews, android tablet, tablet, tablet pc, netbook

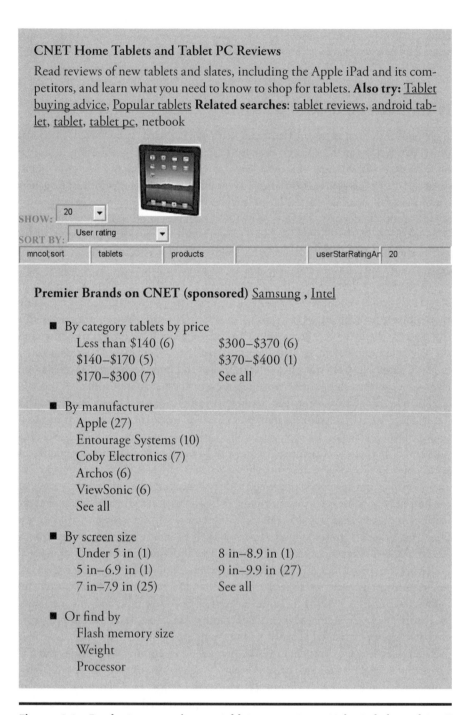

SHOW: 20 ▼

SORT BY: User rating ▼

mncol;sort	tablets	products		userStarRatingAr	20

Premier Brands on CNET (sponsored) Samsung , Intel

■ By category tablets by price

Less than $140 (6)	$300–$370 (6)
$140–$170 (5)	$370–$400 (1)
$170–$300 (7)	See all

■ By manufacturer

Apple (27)
Entourage Systems (10)
Coby Electronics (7)
Archos (6)
ViewSonic (6)
See all

■ By screen size

Under 5 in (1)	8 in–8.9 in (1)
5 in–6.9 in (1)	9 in–9.9 in (27)
7 in–7.9 in (25)	See all

■ Or find by

Flash memory size
Weight
Processor

Figure 6.4 Product comparisons—tablet computers. (Adapted from http://reviews.cnet.com)

through massive databases crammed with up-to-date information about orders, promotions, product revenues, and stock levels in warehouses and stores, revealing to companies, among other things, when to start discounting. The Casual Male Retail Group used a system developed by ProfitLogic to provide guidance on what to discount and by how much. The software led the Casual Male to discount less, but a lot sooner.

Granted, the transparency of the Web will certainly expose price differentials; companies can and should respond by personalizing their products and services. Dell is probably the best example of how to avoid "commodity selling" on the Web. Dell largely achieves its differentiation by maintaining direct contact with its accounts, allowing its salespeople to customize solutions to match its clients' particular needs. "Dell's helping to define what customers are buying," says Jeff Gans of Easton Consultants in Stamford, Connecticut.[14]

Dell also sets up customized "intranet" sites for its large customers. Shell Oil, for example, has been using a customized intranet site, otherwise known as a premier page, to purchase computers from Dell. The site keeps purchasing managers up to date on product and pricing changes while also tracking the order status of Dell computers purchased on the Web. If Shell needs personal assistance, it can readily contact any Dell marketing or technology employees who service its account.

Image—The Other Communicator

What comes to mind when you hear marketers or consumers discuss image? Perhaps, you associate this word with a related term: *imagine.* Apple, Disney, and Zynga (maker of Farmville) enable customers to cocreate value by giving them the ability to do things they previously could not do (e.g., design professional graphics materials, manage vast music libraries, or instantly share photos and experiences with others overseas) or be magically and emotionally transformed to another time or place. Speaking of place, some of the best image marketing campaigns have been tied to geographic areas: Remember "I Love New York," "What Happens in Vegas Stays in Vegas," and "Virginia is for Lovers"?

One distinction that helped create the Starbucks atmosphere, experience, and customer connection is store design. Each store is carefully conceived to fit the character of a store's local neighborhood, to be inviting, and to be environmentally friendly. Starbucks uses four store-design concepts:

1. *Heritage* coffeehouses reflect the mercantile roots of the first store in Seattle's historic Pike Place Market. These stores feature worn wood, stained concrete or tile floors, metal stools, and factory-inspired lighting. Large community tables, club chairs, and wood blinds evoke a turn-of-the-last-century feeling.

2. *Artisan* stores echo the industrial past of urban markets, taking inspiration from the Modernism of the 1930s. This motif celebrates simple materials like exposed steel beams, masonry walls, factory casement glass, and hand-polished woodwork in a creative gathering place for culture and the arts.
3. *Regional modern* embodies a trend-setting style that is comfortable and welcoming. The design uses bright, loftlike, light-filled spaces punctuated with regionally inspired furniture and culturally relevant fabrics to create a calm and contemporary respite from the clamor of the fast-paced world.
4. *Concept* stores are unique environments created by designers to explore innovations within the coffeehouse. Starbucks calls these stores *design sandboxes* because they purposely convey a sense of exploration that is extended to everyone who visits, through daily coffee and tea cuppings, artistic events, and community gatherings.[15]

We often associate image with entertainment, fashion, and technology markets. A successful image can be a key driver in organizational success. The British classic rockers Queen, the band behind such legendary stadium anthems as "We Are the Champions" and "We Will Rock You," struggled in their early days until they created the right image. Consider this interesting anecdote from the music industry:

> In 1973 it happened. Their debut album was released…. It was three years in the making and it got good reviews. But nobody bought it. What did it matter that Eric Clapton would later call Brian (May) the best guitarist in the world if no one else heard him? How did it help that Freddie Mercury was hailed as the most energetic stage performer since Mick Jagger if audiences didn't know his name? What was the point of being glam if no one could see you glitter? Queen had the looks, the dynamic front man, the pretty boy drummer, the songs, the question-marked sexuality, the drive, the intelligence and above all the talent. But they didn't have an audience. They needed help. They needed exposure. They needed an image. They needed fans to know they were out there. That they were part of the Scene.[16]

Corporate image is the aggregate perception or reputation of an organization as viewed by its various stakeholders: shareholders, managers/employees, customers, business partners, media, communities, etc. All companies have an identity that is its unique corporate personality and that differentiates it from its rivals. The marketing communication challenge is, over time, to manage and enhance the firm's image.

Using customer opinion and financial performance data, the sixth annual BrandZ Top 100 Most Valuable Global Brands (2011) conducted by Millward Brown Optimor, New York, identified the top brands in the world. According to the study, the 10 most powerful brands were Apple, Google, IBM, McDonald's,

Microsoft, Coca-Cola, AT&T, Marlboro, China Mobile, and General Electric. An overview of the top quartile of companies offers the following highlights:

- Almost two-thirds of the companies were technology firms: Apple, Google, IBM, Microsoft, AT&T, China Mobile, GE, Vodafone, Verizon, Amazon.com, Hewlett-Packard, Deutsche Telecom, Oracle, SAP, Movistar, and Blackberry.
- Service leaders are well represented: McDonald's, Industrial & Commercial Bank of China (ICBC Asia), Amazon.com, Walmart, Wells Fargo, UPS, VISA, and China Construction Bank.
- Classic global brands are still important: IBM, McDonald's, Coca-Cola, and Marlboro.
- Chinese companies are rising: China Mobile, ICBC, and China Construction Bank.[17]

As Figure 6.5 illustrates, a perceived image is based on two major components: (1) what the company does and says, and (2) what the customers and market say about the organization (this is more important). Companies manage their image via an IMC (integrated marketing communication) program, which consists of advertising; selling; sales promotion; and direct, online, and public relations activities. Customer-initiated communications such as social media (Facebook, Twitter, etc.), blogs, and online communities can dramatically impact organizational performance. Dellsucks.com and the YouTube viral video called "United Breaks Guitars" showed the amazing power of the Internet, which was devastating to Dell, Inc., and United Airlines, respectively.

Perhaps your company is not a global giant and you're wondering if image research still makes sense for your organization. Clearly, it does. It can provide

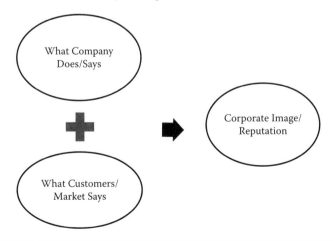

Figure 6.5   Evaluating corporate image.

a practical tool to guide promotional strategy. Let's assume that you are a restaurant entrepreneur and recently opened a trendy sports bar and café. How can you assess your corporate image in the local community? Using image analysis, a simple two-dimensional plot of customer perceptions can be evaluated. Familiarity ("not familiar with" to "know very well") and favorability ("very unfavorable" to "very favorable") scales for your firm and for your direct competitors, casual dining establishments, can be examined within your primary trade area (PTA). The PTA is often a geographic radius (in this case, let's say 5 miles), where a company will generate about 70% of its business.

Following an initial image study, data should be collected within your PTA about indirect competitors such as casinos, clubs, hotels, and sports sites. The results of such image research can result in a four-quadrant analysis of a market. Using the health-care industry as an example, there are four strategic outcomes possible:

1. Leading brands (high favorability, high familiarity): Johnson & Johnson
2. Promising brands (high favorability, low familiarity): C.R. Bard
3. Rebounding brands (low favorability, high familiarity): Aetna
4. Challenged brands (low favorability, low familiarity): UnitedHealth.[18]

Image-Based Differentiation and Positioning

Differentiation means having an advantage over the competition. This advantage can be real (a more durable product, better service, or lower price) or perceived (based on the image component of the S-Q-I-P framework). While companies can actively reposition themselves via changing the product or service mix, image-based positioning is more often the approach through which unique market identities are created.

As Ries and Trout note, positioning is often done in the minds of the customers.[19] In our overcommunicated society, those companies that can best break through the "noise clutter" with clearly focused and often humorous promotional campaigns (insurance examples include GEICO and Progressive) will strike responsive chords with their target markets and succeed in the marketplace.

Apple Computer is a good example of a firm that was a product innovator in the 1980s, fell on very hard times in the 1990s, and has soared to great heights since the early 2000s. Steve Jobs, architect of the firm's successes in the early days, was essentially banished from the company during the difficult times and reenergized the company via the iPod, iPhone, and iPad launches, and Apple became one of the most successful and admired companies worldwide. Since value creation is a dynamic process, image repositioning must be ongoing. There are three levels of product positioning: the core, extended, and total product.[20]

The core product is short-term positioning and typically works for a year or less. In this phase, companies focus on the tangibles: price, quality, and technical specifications. Packard Bell used its borrowed name recognition (from Hewlett-Packard and the Bell phone system) and price-leadership philosophy to become a dominant force in the low end of the retail personal computer market before its lack of product quality made the company crumble. While the core product variables are relatively easy to adjust, competitors can quickly emulate a low-price or comparable-quality strategy. Hence, it is difficult to own short-term market positions.

A more effective approach is building the extended product. In this phase, firms create the necessary infrastructure to develop strong marketing relationships with channel members, suppliers, and, of course, customers. This strategy tends to last in the intermediate term, one to five years. Hewlett-Packard's diverse product line can be found in computer stores, office-supply superstores, department stores, and other retail outlets. Dell's direct-marketing machine enables it to effectively serve *Fortune* 500 firms and other business users. Extended product positioning takes time, money, and process innovations.

Companies that position themselves at the total-product level have clearly identified who the company is and what it stands for. Firms that have garnered a long-term position (lasting more than five years) have clearly won the market's respect. Johnson & Johnson's reputation for quality health-care products and IBM's service excellence have been established over the decades. These companies have well-earned reputations that stress positioning on the intangibles. A total product image gives these companies the benefit of the doubt if they occasionally stumble. Remember IBM's PC Jr. fiasco? The "halo effect" enabled them to quickly recover from this misguided marketing move. A less-respected firm may have found it difficult or impossible to recover from such a market blunder.

"Cool" Companies

Amazon.com, Apple, Ben & Jerry's, Best Buy's Geek Squad, Facebook, Google, Harley-Davidson, IKEA, Intel, JetBlue, Nike, Starbucks, Target, Whole Foods, Virgin, and Zappos are often cited as "cool" companies. Many consumers (particularly Generation X and millennials) aspire to be cool, and their product choices often reflect their self-concept. In addition to age, coolness is impacted by lifestyle, media, reference groups, society, technology, and time.

According to recent research, brand coolness is a multidimensional construct consisting of five components: uniqueness, excitement, innovation, authenticity, and self-concept reinforcement.[21] In their trendy book, *Chasing Cool*, Kerner and Pressman express this idea from a clearly nonacademic perspective. They state that the characteristics of companies/brands that are cool emerge from: the unexpected, a general natural expression, luck, when preparation meets opportunity, intelligence, and a philosophy of "the middle finger to everyone else." Ultimately, they ask this intriguing question: "How can you create the iPod of your industry"?[22]

Coolness or "being hip" is an elusive attribute that is based around overall image but assumes that the other value-proposition ingredients (service, quality, and price) are satisfactory to superior. In fact, there's been some research support for renaming image as *integrated* in a revised S-Q-I-P model. Few companies can solely compete on image and build on an amalgam of customer value inputs, including (S-Q-P). Virgin Group is a classic example of a company that has earned its long-term reputation based on innovativeness, coolness, and corporate image, as seen in Customer Value Insight 6.

Customer Value Insight 6:
How Virgin Group Competes on Image

How much does image matter to an organization? In the case of the Virgin Group, market perception or image defines its essence. Richard Branson's business empire now extends into airlines, books, cell phones, music production, music retailing, radio stations, travel, and other youth-oriented products, leveraging this powerful brand name and global image. Branson's latest venture is Virgin Galactic, which commercializes space travel. Reportedly, the space venture has already received more than 400 deposits for the $200,000 short flights into outer space. For this fee, "astronauts" will get three days of training, a stay at the spaceport, and the trip into space (you free float around the cabin).[23]

Ben & Jerry's and Harley-Davidson's cultlike followings are attracted to the ice cream and the motorcycles as well as what each of these organizations stand for—their image. Is it any wonder that image is a key part of the value proposition (S-Q-I-P)?

QUESTIONS TO THINK ABOUT

1. Do you agree with Virgin's market diversification strategy? If so, what other markets should the company pursue? If you disagree, what should be the business focus?
2. How about some other examples of companies that have built their value proposition around the image variable?

Summary

In this chapter, we discussed the communicators in the value proposition—price and image. These strategic factors do not communicate value alone, but, rather, in conjunction with the presence of perceived product or service quality. That is, price only has meaning when it is paired with the benefits delivered. Buyers will use price as a cue, especially in the absence of other marketing cues, such as a well-known brand name. Firms can become more strategic in their pricing by creating a price position in the company, using value maps, relating price to elasticity of demand, and ensuring that price reflects perceived—not simply delivered—value. Six different market-based pricing methods were introduced, and a process for making good pricing decisions was explained. The image construct was explained, relevant research was presented, and multistage positioning was revisited. The chapter concluded with what it means to be a cool company. Our next chapter explores the world of e-commerce.

Customer Value Action Items

1. How well understood is the pricing function in your company? Discuss.
2. How much does price and image contribute to an offering's perceived value?
3. Discuss the relative importance of price and image in each of the following purchase situations:
   a. Automobile
   b. Life insurance
   c. Graduate education
   d. Haircut/style
   e. Health care
   f. Symphony tickets
   g. Travel
4. Select an industry and create a value map that shows individual brands and how they compare to one another on price and performance (see Figure 6.1).
5. Price customization involves setting prices based on differences in customers and how they use the product/service as well as when and where the offering is used. Give several examples of how price could be customized in each of the following situations:
   a. Car rental
   b. Consulting services
   c. Internet service provider
   d. Restaurant meal
   e. Sporting events
6. Suppose a local used-car dealer was faced with the threat of an AutoNation opening up a dealership a few miles away. Which price differentiation strategy would you recommend and why?
7. Determine your "reference price" for each of the following products/services:
   a. 1-liter bottle of water
   b. Best-selling book (digital and hardcover)
   c. Oil change for your car
   d. 1-hour massage

8. Consider the following managerial marketing issues in setting a price for one of the following services: (a) Sirius/XM satellite radio, (b) Hulu video streaming, (c) prepaid cellular phone service, (d) digital media consulting, or (e) take-out food delivery service.
   - Objective: profitability, volume, meeting competition, prestige?
   - Importance of 3Cs (rank 1, 2, 3): cost, customer demand, competition?
   - Pricing strategy: beat, meet, do not compete, retreat?
   - Penetration, skimming, competitive?
   - Discounts: cash, quantity, promotional, rebates?
   - How much? (set the price)
   - How does the price impact the other 3Ps (product, promotion, place)?

9. How can you apply the ideas in the chapter on enhancing image for your organization?

10. Is "coolness" always desirable as an image strategy? Provide a pro and con example in consumer and business markets.

EXCELLING IN THE MARKETSPACE

Chapter 7

E-Commerce— Opportunities in Marketspace

Everything we ever said about the Internet is happening.

Andrew Grove

Organizations that have survived [the industry] meltdown have one thing in common—they learned quickly to embrace the e-service paradigm.

Roland Rust and P. K. Kannan

Can you imagine getting a $6-billion buyout opportunity and spurning it? Then, we must be talking about Groupon, who said "no thank you" to Google's proposal. This deal-of-the-day online marketer is selling boatloads of 50%-off restaurant meals and related products and services to its millions of followers enticed by getting great prices—if they act immediately. How popular are these daily special offers? LivingSocial, a major competitor of Groupon, sold more than 1.1 million $20 Amazon gift-card vouchers for $10 in a single day.

A major change in 21st-century marketing involves a shift in emphasis from products and transactions to service and relationships. Advanced technologies and ever-expanding electronic networks (e.g., the Internet, wireless technologies, mobile devices, and kiosks) are shaping customer expectations on where, when, and how to choose a service provider. E-service quality is defined as the extent to which e-commerce providers effectively and efficiently manage customer interactions involving searching, shopping, purchasing, and order fulfillment. This chapter reviews some key research findings involving online customer satisfaction and service, explains how to operationalize e-service quality, and provides guidelines for firms to improve their customers' online experiences.

E-Commerce and Customer Satisfaction

Online retail sales in the United States for 2009 were projected to be $156 billion, an 11% annual increase but half the growth rate for most of the decade. The great majority (80%) of e-tailers said the Web was the best marketing channel to use in a tough economy, with conversion rates of about 3%.[1]

Service providers have come to realize that the Internet presents great opportunities as well as challenges in serving customer needs. The new e-consumer is more informed and expects more from the service provider—traditional or online. Online buyers want to do business with companies that are responsive to their requests, track their orders, and offer easy, hassle-free returns, if necessary (think Zappos.com). Others may prefer the integration of bricks-and-clicks, i.e., ordering online and being able to pick up the products at the retail store site, such as Best Buy.

One of the most successful Internet pure-plays is eBay. This virtual firm has gone from a funky online garage full of Beanie Babies and collectible Elvis prints to a powerful global marketplace featuring billion-dollar markets such as used cars and its business industrial site. The beauty of the eBay business model is that the company has no real cost of goods—customers hold the inventory, ship the products, and do the marketing—and customer acquisition and retention is largely driven by word of mouth and the "buzz factor." eBay has created a powerful value proposition by creating a fun, fast, efficient trading environment where buyer-seller risks are kept to a minimum.

The real genius of eBay is that it has figured out how to tap into the social capital created on its site by the millions of people who trade there daily. A primary source of its social capital is its feedback system, which indicates whether users are legitimate sellers or whether a user has had a bad experience with an online seller or buyer. Buyers can enter feedback—positive, negative, or neutral ratings—about sellers and vice-versa. Sellers also achieve star ratings based on the number of positive "votes." On eBay, sellers are forced to wear their reputation on their sleeves. Sellers go to great lengths to avoid negative comments, as negative feedback causes sales to go down. In fact, sellers are often brutally honest about their wares in order to avoid negative feedback. eBay also features community-related tools that create a self-governing and self-policing body of customers. Those sellers that have built solid reputations with buyers are rewarded by higher-than-average prices for their auctioned goods.

eBay is one of 50 companies featured in the *USA Today* Internet Index (see Customer Value Insight 7 for further information). Another innovative life-stage company on the *USA Today* Internet list is the Knot, Inc. It is a leading source for engaged couples via its core Web site www.knot.com. This master site directs clients to dozens of wedding-related sites and services. Two other related Web sites are for newlyweds (www.thenest.com) and pregnant women (www.thebump.com).

Customer Value Insight 7:
USA Today's *Internet Index*[2]

USA Today created the Internet Index on August 9, 1999, in an effort to allow readers and investors to track the ups and downs of the fastest-growing segment of the U.S. economy. *USA Today* considers its index as the broadest, most comprehensive measure of the emerging technology companies' stock performance. The index provides new analytical tools that help assess the forces of economic change.

The original Internet 100 was divided into two subindices: the e-Consumer 50 and the e-Business 50. The e-Consumer 50 consisted of online vendors of goods and services that connect directly to the consumer. The e-Business 50 originally consisted of companies that support the Internet's commercial development. In June 2003, the Internet 100 was renamed the Internet 50, reflecting 50 firms that have weathered the dot.com implosion. The Internet 50 continues to be split 50-50 between the new e-Consumer 25 and the e-Business 25. Index membership requirements are: Companies must derive at least 50% of their revenues from the Internet; share value must be at least $12; the minimum capitalization is $200 million; and all companies must have a minimum 90 days of public trading, be headquartered in the United States, and do a majority of business in this country.

Go to the *USA Today* Internet Index (50 leading new-economy companies) and select a B2C (consumer) or B2B (business) company and evaluate its customer-value strategy (www.usatoday.com/money/markets/internet50.htm). Review the company Web site and/or other sources.

Questions to Think About

1. How do these companies create value? Are they emphasizing service, quality, image, or price? Provide a rationale for your response.
2. How much emphasis do these companies place on customer satisfaction? Discuss their e-commerce strategy, in particular, their customer service approach and policies.
3. Critique their e-service quality strategy. Comment on the companies' use of incubative and active dimensions (see Table 7.2).

Internet buying now extends way beyond books, clothing, and electronics. Many consumers are now buying everyday household staples or personal care products such as cosmetics, detergents, shampoo, trash bags, vitamins, and so forth from online merchants. The most successful of these Web sites tend to focus on a singular attribute in the value proposition. For example, Alice.com is a price leader, while Soap.com stresses outstanding customer service and offers free overnight shipping to most of the country. And, Drugstore.com is all about product selection, with more than 60,000 items available.[3]

About two-thirds (68%) of respondents said that offering a reasonable price is the main factor that drove them to visit one Web site over another. The other two most important motivators were having a user-friendly site (easy to research, browse, and buy goods or services) and providing instant access to live experts via click-to-call or click-to-chat technologies. Currently, most of the customer service for online companies is based upon e-mail inquiries or FAQ (frequently asked questions) pages. Yet, three in five (59%) customers do not believe that these initiatives are useful.[4]

Service has become even more important when doing business online. At times, online customer service has failed to live up to customers' rising expectations, especially regarding Web page speed and responsiveness. Google now evaluates site speed as one of its criteria in its search-ranking algorithm. Online customers' patience is quite short-lived. Users will quickly abort online activity if they become frustrated while navigating a site or attempting to place an order. In fact, consumers expect a Web page to load in one second or less and will often decide whether a Web site is relevant to them in less than three seconds.[5]

The major factors, in order of importance, contributing to online customer satisfaction (operationalized as Internet service quality) were

1. Performance—order fulfillment and transaction efficiency
2. Information quality/credibility and quantity on Web sites
3. Security

4. Access—product selection
5. Sensation—aesthetic value of Web site, which includes the overall shopping experience (e.g., live chats, graphics, testimonials, virtual product demonstrations, etc.)[6]

The annual American Customer Satisfaction Index (ACSI) examines perceived value (including quality and customer expectations), customer satisfaction (including customer complaints), and customer loyalty. National customer satisfaction data is captured for 12 sectors and 47 industries. The overall ACSI index average in 2011 was 75.7 (100 maximum). The e-commerce sector consisting of Internet brokerage, retail, and travel exceeded the average by nearly 4 points (79.3). In contrast, the e-business sector comprised of Internet news and information, portal and search engines, and social media fared slightly below average at 75.4.[7]

This implies that e-commerce companies are doing a good job satisfying their customers, while the e-business providers need to do a better job in this area. Internet leaders in customer satisfaction include Amazon and Netflix, with ACSI scores of 85+. It is no surprise, perhaps, that Netflix recently surpassed 20 million customers, and Amazon now sells more Kindle e-books than traditional books.

Going Mobile and New Technologies

Mobile marketing is the second-hottest trend in marketing today (behind only social marketing, to be discussed in Chapter 8) according to a study of American Marketing Association members.[8] U.S. mobile ad spending has recently surpassed $1 billion and is projected to increase to more than $2.5 billion by 2014.[9] In fact, a Cisco study predicts there will be 7.1 billion mobile interconnected devices by 2015, which is equivalent to the world's population forecast. Overall, Internet traffic via mobile devices is expected to increase 26-fold by 2015![10] As Table 7.1 shows, the top five reasons for going mobile are increasing customer engagement, improving customer satisfaction, appearing to be innovative, building loyalty, and generating revenues.[11]

Mobile messaging is a powerful medium for customer care. Text messages have an open rate of more than 90%, and e-mail readership on mobile devices is on the rise—currently estimated at 40% overall, but much higher for Generation X and millenials.[12]

The Starbucks mobile iPhone and Blackberry applications assist customers in finding the closest store, ordering their beverages over the phone, and paying for their coffee, tea, and food items. This is a nice complement to their use of free Wi-Fi, which the company learned is a great way to get repeat business, keep patrons in stores longer (to purchase more), and excite new customers to join the Starbucks movement. McDonald's, Panera Bread, and Einstein's Bagels have also discovered the value of free Wi-Fi in their restaurant operations.

Table 7.1 Companies' Top Objectives for Mobile

Objectives	% Use
Increase customer engagement	52
Improve customer satisfaction	36
Appear as innovative	30
Build loyalty	28
Generate direct revenue/sales	26
Increase brand awareness	24
Test and learn	23
Drive traffic/sales in other channels	22
Acquire new customers	22
Reach particular consumer segments	20
Reduce operating or marketing costs	10

Source: Forrester Research, *Global Mobile Maturity Online Survey,* Quarter 3, 2010.

Small, lightweight technology introduced in the tablet subcategory (such as iPads and Samsung Galaxies) and netbooks have made it much easier for consumers to always have access to their computers and use them to satisfy consumption needs. E-commerce has also gone social, as Facebook fanatics are now buying goods and services without ever leaving the platform. Trailblazers in this area include Pantene, The Limited, and 1-800-Flowers.com.[13] To broaden their product line and appeal to their target market, 1-800-Flowers has partnered with numerous online gourmet retailers such as Cheryl's Cookies, The Popcorn Factory, Fannie May Chocolates, and Winetasting.com.

One challenge that companies competing in the marketspace face is an effective staffing plan for the digital world. Fewer than 20% of marketing executives believe they have the right people on their team to meet organizational objectives and be prepared for the trends and technologies affecting their businesses. The need for e-marketing managers has been identified in seven key areas: search-engine optimization (SEO), search-engine marketing (SEM), usability analysis (tracking customer experiences and sales conversion performance), e-mail marketing (eMM), mobile Web marketing (MWM), social media marketing (SMM), and Web analytics.[14] Does your organization have the requisite e-commerce expertise and marketing talent onboard to win in highly competitive global markets?

Defining E-Service Quality

In the previous chapter we examined the key determinants of service quality. Zeithaml and her colleagues conducted research examining whether traditional service quality dimensions differ from e-service quality determinants. Based on a series of focus groups concerning e-service quality, they proposed a model and 11 major dimensions of perceived e-service quality (E-SQ), including the original dimensions of reliability, responsiveness, access, assurance, and empathy, which are still relevant in e-commerce. However, several new dimensions of e-service quality emerged from their research, including ease of navigation, flexibility, efficiency, site aesthetics, price knowledge, and customization/personalization.[15]

Price knowledge refers to the ability of online shoppers to determine shipping price, total price, and comparison prices. In fact, an interesting finding of their study was that, contrary to conventional wisdom of how value is framed, price and quality were more strongly intertwined in online shopping. Data collected from 271 subscribers to a regional Internet service provider revealed that six e-service quality indicators (reliability, access, ease of use, personalization, credibility, and security) follow closely to the original service quality indicators developed by Zeithaml et al. Reliability was the strongest predictor for Internet purchaser's perceived service quality, followed by personalization, ease of use, and access.[16]

Additional research by Parasuraman, Zeithaml, and Malhotra refined the E-SQ scale and identified two subscales. First, they determined that there was an e-core-service quality (E-S-Qual) scale consisting of four dimensions: efficiency, fulfillment, system availability, and privacy. This measures the service quality delivered by Web sites. Second, an e-recovery service quality scale (E-RecS-Qual), useful in cases of online service problems and inquiries, was composed of three items: responsiveness, compensation, and contact. The second scale is relevant only for nonroutine service encounters or service-recovery situations.[17]

E-SQ and Customer Loyalty

As we have seen, e-service quality is essential in creating customer e-satisfaction, but what about in building loyalty in the online environment? It has been estimated that it costs an Internet retailer about $82 to attract an online shopper, which is about 2.5 times what it costs brick-and-mortar retailers.[18] Customer acquisition costs for pure-play online apparel retailers are 20%–40% higher than for traditional brick-and-mortar apparel retailers with both physical and online channels. Customers must continue doing business with most online firms for at least two years just for them to recover their initial acquisition costs. Yet, in future years, profit growth accelerates at a faster rate; in apparel e-tailing, repeat customers spend more than twice as much in months 24–30 of their relationships than they do in the first six months.[19]

Online customers continue to patronize particular e-retailers because of various attachments: constraints (they have to), desire (they want to), customization (they can specify modifications), or community (they flock to). It was found that community attachments were the strongest and that customization was the weakest bond impacting repurchase intention.[20] How do Web site characteristics impact the business performance of the site? Web sites that are secure, frequently updated, fail rarely, respond to inquiries expeditiously, and are content-rich and relevant to users correlated positively to four measures of site effectiveness—number of visitors, repeat visits, average time spent per visit, and sales conversion ratio.[21] Another study among webmasters from *Fortune* 1000 companies identified information quality, system use, system design quality, and playfulness as four major determinants for the future visits to company Web sites. Company webmasters can improve service quality by focusing on the way in which customers use their Web site. It is the customers rather than business organizations who should control the online transaction process.[22]

Dell Computers, a leading personal computer company, has created a loyal customer base of corporate users. The company has determined that its major loyalty drivers are: order fulfillment, product performance, and postsales service and support (once a trouble spot that has been remedied). Dell then determines the optimal measure of each one of these key drivers. Success in order fulfillment, for example, is measured according to "ship to target"—a measure of the percentage of orders delivered accurately and on time.

Improving E-Service Quality

Given the dismal record of many e-commerce providers, what should firms do to improve customer service? Realize that the fundamentals of customer service for e-marketing are the same as in traditional marketing. Most consumers today are looking for convenience and ways to streamline their shopping—to get it done quickly without compromising price or quality. The online shopping experience needs to be both simple and efficient or shoppers will click-and-run. Many companies mistakenly view technology as a cure-all to customer service problems. However, no amount of sophisticated technology can make up for the lack of a customercentric culture.

Research has proposed that the five following components be considered in delivering e-service quality:

1. Core service
2. Facilitating services
3. Supporting services
4. Complementary services
5. User interface through which the customer accesses the services[23]

Core services represent the reason for being and are those that are designed to meet the primary demand need of a specifically described target market. Using the example of online book retailers, a core service would be displaying information on new products and offering recommendations. Facilitating services make it possible to use the core service and, without them, the core service collapses. In the case of online book retailers, a facilitating service might be archiving and searching capabilities. Support services do not facilitate using the core services but, rather, add value to them; support services might include the availability of useful links or virtual book clubs. Complementary services are services that accompany the core service and support its acquisition and use or disposition. For online booksellers, a complementary service might represent book reviews or its shipping capabilities. Finally, the user interface is a means of communication between the e-service marketer and the potential customer. What information appears on screen, how it is organized, and how users access the information define the user interface. Limited menus, poorly designed navigation systems, and difficulty comparing multiple products on different screens all have adverse affects on electronic shopping.[24]

Even with the shift of business activity to the Web, the fundamentals of marketing exchange remain the same: to create enduring and profitable customer relationships. A key factor in establishing and maintaining profitable customer relationships is trust. As the eBay example earlier in the chapter illustrated, sellers with high credibility can command price premiums, at times, versus other vendors that do not have as strong a reputation.

Trust, privacy, and security are major Internet concerns that prevent many users from conducting more transactions and business online. The VeriSign Internet Trust Index is a relative indicator of the overall level of trust Americans have with the Internet. The inaugural 2010 study achieved a score of 61.5 (on a 0–100 point scale), which indicates a moderate level of online trust. Frequent Internet users, long-term online users, college students, connected homemakers, and sports fanatics all report trust scores of 80+; in contrast, infrequent users, those with limited technological skills, and retirees had trust scores of less than 40.[25]

Following is a list of some of the keys for building Web site trust:

- Maximize cues that build trust on your Web site.
- Use virtual-advisor technology to gain customer confidence and belief.
- Provide unbiased and complete information.
- Include competitive products.
- Provide open and transparent organizational communication.
- Keep your promises.[26]

Realize that e-service quality mirrors many of the service-quality dimensions discussed in Chapter 5. While consumers may use their brick-and-mortar service quality experiences to form expectations when shopping online, their "zone of tolerance" may be considerably narrower—competitors' storefronts are only one click away.

Table 7.2 E-Service Quality Dimensions	
Incubative Dimensions	*Active Dimensions*
Ease of use	Reliability
Appearance	Efficiency
Linkage	Support
Structure and layout	Communication
Content	Security
	Incentives

Source: Adapted from J. Santos, "E-service quality:
a model of virtual service dimensions,"
Managing Service Quality 13 (2003), 239.

Table 7.2 provides a two-column list of the major dimensions of e-service quality. The *incubative* dimensions would be considered before a Web site is launched and are largely related to site-design issues and include ease of use, general appearance, linkage, structure and layout, and content. Note, site layout is highly correlated to repeat visits. On the other hand, certain factors (*active* dimensions) need to be considered throughout the period in which a company's Web site remains operational, such as reliability, efficiency, support, communication, security, and incentives. These factors are responsible for increasing customer retention and for encouraging positive word-of-mouth referrals.[27]

Finally, as with service quality in general, the challenge for e-service marketers is to determine the relative performance and valence on each of these various service-quality attributes and devise strategies to improve in these areas. Customer Value Checklist 7 lists some of the major e-service quality dimensions and suggestions on how to improve in these areas.

Customer Value Checklist 7:
Keys for Improving Service Quality

1. *Access*: Give customers access to their accounts to check their profile or track recent activity; also give them numerous ways to contact you. Don't bury the telephone numbers somewhere deep in the Web site. Frontgate (www.frontgate.com) sells outdoor furniture and home accessories and provides the type of access that customers expect today.

2. *Personalization*: When the prospect (or customer) grants permission to be contacted, e.g., "opt-in," thank them for the visit, and subsequent visits should present information based on the customer's earlier preferences, i.e., by using "rules engines." Customers also want the opportunity for detailed shipping, billing, and credit card information as well. Most Web sites offer a section called "my account," which provides such information. H&M's Dressing Room shows women how clothing items and combinations look by "virtually trying them on" on various models at their Web site (www.hm.com). Web sites should also consider using online live chats. Sites that offer online live chat should be sure to give visitors who select this option an expected wait time for a customer service representative.

3. *Responsiveness*: Customers expect a prompt response to their inquiries. At the very least, visitors should immediately receive an automated e-mail response, and a more detailed response to the customer's inquiry should follow. Customers also want to find information and access it quickly, which would suggest offering faster page loading. Finally, keep customers informed when the status of their order changes. Today's e-consumers expect to be updated when a change to their order occurs.

4. *Navigation*: Main links should be clearly visible on the top of all pages, as well as on the side or bottom of the page. Once the prospect has navigated each individual page, second-level links should be visible under the main links. Access to "home" needs to always be present, regardless of tier level that the prospect is at. Your site navigation scheme must be intuitive and easy to follow. By the time your visitors get to the second page, they must understand how your site is set up, and key pages must be clearly labeled in the main menu, and the submenus must be very obvious. If a visitor gets lost in your site, they are much more likely to leave it than they are to try to figure out a confusing navigation scheme. Finally, shoppers want to get in and out, quickly and efficiently. Thus, online retailers should limit requests for information, never ask for the same information twice, and state the return policy clearly.

5. *Assurance*: Involves confidence that service providers will keep their promises and that the information presented is clear, truthful, and secure. A study conducted by Consumer WebWatch, a nonprofit research project organized by

Consumers Union and funded by several nonprofit foundations, recommends that in order to improve credibility with consumers, online merchants should:

a. Disclose the physical location where they are produced, including an address, telephone number, or e-mail address. Ownership, purpose, and mission should also be clearly disclosed.

b. Clearly distinguish news and information from advertising. Web sites should also clearly disclose sponsorships and relevant business relationships, including links to other sites.

c. Disclose financial relations, particularly when the relationships affect the cost to a consumer. Fees for service, transactions, and shipping and handling should be clearly stated.

d. Any posted incorrect information should be immediately corrected, and policies on consumers' rights if a purchase is made based on incorrect information should be clearly stated.

e. Privacy policies should be easy to find and clearly and simply stated. Web sites should clearly disclose how a customer's personal information will be used.[28]

E-sellers should also be able to offer assurances about delivery. One of the major reasons many dot.com businesses collapsed was due to problems with order fulfillment. Customers never gave these e-tailers a second chance when their orders arrived after Christmas!

6. *Price clarity*: Extent to which seller makes clear the final price to be paid. Prices should be clearly displayed alongside the items, and a running total of purchases and shipping costs should be shown as the order progresses. Foreign consumers in particular have been hesitant to buy U.S. goods online when they didn't know what the final cost would be after adding in customs and other fees.

Source: CV Checklist 7 prepared by William C. Johnson, Ph.D.

Summary

As we have seen, service quality is an important driver of electronic commerce. Online customer service expectations such as reliability and responsiveness often mirror offline service expectations. Given the online clutter and the myriad of sites vying for the consumer's attention and loyalty, establishing online trust is critical. E-commerce marketers who regularly assess the relative importance and performance of incubative and active dimensions will be rewarded with loyal customers. It has been proposed in this chapter that an opportunity exists to use online service quality to create high levels of customer satisfaction, repeat Web site visits, and increased overall business performance. With the rapid movement into mobile marketing and new technologies, it is projected that the e-commerce arena will gain even more importance in the next few years. Our next chapter dives deeper into the digital world by examining integrated marketing communications with an emphasis on social media.

Customer Value Action Items

1. Choose two of the following organizations and identify their core, facilitating, support, and complementary services.
   a. Portal (e.g., AT&T, AOL)
   b. University
   c. Large public library
   d. Online brokerage (e.g., Charles Schwab, E-Trade)
2. Visit the Web sites of three major airlines and compare each of them using the incubative dimensions in the E-Service Quality Model (see Table 7.2).
3. As a consultant, you are asked to advise a client in setting up a food catering and delivery business in a large metropolitan area. The client anticipates that 75%–90% of the orders will be placed online. Thus, your client is interested in learning the following: (a) which service dimensions will be most critical in creating ongoing customer value; (b) how to design the business and in particular the Web site to maximize customer service; and (c) how to assess service quality once the business is operational. Write a one-page plan for the client that addresses these needs.
4. Simplicity marketing gives consumers choices but in new ways that reduces the stress associated with making purchases. Leaders in this area include Apple, Honda, Office Depot, Southwest Airlines, and Target Corporation. Given what you know about customer value (CV) and e-service quality, identify an Internet company that practices simplicity marketing and briefly describe how it implements this strategy successfully.
5. Across the Web, companies are seeking revenue-producing strategies from information. In recent years, Yahoo has rolled out dozens of paid consumer services. The various apps stores offer hundreds of thousands of choices, free and low cost.
   a. How do you feel about paying for online services?
   b. What types of online services are you willing to pay for? How much will you pay?
   c. What are the customer-value implications of this trend?

6. Amazon, eBay, and Google make it easy for consumers to find information that they need to solve problems (creating value from knowledge). How can a start-up company use lessons taught by these Internet giants to design an effective Web site and e-commerce strategy?

7. Scenario: A Retail or Virtual Shopping Experience?[29]

Situation: Customer A has an urgent need to buy an all-in-one printer—copies, scans, faxes, and prints. He drives to the electronics superstore, where he has bought products previously. Nobody helps him, but he finds a model that may suit him. He asks a question about a feature and is told that it is not available, and that's just the way it is. He still wants to buy, but it is out of stock and he is told to try back next week.

Discuss:

a. How did the store lose its three possible competitive advantages: press its buttons (product), press his buttons (immediate customer gratification), or press the flesh (customer service)?

b. What should have happened to create superior customer value?

c. How could an e-tailer overcome these potential competitive disadvantages advantages: press its buttons (product), press his buttons (immediate customer gratification), or press the flesh (customer service)?

d. What additional advantages and disadvantages occur in the e-commerce arena? How do these factors impact the creation of customer value?

e. Comment on customer retention/relationship marketing threats and opportunities.

Chapter 8

Integrated Marketing Communications and Social Media

Unless your campaign has a big idea, it will pass like a ship in the night.

David Ogilvy

Conversations among the members of your marketplace happen whether you like it or not. Good marketing encourages the right sort of conversations.

Seth Godin

A large part of Barack Obama's success in winning the presidency in 2008 was due to his marketing campaign. President Obama's coordinated promotional strategy stressed the use of the Internet and social networking tools. In addition to his electronic town halls and public appearances, Obama was able to emotionally connect and energize the youth of America via his Web site, e-mail newsletter, blog, and leading social media such as Facebook, Myspace, and Twitter.

Building on the value proposition (VP) idea introduced in Chapter 4, this chapter emphasizes how a progressive marketing communications program adds value to customers. Specifically, we explore the concept of integrated marketing communications (IMC) and the explosive growth of social media.

Communicating Value through an IMC Program

Integrated marketing communications (IMC) means coordinating all promotional activities: advertising, databases, direct marketing, Internet, personal selling, sales promotion, and public relations. The corporate database (marketing information system) is the key to success for IMC.

The objective of IMC programs is to provide a synergistic and consistent message (one look, one voice) that communicates value to targeted audiences. Don E. Schultz, a professor at Northwestern University, has researched and written extensively about IMC over the past decade. Some of this guru's major thoughts on this strategic marketing area are summarized in Table 8.1.

While companies are doing an adequate job of utilizing IMC principles, there is clearly room for improvement. Research has found that about 75% of companies now coordinate all or most of their promotional activities. Retailers do it best (85%),

Table 8.1　Forces Impacting Integrated Marketing Communications (IMC)

IMC Drivers	*IMC Restraints*
Small organizations	Large organizations
Business marketers with a strong sales force—marketing communications is a support technique	Consumer marketers with a brand-management system
Single brand or line of products under one brand name	Multibrand packaged goods companies
A database of customers/prospects and their purchase histories	Limited usage of databases
View marketing communications as an entity	View marketing communications as a segmented process
Acceptance of risk taking	Unwilling to take a risk
Willing to rethink the system of promotional incentives	Locked into traditional rewards for promotional activities
Strong top-down management	Bottom-up management
Less-formal marketing structures, limited marketing history	Formal marketing structures, sophisticated marketing organization
Realization that IMC is a major value creator for the organization	Promotional strategies are just another part of the marketing mix

Source: Adapted from ideas offered by D. E. Schultz, "Integrated Marketing Communications," *Journal of Promotion Management* 1, no. 1 (1991), 99–104.

while service organizations are least successful in their IMC endeavors (55%). Service firms tend to farm out a lot of promotional work to different vendors in the areas of direct response, public relations, and sales promotion, which partly accounts for this discrepancy from the norm.[1] Standardizing promotional campaigns becomes a much greater challenge to marketing managers in service businesses.

While social media have generated most of the hype over the past few years, e-mail marketing should definitely not be discounted. E-mail marketing can work effectively and is a mainstay promotional vehicle for many small and growing businesses. E-mail strategists and list vendors such as Constant Contact and Jigsaw have solid products for maintaining regular communications with prospects and clients and offering precision target marketing for business leads. While e-mail response rates are traditionally low (less than 2%), so are the investment costs, and incremental new business can be generated quite affordably in most industry sectors.

According to Forrester Research, the following media options will experience high annual growth rates/projected dollars expended for 2014 (2009 figures in parentheses):

Search marketing	15%	$31.6 billion ($5.4 billion)
Social media	34%	$3.1 billion ($716 million)
Mobile marketing	27%	$1.3 billion ($391 million)
E-mail marketing	11%	$2.1 billion ($1.2 billion)[2]

Although the integrated marketing communications idea is intriguing, implementation is a major problem for most organizations. Recent evidence of practitioners' satisfaction with IMC is disappointing. In a 2008 survey of members of the Association of National Advertisers, only one-quarter of marketers rated their company's integrated marketing approach as "very good" or "excellent"; this is an improvement, however, from 21% in 2003. The major barriers to successful implementation of an IMC program were the existence of functional silos (59%), lack of strategic consistency across communication disciplines (42%), insufficient marketing budget (36%), lack of a standard measurement process (36%), lack of needed marketing skill sets (33%), and the need to develop the "big creative idea" (32%).[3]

Cisco Systems uses an IMC approach to drive its worldwide event marketing program. The company administers hundreds of events annually, ranging from trade show exhibits to large industry conferences. A key promotional theme emerging from customer research was the need to humanize Cisco's technology offerings and focus on security, responsiveness, and collaboration. For a Federal Office Systems Exposition (FOSE), a leading government trade show, Cisco demonstrated its integrated marketing prowess by creating a trade character called Fred Federal to represent a typical government "worker bee." A strong multimedia promotional campaign, with an invitation to meet Fred at the Cisco booth, included e-mail and print direct mail, marketing materials, Web site promotion, banner advertising, a Myspace page, YouTube videos, and postconference follow-up.[4]

Creating an IMC Program

Here is an eight-point plan for initiating an IMC program in your organization.

1. *Use zero-based budgets.* Most companies use incremental approaches in allocating promotional budgets. For example, if they spent $10 million last year, they may "tack on" another 5% to get this year's figure. Other companies base their decisions on competitive spending, industry averages, or a percentage of sales. A preferred approach is the objective and task approach. Start with a zero budget and force all promotional managers to justify their investment. This might result in a $9-million or $12-million (or many other possibilities) budget for IMC activities.

2. *Primarily focus on current customers.* Many organizations direct 80% or more of their advertising and selling efforts to trying to win new business (conquest marketing). An IMC program recognizes the importance of retention marketing (see Chapter 10) and inverts that ratio so that a majority of the promotional activity is earmarked for relationship building with existing customers. This reduces customer defection, upgrades business relationships, and creates advocates for the firm's services. Sam's Club's eValues program sends customized, targeted "smart discounts" to customers. Using data mining and predictive analytics, Sam's Club is able to achieve 20%–30% response rates from its promotions (typical response rates are 1%–5% for mass marketing and segmented offers, respectively).[5]

3. *Use targeted mass promotion and personalization.* Direct mail, localized initiatives, and the Internet can be used to reach customers effectively. As an example, a Chicagoland Macy's hosts a beach party targeting 65,000 college students from 10 local campuses to buy fun spring-break clothing and encourage them to buy suits for job interviews. Using database analysis, Macy's also mails 30,000 versions of its catalog—ranging from 32 to 76 pages—to customers.[6]

4. *Build marketing relationships.* Strategic partnering is a major part of every good IMC program. In addition to the Internet and intranets (protected corporate information resource centers), progressive companies are creating extranets that link an enterprise's extended family of suppliers, distributors, retailers, and business partners.[7] Hence, customer, channel, referral, and stakeholder relationships can all be nurtured through carefully conceived marketing and promotional strategies.

5. *Note that everything an organization does sends a message.* Image and atmospherics are very important in communicating value to customers. The little things

like stationery, signage, telephone greetings, and Web site design, etc., should all reflect professionalism and a consistent message to the marketplace. A carefully conceived Web site has become an indispensable marketing technology for 21st-century companies. It has evolved into a one-stop, online corporate information source, customer support tool, distribution channel, order taker, product catalog, price list, promotional vehicle, research technique, segmentation source, and a strategic and tactical marketing differentiator.

6. *Two-way dialogue is key.* In an overcommunicated society, the marketing challenge is to establish a meaningful dialogue with customers as to how the firm's service mix can provide maximum benefits/value. Interactivity and involvement on the part of the customer is important for sharing information and creating firmer bonds. The Web is an ideal medium to accomplish this objective. Its selectivity and flexibility creates a customized business experience for each user. The proliferation of social networking (discussed in the next section of this chapter) has accelerated dialogue between companies, customers, and brand communities.

7. *Use cutting-edge communication technologies.* In today's changing marketplace, companies must seek new and better ways to stay in touch with their target markets. Communication options include blogs, custom content, e-commerce (Web sites), e-mail, events, mobile media, point-of-sale promotion, search-engine marketing, social media, telemarketing, multimedia, videos, webcasts, etc. According to IDG Research Services, a projected 2011 media mix for global technology marketers consists of: digital (52%), events (18%), print (16%), broadcast (7%), and other media (8%).[8] (Note that, for most industries, new media still represent less than 20% of the promotional mix.)

8. *Measure promotional effectiveness.* Traditionally, advertising executives competed with sales managers for their "fair share" of the corporate promotional budget. Today, management requires accountability and demands to know and justify the return on investment of limited resources; they will no longer accept the nonmeasurable communications methods used by marketers in the past.[9] A marketing information system/database is the key tool for effectively monitoring and measuring the success of an IMC program. As part of this process, job descriptions and reward systems are likely to be redesigned. In a strong IMC-centered environment, in-house competition is replaced with cooperation/teamwork. Joint rewards help the organization do what's best, rather than just protect individual turfs. Perhaps the sales manager will accept a 5% cut in new hires and the advertising manager will agree to a 10% reduction in advertising expenditures to redirect dollars to needed sales promotion or public relations activities if it is for the good of the organization. Under this scenario, if the overall net effect of the promotional strategy improves through an IMC plan, all key players share in the rewards of their efforts.

Social Media

Twitter—that powerful 140-character, online megaphone to the world—has evolved from the voice of breaking news by celebrities, athletes, and influentials to a mainstay social media tool for businesses of all size. Perhaps, you are at Safeco Field enjoying a Seattle Mariners baseball game and want a cold beer. Since there is no vendor in sight, you send a tweet to Kevin Zelko@Msbeervendor (the smarter beer vendor) on your mobile phone and promptly have your beer delivered right to your stadium seat. Zelko says Twitter vending takes some of the guesswork out of wandering, leads to more satisfied customers who will spend more, and better tips.[10]

According to Antonia Harler, a social media strategist at Paratus Communications, there are seven imperatives for businesses using or planning on using Twitter in their integrated marketing communications programs. To become a "sweeter tweeter," she says companies should:

1. Really listen to their customers
2. Have a clear relationship marketing strategy
3. Offer messages that are credible and authentic
4. Provide quality content
5. Interact and communicate with your customers and prospects
6. Have a consistent communications strategy (including Twitter)
7. Always put your customers' needs first[11]

In addition to Twitter, Facebook, and LinkedIn are very popular social media tools. (Note that there are hundreds of other options, but these will not be explicitly discussed here.) LinkedIn has become the de facto social medium standard of global business professionals. This networking platform boasts more than 100 million users worldwide and is the "go to" choice for sales prospecting, business development, and online relationship building. Using the Answers feature, I contacted my LinkedIn network and posed the question on how marketing professionals use social media effectively. CV Insight 8 provides selected responses to this query.

Customer Value Insight 8: How the Marketing Pros Use Social Media

How do you use social networking tools to promote your business?

■ Dr. R. J. Trasorras—private investigator, Tampa, FL
  I use several sites, Facebook, Twitter, and LinkedIn. But, Facebook and Twitter are the ones I primarily use to inform potentials about my services. LinkedIn is great to connect

with colleagues, and Twitter dumps into the LinkedIn site. Since targeting is key, I use key words in my profile to have people identify topics they are interested in. Hence, I may post about employee theft or background screenings, etc. I also appeal directly to my following and friends on Facebook, asking them for referrals or to spread the word about what I have to offer. Twitter allows me to make short bursts to everyone at once when I am thinking about something. Social marketing is a must do. Consistency in your message is also crucial.

- ■ Nancy Domenichelli—transcription/data entry service, Ludlow, MA
  We are geared toward researchers of all kinds. Our prime target markets are academia and marketing and marketing research professionals. LinkedIn is the only social media used to promote my company, and it has proven an invaluable marketing tool. I can attribute 70+% of new business directly to my activity on LI. I have joined 20+ LinkedIn groups that I know my clients and potential clients frequent and have linked up with members I have gotten to know through those sites. I have over 1600 connections right now. After connecting, I always write a short "thank you for connecting with me on LI" message, adding that I hope the contact will give consideration to using Modern Day Scribe for future transcription or data-entry needs.

  The health-care sector is one of our main areas of expertise. Recently I reviewed my LI contacts in that area that I hadn't heard from in a while. I sent out a version of the following message: "We're connected on LinkedIn, but I thought I'd take a minute to re-introduce you to Modern Day Scribe. Modern Day Scribe has produced transcripts of meetings on a variety of topics including barriers to healthcare, molecular profiling, the pharmacokinetics/ pharmacodynamics of anti-cancer agents, and issues around leukemia/lymphoma treatments. Our broad exposure to a variety of products, industries, and technologies positions Modern Day Scribe as the premier transcription service available. Hoping that if XXX has a need for transcription services, you will consider Modern Day Scribe. Please don't hesitate to contact me for more information about our services." Within three weeks of sending out that message, I had four new clients, all recipients of my follow-up e-mail.

■ Linda Hamburger—public relations, Fort Lauderdale, FL
  On Call PR, The South Florida Public Relations Network
  (SFPRN) works with clients in entertainment production
  and job services. Social marketing tools are extremely
  important in my promotional strategy. I primarily use
  Wordpress, LinkedIn, Facebook, Twitter, Createsend.com,
  and Yahoo Listserve. Wordpress is now merged with
  Twitter and LinkedIn and has becoming surprisingly
  efficient, affordable, and great looking. The moment I
  launched SFPRN using Wordpress and announced it,
  numerous people signed up. It really made the process far
  easier to attract and interest people and expedited word
  of mouth.

■ Steven Cates, DBA, JD—HRM Consulting, Danville, VA
  My company specializes in employment and labor law
  matters. I use LinkedIn and Facebook to network and
  search for new clients. Social media as a marketing tool is
  gaining traction but is still new to traditional businesses, so
  this is one stream of marketing that is used to get my message out to companies as well as individuals who need
  services such as mine. Joining special interest groups puts
  you in touch with those who provide similar services or
  those looking for those services.

■ Estuardo Jo—Internet retailer of office supplies, Miramar, FL
  Databazaar services consumers through our B2C site
  www.databazaar.com and corporate/institutional clients
  through our B2B site www.databazaar.net. Our corporate/
  institutional target markets are small/medium-size businesses, schools, and government institutions. We use
  Facebook and LinkedIn to communicate promotions and
  events. We get more customer feedback from Facebook.
  Social media is not as important as our e-mail campaigns
  in our marketing strategy. We still need to learn how to
  use social media effectively.

Questions to Think About

1. What social marketing tools that you are not currently using
   should you use?
2. What percentage of your promotional budget is in social
   media? Should it be increased?
3. How should you measure the effectiveness of your social
   media strategy?

Online Consumer Typologies

Marketers are now employing powerful segmentation techniques in the market-space. Forrester Research's Social Technographics Profile identifies five overlapping groups of online consumers—creators (content developers), critics (content reviewers), collectors (content acquirers), joiners (social networkers), and spectators (content consumers)—based on how involved they are in the online "groundswell." Charlene Li and Josh Bernoff define the groundswell as "a spontaneous movement of people using online tools to connect, take charge of their own experience, and get what they need—information, support, ideas, products, and bargaining power—from each other."[12] Exact Target's Social Profile identifies 12 online distinct, self-reported personas, and consumers could place themselves in as many as three categories simultaneously (see Table 8.2).[13]

While such profiles or personas can be insightful, a true segmentation basis is preferable. Segmentation is the process of partitioning markets into groups of potential customers who have similar needs or characteristics and who are likely to exhibit similar purchase behavior. Segment-formation criteria include homogeneity within segments (similarities among group members), heterogeneity among segments (differences in the various market segments), and meaningful segment data (practical, usable, and readily translated into marketing strategy).

Consider these amazing findings about the stranglehold the Internet has attained in America:

- 57% of people now communicate more online than in person.
- Two out of five women aged 18–34 admit to being Facebook addicts.
- 15% of moms say that they check Twitter every waking moment.[14]

Viral Marketing

A key benefit and potential risk of social media is that the message is shared among consumers and can spread quickly like wildfire (or a virus). Jennifer Aniston's YouTube spoof of viral advertising for Glaceau Smart Water—featuring dancing babies, puppies, rainbows, and sex appeal—was a huge online hit. In contrast, consider the viral song "United Breaks Guitars" by Dave Carroll, a disgruntled United Airlines passenger; this video generated more than 10 million Web hits and was a public relations nightmare for the company. While reminiscent of the classic American Tourister luggage commercials on television more than 30 years ago, where gorillas destroyed airline passengers' baggage, the broken-guitar video clearly demonstrated the power of user-created content.

For many companies, viral marketing has become an important part of the promotional mix. Research found that 89% of consumers share content, 63% do this weekly, and 75% forward content to as many as six people. In addition, two-thirds

Table 8.2 Online Consumer Personas

Persona	Key Motivator	Preferred Brand Interaction(s)	Online Consumers (%)
Inner circle	Strengthen existing relationships	Facebook	47
Cautious	Selective about who to communicate with	Twitter	33
Info seeker	Find and consume information	Facebook, Twitter	33
Enthusiast	Offline interests and hobbies	e-mail	32
Deal seeker	Promotional content	e-mail, Twitter	30
Shopper	Topic of shopping	e-mail	24
News junkie	Real-time breaking news, current events	e-mail, Twitter	21
Gamer	Latest and greatest in gaming software (casual vs. serious)	Facebook	19
Social butterfly	Make and maintain a lot of online friends	Facebook, Twitter	13
Business first	Use the Internet for business purposes	e-mail	8
Megaphone	Connect, educate, and share resources and information with others	Facebook, Twitter	7
Open book	Uninhibited consumers who freely express their thoughts with the online world	e-mail, Facebook	6

Source: Adapted from Exact Target, *The Social Profile*, 2010. Research can be downloaded at http://www.exacttarget.com/sff. Reprinted with permission.

of U.S. consumer goods are influenced by word-of-mouth communications.[15] In recognition of this trend, companies are now investing more attention and resources to their Web sites as well as increasing their e-mail/video e-mail marketing programs, mobile marketing (smartphones, iPads/tablets), and other online advertising initiatives.

Measuring the Impact of Social Networks and New Media

As part of my study on B2B segmentation in technology companies, I evaluated the effectiveness that companies had in various marketing activities. Only 56% of executives said that their companies were successful in social media. In contrast, they were quite strong in market research, niche marketing, customer relationship marketing, competitive analysis, and targeting and evaluating markets (success rates of 72% to 91%).[16]

Compared to traditional marketing activities, social networking is a rapidly growing, changing, and evolving area of business. Hence, there is a major opportunity to connect better with customers via the right platforms and media for their customer base, whether it be blogs, Facebook, mobile messaging, or video e-mail.

According to Ben Verschuur, a European Internet marketing practitioner with expertise in B2B and B2C markets, there are three key challenges facing social media marketers:

1. Develop an effective strategy
2. Get a measurable return on investment from social marketing campaigns
3. Change social followers into customers

Additional insight on social media marketing (SMM) is provided in Customer Value Checklist 8.

Customer Value Checklist 8: Social Media Marketing Guidelines—A 10-Step Process[*]

1. *Determine your goals.* Social Media Marketing (SMM) will often be part of existing marketing plans. It may be an additional channel for your target audience, or sometimes SMM is used exclusively. There are several reasons for this: budget, image, experiment, or nature of the campaign. In all cases, you will have to formulate a goal, whether it is fixed in the marketing or SMM plan. From my experience, there are four major objectives: (a) setting up a clear social media strategy, (b) getting a good return on investment (ROI) out of social media campaigns, (c) increasing traffic for your Web site, and (d) increasing brand awareness and brand engagement.

---

[*] Prepared by Ben Verschuur, an Internet marketer and social media expert in the Netherlands. Mr. Verschuur can be reached at benverschuur@hotmail.com. Feel free to add him to your network on LinkedIn: http://nl.linkedin.com/in/benverschuur.

2. *Define your target audience.* Who is your audience? What do you know about your target audience? Why would they share your information with their connections? What networks are you targeting? Which influential blog, social media, and people can you identify? How active are your competitors with social media? What does your target audience know about you, your organization, and your product or service (nothing at all, heard about us but never took action, have taken action, have taken action and are enthusiastic, or are true advocates)? Browse through content-sharing sites like YouTube and look at Facebook fan pages that are relevant to your business. See if you can identify key persons on Twitter who publish, and read what they publish. For online consumer typologies within your target audience, use the *Social Technographics Ladder* by Forrester Research as a tool.

3. *Clarify your value proposition.* With a distinctive value proposition, you are able to add value to your target audience. Many companies create value propositions, but often it is not suitable for online use. So, make sure that your value proposition is simple and understandable. Besides that, ensure that your value proposition fits the perceptions of your target audience.

4. *Determine your budget.* Social Media Marketing can require less money than traditional marketing. Nevertheless, it is important to establish your budget. Consider these two reasons: (a) spending a lot of time on SMM happens quickly but can be avoided if you use the right tools, planning, and partnership agreements, and (b) you want to know your expected ROI.

5. *Track the results of SMM.* You have to design a system that enables you to follow your target audience. Monitoring what is said about your organization or brand is crucial. A good monitoring system consists of automated searches, alerts, and ranking figures, all put together in one user-friendly, customercentric dashboard.

6. *Integrate SMM into your IMC program.* Create a strong reference point like a Web site that explains your value proposition. People will search for information about your company before sharing. This should be a clear story that is exciting and adds value to existing knowledge. It is also important that information on the profile page, Web site, blog, and other Web sites are congruent with each other and with what you say via social media.

7. *Set up a calendar for publishing your content.* Does SMM consume too much valuable time? Companies are concerned that this is the case, but if you map your ROI in a structured way, it will not be a waste of money. Use the best online tools to partially automate your online presence and you will decrease a lot of the workload. For instance, you will only need a few input systems to distribute the output among numerous other systems. To ensure social media success, you need to treat this promotional avenue as an investment. At the companies where I have worked, we budgeted based on staff salaries and expenses that came along with the staff. A few rules for interacting with your target audience: Abide by the code of conduct of your target audience on social media Web sites; be authentic; build relationships; listen to your audience; add value; give credit; and plan your communication.

8. *Engagement.* If you have implemented the above elements, you are ready to interact with your target audience. You need to react quickly and effectively on actions taken by your target market. Show your appreciation for your consumer's interaction. Here are some additional helpful pointers:

   ■ *Social networking platforms.* Be active in discussions, groups, and forums. Interact with your target audience and initiate your own topics. Monitor reactions of commentators. Use powerful sentence headings and phrases, but don't overdo it.

   Facebook: Post messages and polls with visuals that will likely be shared by your target group. Use contests that are engaging and shareable.

   LinkedIn: Search for interesting people in contacts of your first-degree contacts and make sure you are introduced by them.

   ■ *Micro-blogs (Twitter).* Handle all messages properly; keep sharing relevant knowledge with your followers. Potential followers will see your shared knowledge and decide whether they will or will not follow you.

   ■ *Blogs.* Keep your blog up to date with relevant content, comment on topics, and see if you can contribute to other blogs.

   ■ *Content-sharing Web sites (YouTube and SlideShare).* Make sure you respond quickly to positive or negative comments.

9. *Set up an effective call to action!* Eventually, you want your potential customers to take action. You may want to influence their attitude, promote your business, let them buy your products, or share content within their network. You need to create an effective call to action. A call to action is a textual and visual trigger to give an incentive for consumers to take action. This occurs through successful viral campaigns.

10. *Measure your efforts.* After you implement Social Media Marketing, you want to assess if your strategy is effective and determine your ROI. Therefore, your dashboard should include measurable Key Performance Indicators (relevant metrics are illustrated in Table 8.3). The ROI of social media is difficult to determine. In my opinion, you can measure conversations, comments, tweets, etc., but to actually assign values to those inputs is very difficult. What is a "tweet" worth on Twitter, or how do you quantify the impact of a fan on your Facebook page? Some of my preferred metrics for SMM include: number of visitors referred to our Web site; conversion rates; the reach of subscribers, followers, and fans; leads generated; and ranking of our Web sites in search engines.

Research of the *Fortune* Global 100 companies by Burson-Marsteller ("The Global Social Media Check-Up") found the following usage of the major consumer social media tools in the United States: Twitter accounts (72%), Facebook fan pages (69%), YouTube accounts (59%), and corporate blogs (34%). Across the board, the numbers were down for Asian companies by about 40% with the exception of blogs, which are used by half of the companies.[17]

The top small-business tools were Twitter (88%), Facebook (87%), LinkedIn (78%), blogs (70%), and YouTube/other video (46%). Companies that spent six hours or more per week on social media achieved the best results. While only one-third of small-business owners said that social media helped them close business, other tangible benefits were cited such as: increasing Web traffic, opportunities to build new partnerships, generating good sales leads, creating buzz for their business, a rise in search-engine rankings, and a reduction in overall marketing expenses. Blogs were the area of choice to spend more time on by small-business marketers.[18] A list of 18 Internet and mobile advertising platforms based on current usage is shown in Table 8.4.

Table 8.3   Relevant Metrics for Social Media Applications Organized by Key Social Media Objectives

Social Media Application	Brand Awareness	Brand Engagement	Word of Mouth
Blogs	Number of unique visits Number of return visits Number of times bookmarked Search ranking	Number of members Number of RSS feed subscribers Number of comments Amount of user-generated content Average length of time on site Number of responses to polls, contests, surveys	Number of references to blog in other media (online/offline) Number of reblogs Number of times badge displayed on other sites Number of "likes"
Microblogging (e.g., Twitter)	Number of tweets about the brand Valence of tweets ± number of followers	Number of followers Number of @ replies	Number of retweets
Cocreation (e.g., NIKEiD)	Number of visits	Number of creation attempts	Number of references to project in other media (online/offline)
Social bookmarking (e.g., StumbleUpon)	Number of tags	Number of followers	Number of additional taggers

Continued

Table 8.3 (continued)   Relevant Metrics for Social Media Applications Organized by Key Social Media Objectives

Social Media Application	Brand Awareness	Brand Engagement	Word of Mouth
Forums and discussion boards (e.g., Google groups)	Number of page views Number of visits Valence of posted content ±	Number of relevant topics/threads Number of individual replies Number of sign-ups	Incoming links Citations in other sites Tagging in social bookmarking Offline references to the forum or its members In private communities: number of pieces of content (photos, discussions, videos); chatter pointing to the community outside of its gates Number of "likes"
Product reviews (e.g., Amazon)	Number of reviews posted Valence of reviews Number and valence of other users' responses to reviews (±) Number of wish-list adds Number of times product included in users' lists (e.g., Listmania! on Amazon.com)	Length of reviews Relevance of reviews Valence of other users' ratings of reviews (i.e., how many found particular review helpful) Number of wish-list adds Overall number of reviewer rating scores entered Average reviewer rating score	Number of reviews posted Valence of reviews Number and valence of other users' responses to reviews (±) Number of references to reviews in other sites Number of visits to review site page Number of times product included in users' lists (e.g., Listmania! on Amazon.com)

Table 8.3 (continued)   Relevant Metrics for Social Media Applications Organized by Key Social Media Objectives

Social Media Application	Brand Awareness	Brand Engagement	Word of Mouth
Social networks (e.g., Bebo, Facebook, LinkedIn)	Number of members/fans Number of installs of applications Number of impressions Number of bookmarks Number of reviews/ratings and valence ±	Number of comments Number of active users Number of "likes" on friends' feeds Number of user-generated items (photo, threads, replies) Usage metrics of applications/ widgets Impressions-to-interactions ratio Rate of activity (how often members personalize profiles, bios, links, etc.)	Frequency of appearances in timeline of friends Number of posts on wall Number of reposts/ shares Number of responses to friend-referral invites
Video and photosharing (e.g., Flickr, YouTube)	Number of views of video/ photo ratings ±	Number of replies Number of page views Number of comments Number of subscribers	Number of embeddings Number of incoming links Number of references in mock-ups or derived work Number of times republished in other social media and offline number of "likes"

Continued

Table 8.3 (continued)   Relevant Metrics for Social Media Applications Organized by Key Social Media Objectives

Source: Donna L. Hoffman and Marek Fodor, "Can You Measure the ROI of Your Social Media Marketing?" *Sloan Management Review*, Fall 2010, 44. Reprinted with permission.

Note: This table organizes the various social metrics for social media by classifying them according to social media applications and social media performance objectives. While it is not exhaustive, it should give marketers a usual starting point for measuring the effectiveness of social media efforts because all of the metrics listed are easily measured.

In addition to "What they are using?" the next big question that senior marketing executives have today is "How do you measure the return on investment?" in social marketing initiatives. The traditional reach and frequency approach that thrived in a mass-promotion world is no longer relevant in an interactive environment.

Some argue that consumers (not companies) now own every brand, since they have the ability to praise or criticize their product/service experiences and tell the world their opinions. In addition to comments, they can add articles, link to Web sites, and provide video content. As Jaime Cohen Szule of Levi Strauss & Co. said: "We no longer control the message. We manage the dialogue."[19]

In response to an upside-down marketing communications transition, Hoffman and Fodor offer a new media measurement approach:

> Effective social media measurement should start by turning the traditional ROI approach on its head. That is, instead of emphasizing their own marketing investments…begin by considering consumer motivations to use social media and then measure the social media investments customers make as they engage with the marketers' brands.

The authors add that consumer investments include the number of visits and time spent with the application, including user comments (e.g., a blog), Facebook updates, or Twitter pages about the brand. The goal is to measure changes in awareness, brand engagement, and word-of-mouth promotion. A comprehensive list of relevant metrics for measuring the effectiveness of the major social media is shown in Table 8.3.[20]

Summary

Service organizations must rethink the way that they promote their value edge. First, an integrated marketing communications (IMC) philosophy was introduced, and an eight-point plan for implementation was presented. The second part of the

Table 8.4   Usage of Social Media Platforms

Platform	Example	Percentage Using
Search engines	Google	89
Social media	Facebook	84
Microblogs	Twitter	72
Video sharing	YouTube	70
Content sites	ESPN.com	50
Blogs	Gizmodo	49
Content portals	Yahoo!	46
Presentation sharing	SlideShare	44
Mobile apps	Droid Market	39 (42% plan to use)
Social bookmarking/news	Digg	36
Advertising networks	Glam Media	31
Live streaming	Ustream.tv	29
Photo/video sharing	RockYou	28
Reviews	Yelp	27
Location based	Foursquare	23 (35% plan to use)
Music/audio sharing	Blip.fm	19
Online games/in-game advertising	Farmville	8
Virtual worlds	Second Life	3

Source: Adapted from Extra Mile Audience Research, *Research Report: Marketers' Current and Future Use of Social Media,* October 17–19, 2010, New York: Pivot Conference, 11.

chapter explored the burgeoning world of social media as a solid extension to a strong IMC program. Among the major considerations addressed were online profiles, viral marketing, and the use and measurement of social media tools. The next chapter explains how service companies can strengthen customer relationships.

Customer Value Action Items

1. How does your firm differentiate itself from its rivals?
   a. Describe your real and perceived competitive advantages.
   b. Discuss your current value proposition.

   c. Using an integrated marketing communications (IMC) campaign, how can you develop an even stronger image and simply but elegantly communicate maximum value to your target market(s)?

   d. What social media tools should be part of your promotional mix?

2. Which of the online consumer personas in Table 8.2 best represent your target market(s)? Does your social media strategy mesh with consumers' preferred modes of brand interactions?

3. You were recently hired to manage a new casual dining establishment that will compete with Chili's, T.G.I. Friday's, Ruby Tuesday, and other national and regional restaurant chains. Based on what you know of the groundswell, how can you attract and retain customers that may be *creators, critics, collectors, joiners,* and/or *spectators*? What social media applications will you use and how will you measure success (compare and contrast two groups)?

4. Given the list of social media platforms in Table 8.4, which techniques are your company:

   a. currently using effectively

   b. could use more effectively

   c. not using but should be using

5. Assume you are a consultant brought in to advise a local, alternative/pop-culture newspaper on how to design and deliver superior customer value. What would be some of your recommendations on how this newspaper publisher could add value and communicate more effectively with its readers and information seekers?

6. On a 5-point scale, where 1 is "not very successfully" and 5 is "very successfully," how good a job does Disney do with respect to practicing IMC? Provide a rationale for your response.

7. IMC can be used as a foundation for communicating customer value and strategic promotional planning. Select a "basic" product in one of five product categories: consumer good, consumer service, industrial good, industrial service, or Internet service. How can you differentiate your basic product (e.g., tablet computer, overnight delivery service, travel Web site, etc.) to gain a moderate or strong competitive advantage.

   a. Based on the S-Q-I-P (service, quality, image, price) model introduced in Chapter 4 and the promotional strategies discussed in this chapter, how will you create value for customers?

   b. Devise an ad theme, list key selling points, and outline a media plan (including the Web) to market the differentiated product/service.

   c. How can you apply IMC concepts to your promotional campaign?

8. Zappos.com recently added videos (featuring company employees) to its product information to support sales of its shoes, handbags, and accessories. Initial results were positive, generating a 10% increase in sales versus no videos. Critique the Zappos strategy of not using professional models in its promotions. Discuss the effectiveness of Zappos's IMC program and social media strategy.

RETAINING CUSTOMERS— ANALYSIS AND STRATEGY

Chapter 9

Creating Value through Relationship Marketing

The value of a relationship is in direct proportion to the time that you invest in the relationship.

Brian Tracy

Business is not just doing deals; business is having great products, doing great engineering and providing tremendous service to customers. Finally, business is a cobweb of human relationships.

Ross Perot

The complex nature of buyer-supplier interactions today is dependent on relationship creation and management. A business relationship is like a marriage: Success is achieved not just through good intentions, but also through hard work and close attention to the other party's needs. Hence, a key to success is the ability to get things done with similar-minded others. Collaboration and social business networking (e.g., LinkedIn) have risen in prominence. The goal is to identify and create new value with individual customers and their community of contacts.

Amazon.com masters online relationships via a personalization technology known as collaborative filtering. For example, once a customer buys a book, Amazon recommends other books by comparing that purchase to those of fellow book buyers with similar taste. Apple's iTunes Genius list provides a similar function in recommending possible musical purchases based on one's library of existing music on his or her iPod.

This chapter explains how to preserve and grow the customer base using relationship marketing principles. A major thrust of the chapter is building online relationships. First, relationship marketing is reviewed. Second, the buying cycle explores relationship marketing at various stages of the sales process. Third, value-chain concepts such as the vertical (extended) value chain and value web are examined to better understand supplier relationships. Fourth, customer relationship management (CRM) and marketing automation are discussed as key tools for evaluating customer relationships. Finally, some strategies for practicing successful relationship marketing are provided.

What Is Relationship Marketing?

The cornerstone of marketing is getting close to customers to better identify and satisfy their needs (and wants). Realize that marketing is responsible for more than just getting the sale. We have witnessed a significant change in how business is conducted, with the focus shifting from the transaction to the relationship. This is particularly true for services marketing, where it is difficult to separate service operations and delivery from relationship building.

The traditional marketing paradigm (the 4Ps: product, price, promotion, and place) has lost some of its influence in the digital world. This approach focuses on the transaction and the core product, taking a short-term perspective; customer attraction (conquest marketing) is the overriding goal. This perspective is no longer sufficient, as the powerful forces of industry globalization, the value movement, rapid advances in technology, and a shift in the balance of power toward customers have coalesced to change the rules for business success.

Relationship marketing represents a fundamental transformation, where relationships shift from adversarial to cooperative, and the goals shift from market share to share of customers. In the new economy, products do not matter as much as the relationship between company and customer. Managing customer relationships is paramount, yet so is the growing importance of managing business relationships with suppliers and resellers, as well. An overview of how traditional marketing differs from relationship marketing is presented in Figure 9.1.

Think for a moment about the purpose of a business. Ask most businesspeople and they might reply "to make a profit" or "to grow shareholder value." As commendable as these goals are, should they be the primary focus of an enterprise? What about creating and satisfying long-term customers? Given the strong interest in relationship marketing, a number of useful definitions have been proposed by service gurus such as Berry, Gronroos, and others.[1] While these definitions are useful, arguably, Gordon's view of relationship marketing expresses the essence of relationship marketing best:

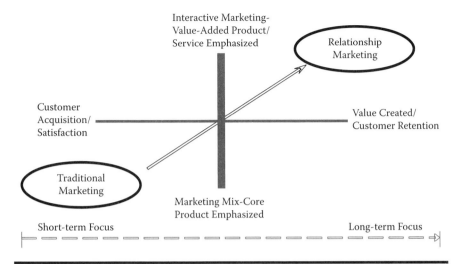

Figure 9.1 Traditional versus relationship marketing. (Adapted from J. Sheth, AMA Faculty Consortium/Evolution of Global Marketing and Relationship Imperative, Scottsdale, AZ, 1996.)

> Relationship marketing is the ongoing process of identifying and creating new value with individual customers and then sharing the benefits from this over a lifetime of association.[2]

Relationship Marketing Success

Prior to the 1990s, companies focused most of their marketing efforts on acquiring new customers. Little attention was given to existing customers. With the cost of customer attraction rising and brutal competition in most markets, companies are paying much more attention to holding on to their existing customers. For example, SunTrust found that online customers cost less to acquire, are less costly to serve than in a branch or over the phone, and the five-year profitability of avid eBill users (those who view three or more bills online per month) is about 2.5 times that of the average bank customer.[3]

In the mid-1980s, Ryder Systems began a relationship with one of the large Bell operating companies via a short-term truck rental program. Over time, the company provided more value to the customer, including full-service equipment leases, drivers, a full outbound delivery network, and logistic solutions. Ryder also assumed operation of all inbound transportation and distributor-center packaging/shipping/cross docking and storeroom operations, all staffed and operated by corporate personnel.

Later, Ryder introduced *e-Channel Solutions*, which offered a global network of e-commerce capabilities for on-demand delivery to consumers that facilitates online replenishment from distribution centers to a network of neighborhood depots, then unattended or attended delivery to a consumer's home. The company will manage the entire fulfillment channel for its clients—operating the distribution centers, managing the transportation of goods to the neighborhood depots, coordinating the last-mile delivery through Ryder's network of couriers, and leveraging the infrastructure to facilitate returns.

Realize that when taking into account lifetime value, the financial toll of losing customers is staggering. One Ryder manager recently said that a typical customer was worth $9 million ($3 million a year revenue for three years). Hence, customer relationships are assets that should be evaluated and managed as rigorously as any financial or physical assets.

In relationship marketing, value is created in the relationships that companies have with their customers. (Are customers getting the best deal, the best product, or a best friend?) Although the primary responsibility of most employees may be non-marketing, i.e., technical support, back-office, or front-line workers, all are value-creators and may perform crucial marketing tasks. Remember, customers evaluate value at every point of contact in the organization to determine if they received what was expected and promised.

If the goal is to create more value through interdependent, collaborative relationships with customers, the outcome is customer retention. Relationship marketing is ongoing—a constant search for finding opportunities to generate new value. AT&T trains its service reps to act as small-business consultants and work with their customers in addressing communications as well as business needs. Many small-business clients have limited marketing budgets and appreciate the bundled solutions offered by AT&T, such as phone plans and Web services.

The online shopping experience is unique, especially as it relates to the exchange process. In traditional marketing, the seller's actions (i.e., communication activities) tend to be unidirectional and largely influence the exchange process. However, in the new economy, the communication activities are often bidirectional, and not always just between the buyer and seller. In addition, many online communities serve as forums for consumer-to-consumer exchange of common interests, e.g., evaluating past service experiences. Furthermore, consumers often initiate the conversation with the seller rather than passively attend to the seller's messages. For example, in reverse auctions such as Priceline.com, the prospect initiates the exchange process by submitting a bid on a flight or hotel room; Priceline then tries to locate sellers interested in accepting the bid.

Building Strong Customer Relationships

You may recall an American Airlines TV commercial a few years ago where a senior manager is gathered with his subordinates, lamenting that "we just got fired by our best customer." He reminded them that they used to conduct business with a visit and handshake—now it's by fax or voice mail. He proceeded to hand out airline tickets to each person present in the meeting, instructing them to pay a personal visit to each of their key customers. He, of course, was going to visit the customer who fired them. The message was simple: Never take customer relationships for granted!

It is the seller's responsibility to nurture the relationship beyond its simple dollar value. Sellers can resist this natural tendency toward decline and complacency by developing the two crucial relationship enablers—trust and commitment. Both of these factors were found to directly correlate with business performance.[4] In a study of global high-technology firms, trust and commitment were consistently ranked higher when marketing personnel from these companies were asked to consider what factors were most important in maintaining strong business relationships.[5] Three secondary relationship enablers are cooperation, dependence, and information exchange.

First consider the effect of trust. Trust is an important factor in the development of marketing relationships and exists where there is confidence in an exchange partner's reliability and integrity. A seller can create confidence in the eyes of the buyer by being credible and following through on what the seller promises.

FedEx dominates the market for overnight delivery because it promises to have the customer's package there "absolutely, positively, overnight." FedEx's customers rest easy at night knowing that this statement is not simply an advertising slogan, but a pledge to deliver on what the company has promised (see the FedEx case study in the Appendix at the end of this book). One of the best tools for establishing trust is effective communications. It is important to be open and honest, as well as clear and thorough. Establishing a good channel of communication can help you avoid countless potential disasters and loss of customer trust down the road. Remember also that trust is a "bank account" where deposits and withdrawals are made over time. The trust account accumulates interest only when the sellers' messages and actions are clear, consistent, and reliable. There is evidence that trust plays a critical role in building durable online relationships and has been called the most important factor for customers in choosing online suppliers.[6]

Another important relationship enabler is commitment. Where trust involves a reliance on the seller, commitment is an implicit or explicit pledge of maintaining and supporting the relationship. Although we make a distinction here between trust and commitment, research has found that trust actually leads to commitment.[7]

A high level of commitment encourages both parties in a relationship to pursue their individual and joint goals. UPS and J.C. Penney formed a $1-billion partnership in which UPS became Penney's sole mail-order carrier as well as their logistics carrier, bringing their equipment and expertise to the partnership. Such a commitment signals a willingness by each player to modify their existing systems to fit the other, inextricably binding these companies together.

Cooperation involves coordinated activities between buyer and seller aimed at producing desirable results for both firms. The gains experienced by cooperating can more than offset the loss of autonomy in a relationship. Furthermore, cooperation frequently involves a willingness to develop joint goals and even share resources. Take Procter & Gamble for instance. P&G actually manages Walmart's inventory, and it is P&G's responsibility to decide when Walmart needs shipments. To do this, P&G has complete access to Walmart's inventory. It manages everything and makes decisions on its own shipments. This arrangement is beneficial for both parties; Walmart can charge less because it doesn't have the cost of tracking or storing inventory, while P&G has a much bigger share of business and it doesn't have to compete with other suppliers. Competitors can also benefit from cooperation as practiced in the airline industry through code-sharing of frequent-flier programs and access to airport lounges.

Dependence is the willingness to invest time and dedicate resources for the purpose of establishing and strengthening business relationships. Nypro, a plastics manufacturer, worked closely with Gillette in manufacturing Lady Sensor razors. Prior to being awarded the contract, Nypro invested in the necessary equipment and technology and was able to bring the product to market quickly and under budget; they then shared the cost savings with Gillette.

Finally, information exchange is the lubricant that keeps the other relationship enablers from corroding. If price attracts a relationship, information sustains it. When buyers offer more information, sellers in turn are willing to provide more services, creating a win-win situation. McKesson Corporation, a major drug wholesaler representing thousands of independent pharmacies, helps them set up accounting and inventory systems, as well as computer ordering systems (i.e., electronic data interchange or EDI). The retailers gain value from improved stock planning, resulting in fewer stock-outs and more satisfied customers. McKesson benefits by creating "captive" retail accounts who grant McKesson unprecedented access to their sales and financial data.

In summary, each of the relationship enablers will be evident to some degree in most successful buyer-seller relationships. Clearly, some of these factors will become more important over the life of the business relationship. Trust and cooperation, for example, are critical during the initial stages of relationship building; commitment, dependence, and information exchange become more important later in the relationship.

Analyzing Buyer Relationships[8]

The buying cycle model articulates corporate and customer relationships and their linkages. In business markets, this can be clarified through a sales segmentation funnel that examines business objectives, buying stages (the center of the framework), and typical customer responses (see Figure 9.2). From a promotional planning perspective, inbound media (search), outbound media (direct marketing and advertising), and social media are used to communicate with potential buyers at varying stages of the buying cycle.

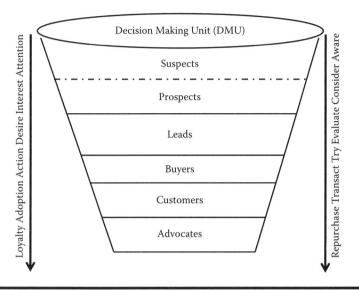

Figure 9.2 Buying-cycle model.

The pool of possible buyers is depicted above the dotted line in the figure. Suspects may buy, but there is little evidence that they even fit the firm's target market profile. Prospects are a much better starting point because they exhibit similar demographics, psychographics, and usage patterns to existing customers. Further qualification of the prospect yields a lead—one that has interest in the offer and the ability to buy. At this point, the company has created desire and mentally moved the individual or buying unit in the continuum from awareness to evaluation.

The bottom half of the buying-stage funnel is where the sales process gets even more interesting. Buyers then act upon the offer and try the goods, services, or ideas. Realize that, for now, this is perceived as a one-time sales transaction. Satisfied "try-ers" quickly become valued, repeat customers. Companies must work hard in the service area to earn customers' trust and loyalty and keep them over the long term. Ultimately, the very best customers become advocates and refer others to the business. Some of the challenges of selling and relationship marketing and their impact on customer value are explored in Customer Value Insight 9.

An example of a promotional plan for a new streaming server illustrates an effective use of the sales-segmentation funnel. A research study for Citrix Systems identified three key segmentation variables: size of the company, relationship with Citrix, and technology preferences. Based on the segmentation analysis, Citrix targeted four market segments (S1 to S4).

The On-Board (S1) were existing Citrix Presentation Server or other Citrix Systems buyers that can be reached through direct selling programs. The Solution Seekers (S2) are existing customers of their Go To product line (e.g., Go To Meeting, Go To MyPC) and are readily accessible, as well. The High Potentials (S3) represent larger companies or government agencies with 250 or more employees. The New Economy (S4) are medium-sized organizations in information, service, technology, or Web-based business sectors. These latter two noncustomer segments (S3 and S4) can be reached via list buys.

Customer Value Insight 9:
Selling and Relationship Marketing

The sales field has changed dramatically in the past few years. It's no longer about pushing unsought goods and products such as used cars, vacation time-shares, or life insurance via cold calls and overly persuasive sales tactics. Today, sales (e.g., pharmaceuticals, technology products, etc.) is a respected business profession often requiring advanced degrees (MBAs) and proven communication, computer, and analytical skills. Marketing students should view sales as a legitimate career option on par with positions in branding/product strategy, marketing research, advertising/public relations, database management, Web design, retail management, and marketing professional services.

A major driver of this transformation in selling practices and sales management is technology, i.e., customer relationship management (CRM) systems and social networking. Sales professionals must carefully manage all of their communications in the marketplace as well as the marketspace via face-to-face interactions; e-mail; blogs; and LinkedIn, Facebook, or Twitter initiatives. Regardless of the medium, the objective is still the same: Create superior value for customers.

How sales professionals relate to all audiences—for example, gender (males or females), age (baby boomers, Generation X, and millennials), different cultures, and multiple buying influences—present additional communication challenges. To succeed in rapidly changing and complex markets, arrogant words or actions and overly aggressive sales tactics must be minimized. Role playing, selling simulations, marketing coursework, and sales training programs can help prevent potentially disastrous transaction blunders with customers and prospects.

Questions to Think About

1. How should a company (provide a specific example) employ relationship selling strategies and tactics as part of a broader marketing strategy to retain customers?

2. Explain how the sales profession has changed during the past decade due to technology. Has this helped or hindered customer relationships?
3. Propose three new developments related to relationship marketing that are likely to emerge as companies strive to be the premier solutions provider and provide exceptional value for their customers?

Improving Supply Chain Relationships

Successful supply chain integration can deliver powerful results to organizations by reducing inventories, lowering costs, and improving quality. The Global Supply Chain Planning Study 2009 found that 29% of managers said that supply chain management (SCM) had a tangible impact on the bottom line, and 16% felt that effective SCM processes provide their organization with a competitive edge. On the flip side, however, 65% of respondents stated that their SCM procedures "need to improve" or they are still "seeking best practice."[9] The sixth annual study by the Gartner Group identified the top 25 supply chains using financial metrics and expert panels. The 10 leaders were Apple (#1 for a third consecutive year), Procter & Gamble, Cisco Systems, Walmart, Dell, PepsiCo, Samsung, IBM, Research In Motion, and Amazon.com.[10]

Just as the opportunity to work with customers in creating new value is important, so is working with supply chain partners to accomplish the same purpose. Firms increasingly recognize that the value added through the supply chain contributes to overall end-customer value. In 2010, Popeyes Louisiana Kitchen achieved a cost savings of $16 million in supply chain costs; this helped franchisees by improving restaurant profit margins by one full percentage point compared to the previous year.[11]

Downstream intermediaries (distributors, wholesalers, retailers) can add value to the offering that the producer cannot easily or economically do. Furthermore, an intermediary can be an enduring source for creating new value with end customers by maximizing speed and minimizing costs and investment. Where in the early days SCM centered on the management of supply within the single company, today the focus is on cross-company planning and implementation, or integrated supply chain management (ISCM).

An integrated supply chain is a connected set of interorganizational resources and activities involved in the creation and delivery of value. The goals of an integrated supply chain strategy are to speed up product development (including time to market), minimize finished goods inventory, minimize investment in resources, improve quality, and reduce response/cycle times.

As such, true integration is emerging in such industries as automotive, computers, telecommunication equipment, and retailing in the form of information sharing, product planning, joint problem-solving/strategic planning, and shared benefits. The effective use of innovative, value-creating distribution options such as Amazon.com's virtual bookstore, Dell's build-to-order direct strategy, the airlines' SkyMall program, and the grocery industry's use of cross-docking are examples of ISCM practices that can provide a strong competitive edge to firms.

Supply chain management revamps channel strategy from an area relatively neglected to an actively managed marketing/logistics function. SCM means that collaboration rather than competition becomes the modus operandi as disparate organizations now jointly focus on satisfying customers by aligning and integrating business processes. All participants in the "extended supply chain network" work in harmony to find new ways to add value at varying points in the distribution cycle. Furthermore, costs may be cut, product/service quality enhanced, delivery time reduced, and overall business performance improved through an effective ISCM system. The United States Postal Service and NCR successfully worked together in revamping post office branches nationwide and reducing operational costs.

In the new economy, competition is shifting to networks of companies cooperating across boundaries to achieve market goals. Firms are increasingly competing as a constellation of collaborating partners, each contributing value in the network. A key factor in making the networked business model work is investing in and coordinating cross-company processes. To succeed in the future, corporations will have to weave their key business processes into hard-to-imitate strategic capabilities that distinguish them from their competitors. Competitors can match individual processes or activities but can't match the integration or fit of these processes between network partners.[12]

Market knowledge provides another opportunity to further leverage ongoing supply chain relationships. Firms should strive to understand their value chain as well as the value chains of their suppliers and customers to create maximum value at the lowest possible costs. The vertically tiered value chain is an important extension from the traditional horizontal value chain advocated by Michael Porter that has been embraced by industry. According to Porter, primary value chain activities include inbound logistics, operations, outbound logistics, marketing and sales, and service. Support activities include procurement, technology development, human resource management, and firm infrastructure.[13]

Comprehending the customer's value chain is the key to vertically tiered value chain analysis, which is a more complete model of value creation (see Figure 9.3).[14] An in-depth assessment of how customers use products or services can provide a strong competitive advantage to the organization. Inclusive and collaborative business networks of all relevant channel participants create a market-driving, relationship-oriented initiative that can lead to increased value for all parties.

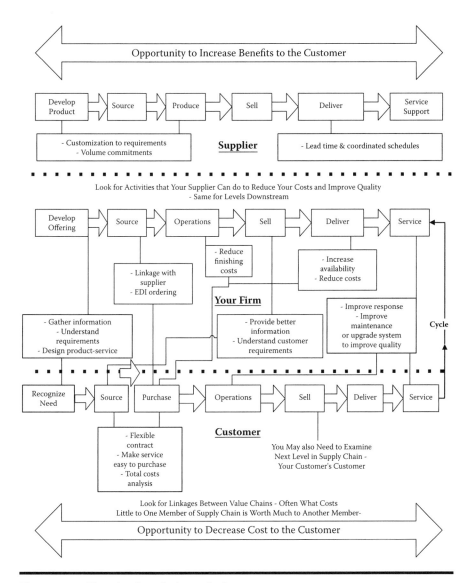

Figure 9.3   Tiered value-chain analysis.

Furthermore, this concept can also be easily adapted and become a virtual supply chain network to facilitate and enhance e-commerce activities.

With the emergence of e-commerce, information is being used to extend and enhance the firm's physical value chain. The *virtual value chain* is the digital, networked, virtual world of information that parallels the tangible world of goods and services or the physical supply chain.[15] Herman Miller, the large office furniture manufacturer, has successfully exploited the virtual value chain when it comes to order fulfillment. When an order is received, it is immediately sent via the Web to a factory in Michigan or California. Once the order has been transmitted, a manufacturing date is set, and space on a truck is reserved that will deliver the order in about a week. The dealer and customer are notified via e-mail confirmation within two hours of both the delivery and installation time.

Suppliers play a key role in the relationship between seller and buyer. As a starting point, there are eight common selection criteria (presented here in no formal order) for choosing the best suppliers. These are: cost, quality and safety, delivery, service, social responsibility, convenience/simplicity, risk, and agility.[16] It should be noted that each customer will value a different set of criteria; hence, each will have its own view of whether or not it is working with a world-class vendor.

There are five evolutionary stages of SCM. In the first stage, the emphasis is on quality and cost control. Customer service is the focus of stage two. Coordinating supply chain processes across the enterprise occurs in stage three. Looking for ways to provide profitable customized products via the extended supply chain is the objective of progressive stage-four companies. Finally, the formation of tightly knit supply chain communities is the aim of stage-five organizations.[17] As companies move toward level-five integration, many are seeking to implement customer relationship management (CRM is discussed in the next section of this chapter).

More companies are now using web alliances to create superior customer value. These value webs now represent the new-economy supply chains. The key to creating superior value today resides in understanding and leveraging the power of supply chain network relationships. Traditional value chain theory assumed a linear flow of supply chain activity. Every product or service produced represents a chain of value-added activities. Value is created (or captured) by a firm moving upstream or downstream in the supply chain. For example, large grocery retailers such as Kroger and Publix have moved downstream by introducing more private-label products, essentially becoming a food producer.

In contrast, value webs reflect how many of the new-economy firms are organized today. A value web can be described as an inchoate network of customers, suppliers, complementors, allies, and competitors whose services either enhance or drain a firm's value. These relationships can be vertical or horizontal (or both) and are less enduring than in traditional supply chains. An illustration of the value web idea in the context of eBay is shown in Figure 9.4.[18]

Unlike conventional supply chains, the 3Com Corporation learned that adding more users to a value web actually creates more, not less, value. Value webs are optimized to the extent a firm understands its relationship with other actors in the web, how its activities will affect the network, and how the other actors will respond. True value creation takes place when several organizations in the value web share common technologies and/or intellectual capital.

Another case in point: Cisco has efficiently outsourced much of its manufacturing to suppliers in its network. Cisco's demand forecasts are visible to everyone

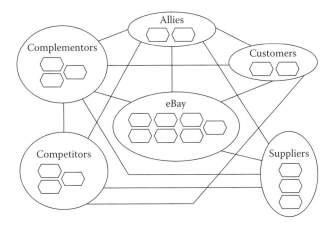

Figure 9.4   eBay value web.

in the supply network, allowing suppliers and manufacturers to better anticipate orders. Even though Cisco acts as the "orchestrator" of its value web, common goals and benefits are shared between members, not just Cisco.

Customer Relationship Management

What is customer relationship management (CRM)? CRM is a business strategy that involves selecting and managing customer relationships in order to optimize the long-term value of a company. The goal of CRM, according to CRM guru and founder of CRMGuru.com Bob Thompson, is to acquire, grow, and retain the right customer relationships—those with the best long-term profit potential.[19] When stated in these terms, customer relationship management is not a new idea; rather, it is about collaboration with your customers and partners in such a way that they receive superior value.

Although CRM programs have been embraced since the 1990s, many companies do not maximize its potential. Consider these surprising findings:

- 90% of the 50 largest CRM users were unable to quantify a return on their CRM.
- Only 30% of companies measured the benefits of CRM.
- Only 37% knew if they shared a customer with another division in their company.
- Only 20% knew if a company ever visited their Web site.[20]

Bain and Company does an annual study of 25 of the most popular management tools. According to the 2009 report, CRM was the fourth most popular business tool used by 63% of companies; average use per tool was 42%. CRM ranked only behind benchmarking (76%), strategic planning (67%), and mission and vision statements (65%).[21]

While the trade and academic press often report high failure rates (around 70%) for CRM initiatives, recent evidence contradicts those conclusions. In fact, CRM programs are successful about two-thirds of the time. The highest success rates are in call centers and e-commerce, with the lowest success rates in field sales projects.[22]

When CRM programs fail, it often is because the project is purely technology focused instead of segmentation focused, with little foresight given to how customers, employees, and suppliers will be affected. The on-demand or software as a service (SaaS) CRM applications are now being supplanted by cloud-based technology led by traditional vendors such as salesforce.com, Microsoft, and Oracle as well as new providers such as Amazon and Sage. While the movement "to the cloud" will enhance firms' data management and analysis capabilities and may reduce costs, one concern may be the further erosion of customercentric business practices.

Some additional reasons why companies' CRM efforts fail include

1. *No focus.* Companies are not sure what they want from their customer relationship management program.
2. *No change-management policies.* CRM ultimately involves change, improving the relationship with the customer, altering the way the firm does business, and changing employee behaviors in the process.
3. *No buy-in.* A huge barrier to CRM implementation is "cultural," requiring involving and educating employees and supply chain partners.
4. *Business unit silos.* There is often a lack of cross-functional planning between departments, particularly IT and Sales.
5. *Complicated procedures.* CRM software will not magically automate and fix processes that are already ineffective.[23]

Many of the problems associated with poor CRM implementation can be avoided by careful planning, appropriate involvement of people in the organization and among supply chain members, customer-driven processes, and a sound platform for introducing CRM software and solutions.

Interactions with customers, regardless of the sales channel (i.e., direct sales, call centers, Web site), should be constantly managed to optimize the value of those relationships. Effective CRM systems provide a complete view of the customer, including the frequency, response (i.e., to promotions), and the quality (i.e., customer satisfaction) of the interactions with the customer. A good CRM system is capable of describing customer relationships in sufficient detail so that management, salespeople, customer service, and even suppliers have direct and real-time access to customer information. The information gathered should help match customer needs with product/service offerings, remind customers of service requirements, predict future purchases, and alert the company when a customer's purchase behavior has changed.

Recall that a key feature of CRM is sharing the customer experience across the organization and supply chain (360-degree view). Companies should continuously gather critical customer data known as BADI: *behaviors* (how often and where customers visit), *attitudes* (customer satisfaction, service quality assessments), *demographics*, and *insights* (share of market, share of wallet). Proper positioning of the company's offer (and value proposition) necessarily involves an understanding of the competitor's value proposition. Marketing knowledge should also include evaluating the customer database by performing an RFM (recency, frequency, and monetary value) analysis; determining customer lifetime value (factoring in customer acquisition costs as well as costs to serve the existing customer base); and tracking customer retention rates—see chapters 10 and 11.

Social Customer Relationship Management

A recent extension to CRM planning has been the integration of social media. This has been expressed quite nicely by Paul Greenberg as "the company's response to the customer's control of the conversation." Case in point, Comcast has used Twitter effectively to respond rapidly to customer complaints about its cable TV service.[24] Recent data indicates that 69% of companies are now testing social customer relationship management (SCRM) applications; 17% are currently using SCRM at the corporate or departmental level; and 14% have no plans to introduce this technology.[25]

An interesting new model to operationalize the social customer relationship management challenge was proposed by Jacob Morgan and is reproduced in Figure 9.5. This adaptable framework is useful in helping firms develop and

Social CRM Process

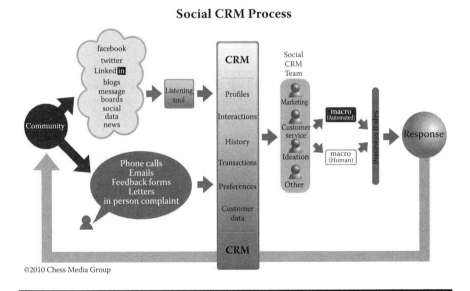

©2010 Chess Media Group

Figure 9.5 Social Customer Relationship Management (SCRM). (Model developed by Jacob Morgan, Chess Media Group, jacob@chessmediagroup.com. With permission.)

implement an SCRM program. First, notice the important role that marketing input (knowledge) from online and offline sources plays in capturing the relevant customer data. Information then drives business decision making. Morgan provides an example of how Southwest Airlines used Twitter, e-mail, and telephone (micro responses) and blogs (a macro response) to deal with controversial publicity generated in light of its policy toward obese passengers.[26]

Marketing Automation

An advanced application of CRM is marketing automation. Frank Jamieson, president of Applied DM Research and a Silicon Valley direct marketing expert, notes that marketing automation software is a hot industry sector today. He explains,

> Customer relationship management (CRM) systems (salesforce.com is a good example) was originally built for sales organizations, which created a problem for marketers who also wanted some form of automation to manage their marketing campaigns. Marketers developed work-arounds with salesforce.com which did not work very well, so an entire industry developed around automating marketing campaigns. Often the marketing automation software can plug into salesforce.com as a cloud computing addition. Marketo and Eloqua are leading examples of marketing automation companies.

In his role as a marketing educator for the Direct Marketing Association of Northern California, Jamieson also designed a webinar and moderated a panel discussion with three thought leaders in marketing automation: Laura Ramos of Forrester Research, Steve Woods of Eloqua, and Debbie Qaqish of The Pedowitz Group. Some of their insightful comments follow:

1. The top two sales objectives are improving lead quality (34%) and lead volume (27%).
2. The marketing challenge is to move from *demand generation* to *demand management*.
3. Lead nurturing means giving potential buyers reasons to stay in touch with you.
4. By really *knowing your customer*, you can deliver superior value.
5. Lead scoring means assessing the *ability* and *intent* to purchase (i.e., there is a huge difference whether your lead is a summer intern or the CEO).
6. Marketing automation can provide a "digital footprint" of the prospecting cycle.

7. LexisNexis is a company that has successfully implemented marketing auto-mation; the CEO regularly tracks marketing dashboards (see Chapter 11 for more on this topic).
8. The number of users of marketing automation systems is projected to grow from 3,000 to 6,000 companies.[27]

Relationship Marketing—Keys to Success

Marketing intelligence forms the basis of a customer relationship strategy. This is driven by: a customercentric orientation (Chapter 2), a clearly defined value proposition (Chapter 4), an alignment with key channel partners, focusing and dominating a market segment, and internal and supply chain process integra-tion. Finally, marketing knowledge and a sound customer value strategy guide the coordination and practice of the relationship management activities—analysis, planning, implementation, and control.

Relationship marketing can be used effectively to attract new customers, retain customers over the long term, and win back former users. This can be accomplished by learning as much as possible about your customers, developing differentiated marketing strategies based on profitability segments, interacting with customers on an ongoing basis, and customizing your offerings to best fit each user's needs.

Relationship marketing represents a shift in thinking about how companies do business. Because relationships are fragile, the attributes of trust, commitment, dependence, cooperation, and information exchange are crucial for enabling and maintaining strong relationships. (These issues were detailed earlier in the chapter.) You should also review Customer Value Checklist 9.

Here are six guidelines for employing a winning relationship marketing strat-egy. First, relationships are strengthened when sellers *create more value* for their customers. Customers are likely to offer their patronage to sellers who supply greater benefits or lower costs, or both. Companies should look for opportunities to offer new features and services, to customize their offering, to unbundle or bundle their services, to enhance product or service quality, and to offer guarantees. Zane Cycles, an independent bicycle retailer in Branford, Connecticut, understands this principle well. The company has differentiated itself from the pack by offering free lifetime service (e.g., full tune-ups, gear and brake adjustments, etc.) and a parts warranty for life for each bike purchased. In addition, new customers can try (ride) a bike for 30 days, and there is a 90-day price protection program to match any competitive price deals.

Second, *do the little things best*. Adding value does not always require doing something for the customer in a grandiose way; sometimes it's the small touches such as Amazon's recommendations or one-click ordering technology that delights customers and intensifies their loyalty. Chances are you have a favorite restaurant and a preferred server at that establishment. While the food is probably great, the service is often better, making for an enjoyable dining experience. The best servers fill your water glass before it is empty and seem to know when you need something even before you do. JetBlue follows this practice in its customer value and retention strategy, which includes providing attributes that distinguish the brand and experience at a relatively low cost, such as comfort (leather seats, extra leg room, and satellite TV at every seat) and customer service (friendly service, punctuality, and low baggage fees).

Third, customer relationships are improved by *quick response to customer needs*. Recall in Chapter 5 that responsiveness was one of the major predictors of service quality. Hartness International designs and manages packaging solutions for industry. For Hartness's customers, time is money, where a down bottling line can cost the customer tens or hundreds of thousands of dollars. Recognizing the importance of this problem, the company hires service technicians who are licensed pilots. That way, whenever Hartness has to fix a machine, technicians are not held hostage to airlines schedules—they can fly one of the company's planes to expedite repairs.

Fourth, companies who successfully practice relationship marketing have mastered *personalization*. Buyers often have individual problems that require unique solutions. Giving customers what they want and how they want it will grow their loyalties. Dell Computers has known this since Michael Dell began custom-building PCs in the mid-1980s. Dell's customer service plan now uses the Internet to automate and customize service much the same way in which they've streamlined and customized PC production. By using the Internet and social media, Dell provides personalized Web pages and is able to answer customers' technical questions with lightning speed. Recent communication initiatives include Direct2Dell (corporate blog featuring news and views); IdeaStorm (forum for sharing product concepts and critiques); and prolific use of Twitter, Facebook, and social media. A main emphasis in Dell's recent marketing strategy has been to build relationships with individual customers.

Fifth, effective utilization of *customer information* is another major factor in building stronger customer relationships. Golf equipment manufacturer Taylor Made has a database of over 1.5 million golfers with their names, addresses, e-mail addresses, birthdays, types of courses played, and vacations taken. The company uses this rich resource to send e-mails and stay in contact with its customers and drive them to its Web site, where new products are announced and special offers are made available.

A final key to practicing relationship marketing is to *track each relationship*. Customer lifetime value (CLV) is simply a projection of what customers are worth over a lifetime of doing business with them. Calculating LTV is important because of the impact of retention levels on profitability. For example, Cadillac knows that a loyal customer is worth about $425,000 to General Motors over the course of their lifetime.

Customer Value Checklist 9: How's the Health of Your Buyer-Seller Relationships?

Choose a major customer (or supplier) and rank the relative importance of each relationship enabler in building the business relationship. Rate each relationship marketing variable on a four-point scale, where 1 is unacceptable, 2 means needs improvement, 3 is good, and 4 is excellent. Explain your rationale for the individual and overall ratings. Propose a plan to strengthen that particular customer relationship. In your response, discuss specific weaknesses, opportunities, competitive advantage, long-term business goals, IMC/social media, cost considerations, product factors, and service requirements.

Relationship Enabler	Relationship Score
a. Trust	
b. Commitment	
c. Dependence	
d. Cooperation	
e. Information exchange	
f. Overall (sum "a" through "e" divided by 5)	

Summary

A massive shift has taken place from marketing to an anonymous sea of customers to developing, nurturing, and managing business relationships with individual customers. Just as the marketing concept focused businesses on seeing customers as the center of the universe, relationship marketing takes a quantum leap forward by concentrating on satisfying and keeping each customer over time. Strong relationships—with the end customer and the supply chain—are necessary for creating and sustaining value.

Business relationships are a fundamental asset that require ongoing investments of time, trust, and commitment. Savvy companies understand that value is created in the relationship they have with their customers—how they connect with them personally and systematically. The buying-cycle model, extended value-chain analyses, and CRM applications are all useful tools to understand value creation and assist in the relationship marketing process. Companies successful at practicing relationship marketing look for opportunities to add value through their business relationships, new offerings, service, and customization.

Customer Value Action Items

1. Compare and contrast traditional and relationship marketing. Discuss how to create win-win relationships with customers.
2. Are there situations where relationship marketing is not advisable? Why or why not?
3. Using a B2B example, explain how the buying-stages model can be used to attract, retain, and win back customers?
4. Given the companies listed below, provide examples of how practicing supply chain management would create more value for their end-user customers:
   a. Best Buy
   b. Toyota
   c. Samsung
   d. Disney
5. Explain how the vertically tiered (extended) value chain can enhance value creation and delivery using the following elements:
   a. Service
   b. Quality
   c. Image
   d. Price
6. A bank customer is angry because of a late fee on his car payment and wants it waived. The customer has an auto loan of $25,000, a checking account balance of $10,000, and a home mortgage of $175,000; his son has two savings accounts for a total of $20,000; and his wife's business does payroll with the bank. How would the bank benefit from a CRM system? How should the branch manager respond in this situation?
7. Critique and improve the Social CRM model offered in Figure 9.5. Provide an example of how a technology company can benefit from this framework.
8. Analyze Travelocity.com's value web by going through each of the following steps:
   a. Collect information on their business model—how and where the company engages in business, who its customers and competitors are, and the major activities Travelocity performs in the course of its business.

b. Determine which activities are internal and external to Travelocity. (Note that these are the activities—processes—that are the basis of their business model and contribute to the value that it adds to its customers.)

c. Identify Travelocity's customers, suppliers, competitors, and complementors—these are the key actors that can help create value, or in the case of its competitors, drain value.

d. Diagram a value web showing the *linkages* between each actor in the web. (Note: Use arrows to show the directions of the resource flows.)

Chapter 10

Customer Loyalty and Retention

Do what you do so well that they will want to see it again and bring their friends.

Walt Disney

A good customer should not change his shop, nor a good shop change its customers.

Chinese proverb

Starbucks got its swagger back. A victim of the Great Recession, the company was forced to close stores and lay off employees. Some said the day of the $4.00 cup of coffee was over. Reenergized, however, by the return of its founder Howard Schultz, today the company is on a roll—making better strategic decisions about its product mix and profitable once again. Recently, it passed Burger King to become the world's third largest restaurant chain behind Subway and McDonalds. A large part of this recent success has been closely connecting with its highly loyal, tech-savvy customers via its Web site (www.mystarbucks.com) and embracing social digital media. Starbucks has built a loyalty program, and more than 1 million customers now carry the Starbucks gold card and earn rewards for their purchases. How about a grande, iced vanilla caramel macchioto with one Splenda, nonfat milk, and whipped cream?

This chapter explains how companies should employ customer loyalty and retention initiatives to maximize long-term value. Specifically, the importance of customer retention (CR) is examined; loyalty initiatives and measures are described; usage segmentation is discussed as a tool to assist in CR planning; an integrated customer retention model is developed; and a five-step process for designing a CR program is offered.

Why Focus on Customer Retention?

Most companies spend a majority of their time, energy, and resources chasing new business. While it is important to find new customers to replace lost business, grow the enterprise, and expand into new markets, this goal should be secondary in importance to the main objective: keeping your customers and enhancing these customer relationships. Custom Research, a Minneapolis-based marketing research firm, was able to substantially increase revenues and profits by focusing on high-volume/high-margin clients. This was accomplished by practicing individualized "surprise and delight" marketing for its core strategic partners, handpicking and growing profitable new accounts, and systematically eliminating dozens of low-volume/low-margin customers.

According to an Accenture 2009 study, 69% of consumers switched one or more service providers due to poor service, which is 10 percentage points higher than in 2007.[1] Customers leave service organizations due to *service reasons* in about two-thirds of the cases. And, realize that these issues (core service problems, service encounter failures, inconvenience, and response to failed service) are largely controllable from the firm's perspective. Pricing, competitive, ethical, involuntary switching, and other factors account for the balance of the switching motives.[2]

Frederick Reichheld, of Bain & Company, is a leading consultant on loyalty management. In his book, *The Loyalty Effect*, he builds a strong case for emphasizing employee and customer retention in business. Service companies must retain the best personnel to win and keep good customers (typically, they lose half their employees in four years). He notes that "it's impossible to build a loyal bank of customers without a loyal employee base." Reichheld also shares these important statistics on the significance of customer retention.

- A typical company has a customer defection rate of 10%–30% per year.
- Raising the customer retention rate by 5% can increase the value of an average customer (lifetime profits) by 25%–100%.[3]

While a study by Marketing Metrics, a New Jersey firm, found that corporations spend 53% of their budget on customer retention, there is still concern that most effort is spent wooing new customers, or the great "one-night-stand." A vice president at that firm urged managers to look at this figure with skepticism. He noted that the definition of retention marketing is so broad that databases, satisfaction surveys, and couponing can qualify as retention activities (often such initiatives do not target existing high-value customers); compensation and promotions are generally based on demonstrating short-term profits (transaction business) at the expense of longer-term paybacks; and retention is viewed by many companies as the "fad of the week."[4]

In reality, 80% or more of marketing budgets are often earmarked for getting new business (or less than 20% for keeping customers). My recommendation is to invest at least 75% of your marketing budget on customer retention and relationship marketing activities. Conventional wisdom suggests that it costs at least five times more to get a new customer than keep an existing one. Three other "well-accepted beliefs" about customer relationship management are

1. Treat individual customers as assets (portfolio models can be useful).
2. Create valid estimates of customer lifetime value.
3. Be willing to *fire* unprofitable customers.[5]

Philip Kotler, the internationally renowned professor at Northwestern University, states that "the key to customer retention is customer satisfaction." He notes that satisfied customers: stay loyal longer, talk favorably about the organization, pay less attention to the competition, are less price sensitive, offer service ideas to the organization, and cost less to serve than new customers.[6] Today's market pressures often mean that satisfaction is no longer enough. So how about this amendment? *The key to customer retention is creating highly satisfied customers.*

Five-point Likert scales (e.g., poor, fair, good, very good, excellent) are industry standards for collecting customer satisfaction data. Research has found that the difference between a 4 and a 5 rating on a 5-point satisfaction scale is significant, resulting in an annual increase in customer retention of 12 percentage points, from 82% to 94%.[7] Given the importance of this information, is it really surprising that Lexus says to call their customer satisfaction specialist directly, if you are unable to give them a 5 for your last service encounter?

Customer Loyalty—Issues, Strategies, and Analysis

Why are few customers completely loyal, many somewhat loyal, and others loyal to no one? How does loyalty impact business performance? Which brands matter the most to consumers? What marketing strategies work best to create loyal customers? Can customer loyalty segments be identified and targeted? These are some of the vexing questions that managers must grapple with on a daily basis.

Limited loyalty means that the organization must strive to increase share-of-customer. For example, an industrial paper supplier may grow Customer Z's annual rebuys from 12% to 18% of category expenditures through consultative problem solving, outstanding service, price deals, or relationship-building/social media usage. Volume pricing, seasonal promotions, and trade shows may be employed to increase situational loyalty for infrequent yet high-volume purchases.

Customer loyalty clearly impacts financial performance. A research study by Accenture found that customer loyalty accounts for 38% of margin, 40% of revenue growth, and 38% of shareholder value.[8] According to the 2010 Brand Keys Loyalty Leaders List, the top 10 brands were Apple iPhone, Samsung cell phones, Walmart, Grey Goose vodka, Apple Computers, Hyundai, Amazon, J.Crew, Blackberry, and Avis. Companies on the rise were Progressive Insurance, Avon, Dunkin Donuts, and Domino's Pizza. Decliners included Toyota, Palm, Tylenol, and BP.[9]

Apple has become one of the world's most valued and respected companies. A large part of its marketing success is due to its highly devoted customer base. Apple's strategy to create loyal customers is based on an 11-point plan: (1) the Apple store, (2) complete solutions and complementary products, (3) the Mac brand identification, (4) strong product line, (5) media hype, (6) targeting the education market, (7) products that excel, (8) limited need for service, (9) consistency, (10) innovation, and (11) attractive products.[10]

Some other innovative loyalty-building strategies include sending salespeople to work at the offices of your best customers, participating in customers events, interviewing your customers' customers, holding a retreat with a major customer to share best practices, inviting customers to participate in training seminars, setting up a customer advisory council, developing a preferred-customer pricing strategy, rewarding customers for referring new business, developing three- to five-year business plans with customers, and partnering with key accounts on industry research projects.[11]

Realize that there are three guiding principles to loyalty management:

1. Most customers buy on a portfolio basis.
2. All customers are not created equally.
3. Loyalty is retention with attitude.

Loyals (involved) and *habituals* (indifferent) are usually the most profitable customers, while *variety seekers* (proactive searchers) and *switchers* (price shoppers) are generally less profitable customers.[12]

Factoring time into the equation results in four customer loyal segments; note that only one of these segments is highly desirable. *Strangers* are short-term, low-profit customers, while *butterflies* have high-profit potential but tend to be short term and disloyal. *Barnacles* stay around for the long term but generate relatively low profits. Finally, *true friends* are both highly profitable and are long-term customers.[13]

Measuring Customer Loyalty

There are many ways to evaluate customer loyalty, such as satisfaction scores and indexes, repurchase intentions, recommendation intentions, etc. (see Chapter 11 for an expanded discussion of customer value metrics). In this section, we look at two frequently used approaches: Net Promoter Score (NPS) and Recency, Frequency, and Monetary Value (RFM analysis). Customer Value Insight 10 shows how to calculate these informative loyalty metrics.

NPS

Due to its simplicity and explanatory power, the Net Promoter Score (NPS) has been widely hailed by industry as the best metric for assessing customer loyalty and a company's ability to grow. Developed by Reichheld, this single-item, 11-point satisfaction scale is now used by leading global companies such as American Express, General Electric, Intuit, Overstock.com, Progressive Corporation, and T-Mobile.[14]

NPS leaders for 2011 by industry sector include USSA (financial services), Kaiser Permanente (insurance), JetBlue (airlines), Metro PCS (telecommunications), Apple (technology), Amazon.com (online services), and Trader Joe's (retail).[15] While the measure has captured the imagination of customer value managers during the past decade, many academics and industry researchers contend that NPS is subject to measurement bias, lacks validity, and is no better than other loyalty metrics.[16]

RFM

Recency, frequency, and monetary value (RFM) analysis is a helpful tool in evaluating customer usage and loyalty patterns. Recency refers to the last service encounter/transaction; frequency assesses how often these customer-company experiences occur; and monetary value probes the amount that is spent, invested, or committed by customers for the firm's products and services.

Consider this example: I purchased less than $100 worth of brochure materials from Paper Direct for a one-time consulting project. This eager vendor immediately placed me into the "preferred" customer category and began sending me expensive catalogs about every three weeks without any follow-up orders. RFM analysis tells us that this is not sound marketing practice, since this company treated all one-time "try-ers" as "best" customers. Note that this transaction fared poorly on all three RFM dimensions: recency (several years ago), frequency (a single purchase), and monetary value (low).

Following the lead of direct marketers who are major users of this approach, online retailers have applied RFM analysis with surprising results. For example, for apparel e-tailers, new customers cost 20% to 40% more to acquire when compared to their brick-and-mortar counterparts. However, online repeat customers spend more than twice as much in the months 24–30 of their relationships as they do in the first six months.[17]

Customer Value Insight 10: Customer Loyalty Metrics[18]

CALCULATING A NET PROMOTER SCORE

1. Following the service experience, ask each customer one simple question:

   Based on your last experience with Company X, how likely would you be to recommend Company X to a friend or colleague?

   Customers respond on a 0–10-point rating scale, where 0 is not at all likely and 10 is extremely likely.
2. Respondents are classified as promoters (9–10), passives (7–8), or detractors (0–6).
3. The percentage of customers who are detractors is subtracted from the percentage of promoters (passives are not considered in the analysis) to obtain an NPS.

Example

JetBlue customers: 72% are promoters, 16% are passives, and 12% are detractors. Jet Blue's NPS is 60. This is then compared to the competitive set. For example, Southwest Airlines's NPS is 59, the industry average is 15, and US Airways is -12.

DOING AN RFM ANALYSIS

1. Access a summary of each customer's RFM transaction history, including most recent purchase, frequency of purchases, and monetary value spent per order.
2. Sort customers by purchase dates in reverse chronological order. Divide the customer list into five equal segments. Tag the most *recent* customer quintile as 1, while the least recent purchases are quintile 5.
3. Sort your customers by *frequency* (number of orders) and apply the same methodology and tagging process as in #2.
4. Sort your customers by *monetary value* (average dollar amount of each order) and apply the same methodology and tagging process as in #2.

5. You now have created RFM scores for each of your customers, from your best customer segment (111) to your
worst (555).

COMMENT

It is likely that you will be able to substantiate Pareto's 80/20 rule
with your best segment(s) (see next section, "Usage Analysis
and Customer Retention"). The goal is to acquire look-alikes of
your best customers and improve your marketing effectiveness
with the other "good" RFM segments.

QUESTIONS TO THINK ABOUT

1. Your boss wants you to obtain "hard data" on how successful you are in your customer loyalty program. Which
of these two measures, NPS or RFM, would you use
and why?
2. Describe an industry sector where you would use NPS
and another industry sector where RFM is preferable.
3. After reviewing your situation, you decide that you want
to use an alternative customer-loyalty metric. Explain why
your proposed measure offers a better way to assess customer loyalty for your business.

Usage Analysis and Customer Retention

Segmenting markets by consumption patterns can be quite insightful for understanding your customer mix. Land's End and L.L. Bean use "customer purchase
patterns to compute the probability of purchase for each of the merchandise lines.
Armed with this information, these firms send the customer only those catalogs for
which the calculated purchase probability exceeds a threshold value."[19]

Differentiated marketing strategies are needed for the various user groups—
first-time users, repeat customers, heavy users, and former users. By classifying
customer accounts based on usage frequency and variety, companies can develop
effective strategies to retain and upgrade customers. There are many highly informative, low-cost applications of usage analysis that should be considered by management. Examples include assessing:

1. Heavy, medium, light, former, and nonusers (A,B,C,D,X)
2. Heavy half segmentation (80/20 rule, see discussion later in this section)
3. Users versus nonusers
4. Competitive users

5. Loyal (degree) versus nonloyal customers
6. Product/service applications by user group
7. Adopter categories—innovators, followers, laggards
8. Geographic comparisons (customer penetration indices, growth)

For example, a hotel grades customers based on the number of rooms booked annually. The key accounts are A1 users: These are large organizations that reserve thousands of room nights and conference facilities. A2 customers also book a high volume of rooms without the conference arrangements. A third category of heavy users is the A3 account that is a solid, loyal customer that annually generates hundreds of room nights. Four descending usage levels of B customers (B1 to B4) are considered medium users. Finally, five types of C accounts (C1 to C5) represent light users. The C5 guest may only visit the hotel once a year.

By classifying customers into usage categories, management can design appropriate strategies to create value for each market segment. The objective is to move customers up the ladder, where possible. The implication of usage analysis is that all customers are not equal—some are clearly more important than other categories. Historically, Neiman Marcus has focused on heavy users. The company identified 100,000 customers who spend more than $12,000 annually in its stores and contribute half of its sales. Research found that the other half is growing, and the retailer is now paying close attention to younger, less affluent customers. The marketing strategy for the "other half" now includes sales training to show customers lower priced options (in contrast to the up-sell approach used for heavy users), adding less-expensive designer brands to the merchandise mix and opening more Last Call clearance centers.[20]

In business and professional service markets, the best customers may be identified as key accounts based on customer ranking (e.g., the 100 most important customers), minimum sales volume level (e.g., $1 million in annual business), or market share (e.g., an annual account exceeds 1% of total business). The Pareto Principle, or 80/20, rule is insightful in this context. Realize that in a typical business, approximately 80% of sales come from about 20% of customers; and generally, about 80% of sales come from 20% of the goods or services offered. It is essential to defend this core business, since heavy users (A accounts) are primary targets for key competitors. These highly profitable customers require frequent advertising, promotions, sales calls, and ongoing communication efforts.

Strategy Consulting Inc.'s usage analysis revealed that 26% of its business (long-term clients) accounted for 84% of its profits. In addition, 22% of its revenues (mergers and acquisitions) yielded 87% of its profits. Operational projects (33% of its revenues) were found to be a losing proposition for the company, and subsequent inquiries in this area were farmed out to specialty consultancies.[21]

Medium users (B customers) form the solid base of your business. Revenue-enhancement strategies such as cross-selling or value-added services can be used to keep these customers satisfied and grow their business. Telephone calls, e-mail, and occasional sales calls are suggested to stay in touch with this group. By knowing who the better customers are (the As and Bs)—through geographic, demographic, psychographic, and benefit research—a profile of "typical users" is established. This information is very helpful in planning subsequent customer attraction/conquest marketing efforts. Realize that the marketing information system, the database, plays a key role in customer analysis and decision making.

For unprofitable customers (many C accounts), the company often needs to find new ways to serve them more effectively. Technology such as ATM machines can be used in this regard. Quarterly contact through newsletters and direct mail or access options such as toll-free telephone numbers and Web sites maintains adequate communication with low-volume users. In some cases, it may even be desirable to sever the relationship with certain unprofitable customers.

An understanding of customers' purchasing patterns helps companies hold on to their key customers and gain a larger share of their business. Share of customer (customer retention focus) has supplanted market share (customer attraction focus) as a relevant business performance dimension in many markets. Share of customer is adapted by industry and goes by such names, among others, as share of care (health care), share of stomach (fast food), and share of wallet (financial services). If a company can increase a customer's share of business from 20% to 30%, this will have a dramatic impact on market share and profitability.

Customers can be classified via usage analysis (as previously described), and differentiated marketing approaches for each target market can be developed. According to Rust, Zeithaml, and Lemon, FedEx categorized its customers internally as the good, the bad, and the ugly based on profitability.[22] These marketing scholars propose a generalized four-tier usage segmentation system, as follows:

1. *Platinum tier*: The company's most profitable customers, typically heavy users, not overly price sensitive, willing to invest in and try new offerings, and are committed customers of the firm.
2. *Gold tier*: Profitability levels not as high as *platinums*, seek price discounts, less loyal, and use multiple vendors.
3. *Iron tier*: Essential customers who provide the volume needed to utilize the firm's capacity, but their spending levels, loyalty, and profitability are not substantial enough for special treatment.
4. *Lead tier*: Customers who cost the company money. They demand more attention than they are due given their spending and profitability, and they are sometimes problem customers, complaining about the firm and tying up resources.

Fast Industries, a plastics producer of label holders, serves leading retail store chains, including Walmart, Target, CVS Drugs, and Michael's Crafts. Although there are over 2,000 retail chains in the United States, it was estimated that fewer than 100 will purchase 90% of the store fixtures components that Fast offers. They did business with 30 of these retailers, and for each of these key accounts, delivering superior and customized customer value is a top priority. Service to one customer might mean high levels of in-stock orders. To another it might mean ease in placing an order. To yet a third, it may be constant attention from a sales representative. Quality as a criterion can be broken down into components as varied as the product's engineering and design, its on-time delivery, and/or its being packed and billed correctly. Implementing this targeted customer retention strategy increased revenues by 20% and profits by 25%.[23]

In sum, usage analysis—which is facilitated through CRM systems—can greatly assist us in our customer retention activities. Think about how to hold heavy users and key accounts, upgrade light and medium users, build customer loyalty, understand buying motives to meet/exceed expectations, use appropriate selling strategies for each targeted usage group, win back lost customers, and learn why nonusers are not responding to your value proposition.

Customer Value/Retention Model

Marketing managers know that it is critical to deliver superior value to their customers: This ensures business profitability. The Customer Value/Retention model offers a good way of explaining the key relationships among the core elements that create value in an organization (see Figure 10.1). As we have seen in Chapter 4,

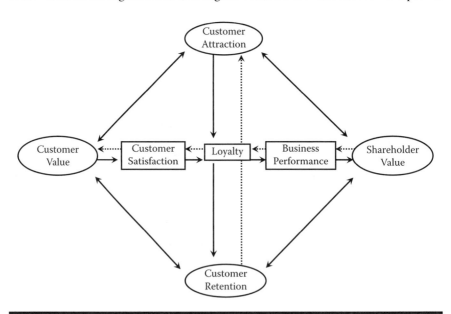

Figure 10.1 Customer Value/Retention model. (Journal of Targeting, Measurement, and Analysis for Marketing, Vol. 10(3), 263 © Art Weinstein 2011.)

customer value is built through the proper mix of S-Q-I-P (service, quality, image, and price)—those elements that attract customers to the organization.

A research study of professional service providers (attorneys, dentists, doctors, financial planners, private investigators, etc.) in the Tampa Bay, Florida, area confirmed strong relationships between customer value and each of the S-Q-I-P components. Furthermore, stepwise regression analyses found that customer value, satisfaction, and loyalty explained 63% of variance for customer retention.[24] Hence, a sharp focus on creating exceptional value, doing what it takes to satisfy customers, and building loyalty programs leads to high customer retention rates.

Realize that a one-time *buyer* is really a *try-er*, rather than a customer. To move beyond the transaction stage, organizational experiences must meet or (preferably) exceed the buyer's expectations. Repeated incidents of high satisfaction are sought through the effective utilization of relationship marketing strategies, leading to higher customer loyalty. While satisfaction may be viewed as largely a passive customer condition, loyalty requires an active or proactive relationship.[25]

Loyalty, in turn (which results from the quality of the customer-company relationship), leads to improved business performance/shareholder value and increased customer retention rates. Furthermore, the ability to successfully retain customers results in increased market values. The vertical customer retention chain shown in Figure 10.1 indicates that, ideally, loyal new customers are retained for many years. Research has shown that companies may expect loyal customers to range from about 40% to 75%, depending on the sector; loyalty, however, does not equate with exclusivity.[26] The business model of Amazon.com is based on retaining customers for a considerable number of years—12 years by some analysts' forecasts—in order to develop deep, continuing relationships that will justify the company's heavy investment in its site.

Feedback loops are also depicted in the Customer Value/Retention model. Strong customer value secures customers over the long term. Similarly, customers (both new and existing ones) want to maintain relationships with well-respected organizations that have high market values.

The customer value/marketing implications of the model are readily apparent. First, the key variables and their relationships to one another are clarified. This provides strategic guidance to management. Second, it stresses long-term relationships (retention) but still realizes that some customer defection and attrition will occur, so customer attraction must remain a priority. Third, the model is interfunctional and systematic: It ties marketing objectives to the big picture, the financial situation.

Designing a Customer Retention Program

To develop an effective customer retention (CR) program, organizations can follow this five-step process.

1. *Determine your current CR rate.* It is surprising how few companies know the percentage of customers that leave (the defection rate) or the percentage of customers that they are able to retain annually (the retention rate). There are many ways to measure customer retention. This includes:
   a. Annual and targeted customer retention rates
   b. Weighted customer retention rates (accounts for usage differences)
   c. Segmented retention indicators (subgroup analysis based on geographic, demographic, lifestyle, product preferences, or other categories)
   d. Share of customer
   e. Customer lifetime value (CLTV)
   f. Recency, frequency, and monetary value (RFM)
   Choosing an appropriate measure(s) provides a starting point for assessing a firm's success in keeping customers.

2. *Analyze the defection problem.* Step two is a three-pronged attack. First, we must identify disloyal customers. Second, we need to understand why they left. According to DeSouza, there are six types of defectors. Customers go elsewhere because of lower price, superior products, better service, alternative technologies, market changes (they move or go bankrupt), and "political" considerations.[27] An analysis of switching motives can also provide insight here. And third, strategies need to be developed to overcome the nonloyal purchasing behavior.

3. *Establish a new CR objective.* Let's assume that your company is currently retaining 75% of its customers. A realistic goal may be to increase client retention by three points annually (to 78% in the first year) and to keep 85% of your clients within five years. Customer retention objectives should be based on organizational capabilities (strengths, weaknesses, resources, etc.); customer and competitive analyses; and benchmarking with the industry/sector, comparable firms, and high-performing units in your company.

4. *Invest in a targeted CR plan to enhance customer loyalty.* Targeted retention planning means that organizations should segment customers by relevant dimensions such as geography, demographic and socioeconomic variables, and other criteria to best understand customer profiles and purchasing patterns. The cost (potential lifetime value) of a single lost customer can be substantial. This is magnified exponentially when we realize the overall annual cost of lost business. Consider the impact of a 25% defect rate (3,750 defections) for a hospital caring for 15,000 patients per year. Assuming an average per-patient revenue of $2,500, this means a loss in revenues of nearly $9.4 million and a dive in profits of more than $700,000 (assuming a 7.5% profit margin). By investing a modest amount in CR program initiatives/patient-retention training, the hospital can dramatically improve its profitability.

5. *Evaluate the success of the CR program.* As an iterative process, the final phase in designing a solid customer retention plan is to ensure that it is working. Careful scrutiny is required to assess the program's impact on keeping existing customers

(see Customer Value Checklist 10 for further guidance in this area). Upgrading current customer relationships may be a secondary business objective. At this point, we gather new information to learn to what extent our CR rate improved. We may need to revisit our benchmarks and further probe isolated causes of defection. CR strategies and tactics will be closely analyzed to determine which methods worked best and those that had little or no impact on keeping customers.

Customer Value Checklist 10: Gathering Customer Retention Data

1. What are your current and targeted CR rates?
2. Given your current defection rate, how often must you replenish your customer pool?
3. Has your CR rate increased during the past three years?
4. What is the lifetime value (CLTV) of a customer?
5. What is the cost of a lost customer?
6. What percentage of your marketing budget is spent on customer retention activities?
7. On average, how much do you spend on current customers annually?
8. What criteria does your company use for developing targeted retention programs by market segment?
9. Do you invest more on high-value (A) customers?
10. How does your firm use NPS and/or RFM analyses?

Customer Retention Approaches

There are literally dozens of methods that can be used to keep customers. Customer retention tactics (for example, promotional incentives) are short term in nature, while CR strategies create lasting value for customers. Customer retention efforts should begin as soon as the firm acquires a customer. These efforts should include learning as much as possible about customer needs, responding promptly to any indications of disinterest, making customers feel truly cared for, resolving complaints quickly and efficiently, and demonstrating a willingness to negotiate with high-value customers who show signs of inactivity.[28]

As the Customer Value/Retention model explained, companies must create loyalty from new customers in order to retain them. Some of the most common and effective approaches for enhancing retention include building a customer database/marketing information system, designing ongoing customer programs (continuity- and loyalty-based initiatives such as frequent-flyer miles), offering long-term services (membership/subscription programs), customizing promotion (using reminder advertising and press releases), focusing on key accounts and heavy users, using newsletters/informational materials to stay in touch with infrequent customers, engaging in social media, attending trade shows, researching customers needs and wants, and welcoming suggestions and complaints.

As we can see, there is a multitude of potential customer retention ideas, tactics, and strategies that can be utilized successfully by value-creating managers. How do we know which approaches should be employed by your company? The following seven criteria provide a useful point of reference:

1. Efficiency (low cost)
2. Effectiveness (likelihood to succeed)
3. Adaptability (strategic fit with your organizational culture)
4. Consistency (works well with your current marketing plan)
5. Competitive advantage
6. Ease of implementation
7. Projected profitability

Hospitals have turned to customer retention planning to keep patients in highly competitive environments. A list of 30 patient-retention ideas in five key areas is summarized in Figure 10.2.

Marketers generally examine past and current purchase patterns in analyzing customer retention. An often-overlooked measure is the customer's future

- *Image/Promotion*—community service, direct mail, educational offerings, health fairs, integrated marketing communications, newsletters, regular contact with patient, useful informational materials, website
- *Service Quality*—continuous quality initiatives, convenience, customer service training, demonstrate that patients are highly valued, mystery shopping, patient representatives/ombudsman, service failure training, smile, treat patients as family
- *Research*—analyze defection rates/reasons, classify customers by usage/satisfaction/loyalty, develop targeted retention programs, "inside-out" (patient-focused) healthcare model
- *Internal Marketing*—loyalty task force, prepare "solutions" to recurring problems, share appropriate patient data with staff, reward and publicize customer care patient of the month
- *Patient-Centered*—"dialogue" marketing, patient bill of rights, patient care councils, understand patient expectations

Figure 10.2   Patient retention tactics.

orientation. Recent research initiatives have identified several useful metrics for evaluation. These are

Expected future use
Anticipated regret
Intent to switch
Intent to remain loyal (return to provider and recommend provider)[29]

Innovative customer value managers should consider these measures to gain additional insight on retention and a potential edge over their competition.

Summary

Companies that deliver superior value to customers on an ongoing basis are able to keep them over the long term. This chapter reviewed the essentials for establishing a customer loyalty and retention focus. By maintaining consistently high levels of customer satisfaction, customer defection becomes less likely. This results in enhanced business performance and increases shareholder value. Relationship marketing is the key strategy to obtain the desired results of retaining more customers, getting better customers, upgrading customer relationships, and using existing customers as advocates for acquiring new customers. The final chapter of the book examines customer value metrics in more detail.

Customer Value Action Items

1. Describe a customer loyalty program that you participate in—in the marketplace and in the marketspace. How do these programs create value for you?
2. Identify two companies that do a good job in retaining customers and upgrading customer relationships.
3. What is the relationship among customer value, satisfaction, loyalty, retention, and business performance? How can a management consulting firm or marketing research company use the Customer Value/Retention model to do a better job getting and keeping customers?
4. In today's fast-changing and highly competitive market environment, customer retention is more important than customer attraction. Do you agree or disagree with this statement? Why or why not?
5. Should companies develop a separate marketing plan for keeping customers?
6. Identify five product or service categories (and organizations, as applicable) whereby you exhibit varying customer loyalty patterns.
   a. Complete loyalty
   b. Situational loyalty—high loyalty for selected purchases

    c. Multiple loyalty—a high degree of loyalty to two or more organizations in a category

    d. Limited loyalty

    e. No loyalty

7. What are the top three reasons that customers leave your company? How can these switching motives be overcome?

8. List some of the customer retention strategies and tactics that your organization uses. What are some additional CR approaches that it should think about using?

9. Does your firm segment its market through usage analysis? Describe your usage segments and explain how you would implement a targeted customer value/marketing program for each key market segment.

10. Choose a company in one of the following industries: business services, technology, B2B distribution, or an Internet pure-play. Answer the following five questions:

    a. Identify approaches that the company should use to retain customers and build long-term relationships.

    b. Rank your top three strategies for the business selected.

    c. Project the lifetime value of an average customer for this company (show calculation).

    d. How should this organization measure long-term customer satisfaction, loyalty, and retention? (Select two key metrics.)

    e. Estimate a Net Promoter Score for this company (percent promoters, passives, and detractors).

11. Best Buy has redesigned its stores to appeal to specific market segments such as high-income men (Barrys), suburban moms (Jills), male technology enthusiasts (Buzzes), young family men (Rays), and small-business owners. The company plans on targeting two of the five segments based on the geodemographics of local markets. Critique this strategy from a customer value, loyalty, and retention perspective.

Chapter 11

Customer Value Metrics*

I know that 50% of my advertising is wasted. I just don't know which half.

John Wanamaker

Everything that can be counted does not necessarily count; everything that counts cannot necessarily be counted.

Albert Einstein

It has been said that "you can't manage what you can't measure." One of the prime challenges that company executives face is choosing the measures (metrics) that matter most. These "right" measures or key performance indicators (KPIs) are used to assess business success and plan future customer value (CV) strategies. And the definition of success, like corporate cultures, varies from one organization to another. Since we cannot measure everything, the challenge is to focus on those metrics that truly impact business performance. As an example, a travel provider in the time-share industry concentrated on four functional areas—operations, production, customer service, and marketing (business development). For the marketing department, one key metric dealt with pitch-rate conversion of weekly unit purchases; the objective was to improve from one-in-seven prospect closes to one-in-six.

---

* This chapter was coauthored by Shane Smith and Art Weinstein. Dr. Smith is an assistant Professor of Marketing at Kennesaw State University, Kennesaw, Georgia. He can be reached at ssmit304@kennesaw.edu. Dr. Weinstein is a professor of marketing at Nova Southeastern University, Fort Lauderdale, Florida. He can be reached at art@huizenga.nova.edu, or visit his Web site www.artweinstein.com.

The final chapter in the book discusses the role of metrics in evaluating the success of customer value-based marketing strategies. Specifically, we address the need for accountability in marketing, a five-step process for measuring customer value (the 5Cs), and the marketing dashboard concept. Throughout the chapter, our intent is to offer practical guidelines for designing and implementing a strong CV-based metrics program.

Accountability in Marketing

According to the CMO Council, customer analytics are the top priority among Chief Marketing Officers (CMOs). More than three-in-five (62%) said their focus is on analyzing customer data to improve target marketing strategy. Nearly half (46%) are investing in digital demand generation and online relationship building. Improved qualifying and tracking lead conversion was cited as a major objective by 44% of CMOs.[1] While data analysis is necessary, information capture transformed into strategic insights is the desired end product—to make better customer-based decisions.

Organizations need sharing of the strategic analysis and plan within the leadership team. A good management information system provides team members access to pertinent knowledge needed in understanding the realities of the internal and external environments. Recognize that information is unique among the factors of production. It gains value through additional perspectives as it is shared for a common good or purpose.

Marketing departments and their CMOs are held more accountable for their actions these days. Boardrooms are asking what the return will be on a marketing expense even before the marketing staff can take the first step toward action. Perhaps, we can chalk this up to a combination of the poor economy as well as tighter restraints on corporations via public outcry since the government's involvement with the TARP (Troubled Asset Relief Program) loans. Nonetheless, CMOs are now more likely to be asked what their actions will mean financially for the organization than ever before.

The problem with this scenario is that most marketers do not know where to begin to measure their business performance, beyond that of the tactical nature. Those that do have a notion of basic metrics often only measure customers' intents, and they cannot convert these figures into meaningful information that relates to the financial health of the organization.

Creating a New Mindset about Measuring Marketing Performance

As mentioned repeatedly in the book, organizations need to become more market oriented. This paradigm shifts the focus from the product and brand toward the customer. Measuring production effectiveness and brand equity is still an integral part of an organization's success; however, this is only done once the strategy gained from being truly customercentric is in place. This new customer-driven reality asks the CMO and all marketers in the organization to consider new measurement tools and approaches.

Since managers are being held accountable for their actions, marketing departments now must justify their budgets (i.e., dollars spent for product development, market research, IMC campaigns, staffing plans, etc.). The boardroom, the CEO, the CFO, and the rest of the C-suite are all expecting greater detail prior to approving marketing plans. Gone are the days of the "blank check and first-class travel," when the marketing department received large expense accounts and resources to perform its duties without having to provide solid evidence to support the proposed initiatives.

Communication with the finance department is sorely needed. As part of a corporate culture of accountability and transparency, the CMO and the entire marketing team must know what the CFO wants in return (and relevant constraints). The quick answer is financial evidence.

Just as international marketers must learn the language of their host countries, corporate marketers must learn the financial language of business and tie their projected performance to dollar equivalents, and not just "soft" measures such as brand awareness or preference.

New metrics that link financial information directly to the customer's actions (or predicted actions) are called for. This allows marketers to demonstrate results in the strategic decision-making process (and provide real input to the executive team) as opposed to only responding to tactical measures (e.g., brand preference or click-through rates). If a measure is already on a strategic level (e.g., brand equity), marketers should consider building a metric that measures the customer more directly (e.g., customer equity).

New customercentric metrics not only help the CMO communicate the marketing agenda to the C-suite, but also play a more active role in shaping future business strategy. The "financial evidence" that CMOs frequently used came from return on investment (ROI). This term was often mismanaged, however. First, the word return is derived from a financial return. Many of the metrics used in the past were not financially linked in a direct manner. Second, the word *return* is referenced to what the organization earns from the investment (payback). Third, the word *investment* was never quite accepted by the C-suite when it came to marketing programs and processes. Instead, the money spent on marketing activities was generally viewed as a business expense and not an investment. This perception is what must change in the new era of customercentricity and customer value-based metrics.

What will be developed are Customer Return on Marketing Investment (CROMI) metrics. The difference in terminology may appear small, semantically, but can be huge to the marketing charge. First, the word *customer* has been added to the return. This puts a focus on the consumer and the value to the organization of individual buyers. Metrics that are able to capture the value of each customer transaction (as well as relationships) allow management to observe and respond to all changes that occur in the marketplace/marketspace. This not only helps to guide the marketing team, but gives them a jump start for gathering business performance documentation, in financial terms. The second word added is *marketing*. Marketing is used to emphasize the investment in the area of customer focus. The phrase "marketing investment" makes it clear that each dollar spent on improving overall customer value is a worthwhile investment, not just an expense (possibly misguided) to be recorded in the accounting books. Based on research by Seggie and colleagues, a set of seven important questions to ask about your metrics is provided in Customer Value Checklist 11.[2] Marketers can use these guidelines to develop more powerful customer value metrics.

Customer Value Checklist 11: Designing Better Measures

1. Do your marketing metrics use the same financial language as the rest of the company?
2. Does your company develop forward-looking metrics taking into account changing competitive dynamics, environmental shifts, and internal initiatives, such as new product launches and brand extensions.
3. Do your marketing metrics adopt a long-term perspective?
4. Do your marketing metrics consider microlevel data (e.g., share of customer) as well as macrolevel data (e.g., market share)?
5. Can you move your analysis from independent measures (e.g., sales or profits) to causal chains (e.g., value creation, satisfaction, loyalty, market performance)?
6. Do your measures consider relative performance (compared to competitors) as well as absolute numbers (your corporate business performance)?
7. Are your metrics based on subjective measures or objective measures (key performance indicators)?

Adapted from Seggie et al., "Measurement of Return on Marketing Investment: A Conceptual Framework and the Future of Marketing Metrics," *Industrial Marketing Management* 36 (2007), 834–841.

The 5C Approach to Customer Value Metrics

A five-step process (the 5Cs) for designing a customer value metrics plan is discussed in this section. These steps are

1. Collect voice of the customer (VOC) data
2. Assess customer lifetime value
3. Assess customer retention
4. Assess customer revenue
5. Establish relevant level of communication

Collect VOC Data

Assuming solid business objectives have been specified, the first step in measuring customer value is getting relevant information to evaluate. A great starting point is to gather Voice of the Customer (VOC) information.[3] The VOC may be obtained from a number of sources, but falls into one of three major categories. The first is direct from the customer, e.g., communications with the actual customer or from employees (such as sales reps) who deal directly with the customer. Such information is often the most recent and most valid. This method is often good at capturing information in real time, and thus if any adjustments are to be made, it gives the organization time to rectify the problem immediately. A downside to capturing the customer's voice in real time is that emotion may overpower rational thought. As we all know, an upset customer can overstate or overreact to a situation and thus negatively bias their responses.

A second form of collecting the VOC is the survey method or other forms of marketing research (depth interviews, focus groups, observational techniques, etc.). Although questionnaires are common and useful, they have some drawbacks. First, a survey is a lagging indicator. In other words, surveys (including e-mail) are often late to the party, as they are sent to the customers after the service experience was delivered. This raises the likelihood that the customer does not remember the exact details of the service encounter. The customer may have lost some emotion, making it difficult to accurately gauge the impact the experience had on the user. At times, the customer may downplay the incident to the organization.

A third approach to collecting the VOC is to utilize data that the organization obtains through other business practices. For example, an organization gathers information on all of its purchases, visits to the store or Web site, the order of pages that a customer visits online, etc. Today, many organizations have sophisticated IT systems in place that coordinate well with marketing reward or affinity programs. These systems are often part of customer relationship management (CRM) systems (see Chapter 9). Such loyalty programs are able to track customers' actions once they have signed in to the Web site or scanned their reward card at the store register. From then on, each move and action is recorded by the organization. Grocery stores are able to recognize that customers who purchase prepackaged salad ingredients are also inclined to purchase salad dressings. Web-based stores are able to track their visitors' click patterns to learn what items they viewed and in what order they viewed them. No matter the industry sector, most companies now have access to a Fort Knox of secondary data that they routinely compile through the course of doing business.

In combination, the three VOC sources can give a complete profile of the customer. The more good sources of information that are available, the more likely the organization is able to truly understand customer preferences. This helps companies design winning strategies to satisfy and delight customers, over time. CV Insight 11 delves deeper into the issues of what type of and how much information to collect.

CV Insight 11: What to Measure

As we have seen, top executives, board members, and shareholders are now demanding accountability for new and established marketing programs. A major issue for debate in an organization is what metrics to collect and evaluate. (A secondary issue is how frequently to obtain the data.) The choices are wide ranging—from a single metric such as Net Promoter Score (NPS), which was discussed in Chapter 10, to literally hundreds of potential marketing and performance variables. For example, one leading book on the subject claims that there are 50 relevant marketing metrics related to the marketing mix, profit margins, customer profitability, share of market, the Web, and other key areas in business.[4]

We prefer the handful approach—choosing a few strong measures that make the most sense for a particular organization within the context of a customer value metrics framework (review the 5C approach). In line with this more parsimonious thinking, Kokkinaki and Ambler concluded that marketing metrics can be summarized into six major categories:

1. Financial measures: turnover, contribution margins, and profits
2. Competitive measures: share of market, advertising, and promotion
3. Consumer behavior: customer penetration, loyalty, and new customers
4. Consumer intermediate measures: brand recognition, satisfaction, and purchase intention

5. Direct customer measures: distribution level, intermediary profits, and service quality
6. Innovativeness measures: new products launched and the percentage of annual revenue from these new products[5]

Arthur M. Hughes, a database expert, prefers to keep it simple by stressing three key measures of business performance: return on investment (ROI), profitability, and lifetime value. Hughes recommends using all three of these measures, particularly in direct-marketing applications.[6]

Sometimes the use of a single metric requires the collection of multiple inputs to obtain the necessary data for the analysis. For example, in measuring customer lifetime value (CLV), you will need to know: the average amount spent per purchase, number of purchases made per year, average gross profit margin per customer, customer-acquisition costs, marketing expenditures per customer, discount rates, and customer-retention rates (see step 2 in the 5Cs). A CLV application or spreadsheet can facilitate this computational process.

Metrics are also industry specific. In the case of retailers, seven categories of metrics are most important: brand equity, customer lifetime value, word-of-mouth referral value, customer acquisition and retention, cross buying and up buying, multichannel shopping, and product return.[7]

QUESTIONS TO THINK ABOUT

1. NPS—used by Enterprise Rent-A-Car, JetBlue, Intuit (manufacturer of TurboTax software), and thousands of other companies—is a valuable and easy-to-use metric. Critique this metric as the primary tool for monitoring business performance.
2. A marketing dashboard consists of a battery of measures of business performance. As a consultant to a consumer packaged-goods company, identify five key CV-based metrics that should be part of the dashboard.
3. As an entrepreneur starting a Web-based company selling restaurant supplies, what metrics would matter the most to you?

Customer Lifetime Value (CLV)

The customer lifetime value (CLV) formula is the actual measure of a customer's worth to a company.[8] Based on this computed measure, organizations can focus strategic decisions and communicate them to the value providers (employees). CLV implies a quantifiable, financial value for each customer, each of whom is treated as a business investment. The more customers are attracted and retained by the organization, the higher the cumulative investment will grow. Customers that are lost to the organization represent a loss of investment. Prospects that have not done business with the company can be viewed as money left on the table (lost revenue opportunities).

By utilizing the information collected from the VOC, forward-looking projections of what a customer is worth financially to the organization can be established. In other words, past knowledge can be used to predict future outcomes. Let's consider this example of CLV:

■ Each customer who bought from us in the past has remained with us for an average of Y years.
■ Each year, they visited the store and purchased from us, on average, T times.
■ Each time they purchased from us, they spent on average, $ dollars.
■ There are N customers that fall into this category.

Therefore, $Y \times T \times \$ \times N$ equals not only value of the past and existing customer base, but can also be used to represent the future customer value. By this definition, the CLV can be viewed as the net present value of the likely future profit stream from an individual customer. Combined with all customers, this stream represents the entire value of customers to the organization.

To determine the CLV of a customer, one follows four basic steps. The first step is to collect data from the organization's customers. This marketing information includes purchase history, the amount spent, the number of purchases made in a specified period, the cost of generating business (product, marketing, etc.), and profit margins. Note that not all customers are alike. Companies should segment their customer base by customer type to determine the higher value customers.

The second step is to determine the customer's likelihood of retention. How long does a typical user in a particular segment remain a customer? Depending on the type of business, this may be based on months or years. The length of time that a customer remains with a company is easy to determine with CRM programs, since this information is routinely monitored. If there is no CRM system in place, a simple research survey can be conducted.

The third step is to determine a financial discount rate used for current investments. This can easily be obtained from your finance department. In fact, this part of the process offers an excellent opportunity for the marketing and finance areas to work together to achieve organizational objectives. (The importance of such a collaboration will be discussed later as the fifth C of customer value metrics—communication.)

The fourth and final step of measuring the CLV is the calculation. While the formula may appear complicated, it is a basic calculation of the previously collected information. The company will determine the revenue the customer brings in over a designated time period minus the costs of product, customer service, marketing expenditures, and other costs, thereby providing a margin. This margin is then projected out over a predetermined period of time, and the discounted cash flow is then applied to recognize the time value of money. The result is a financial value that can be used to estimate what each customer is worth to the company.

Customer Retention

Once we understand CLV, we know what it costs to keep a customer as well as how much it will cost us if we lose an account. We also need to understand who our most profitable customers are and which customers are least profitable. Customer retention plays a key role in making strategic decisions. Chapter 10 provided an in-depth review of this topic.

Using the CLV metric, we can apply customer retention analysis to all types of customers. Knowing that we have customers of varying attributes, we may recognize that some are worth keeping while others should be fired. Yes, you are allowed to fire a customer if that account costs more to service than it generates in revenue and/or that client is difficult to work with (e.g., has a bad attitude, harasses your employees, is frequently late paying invoices, etc.).

Begin by organizing the data into customer types. For example, a large retailer may notice that certain customers from a specific zip code have a higher CLV than most other customer types. Therefore, the marketing department could direct more of its attention toward targeted residents in that zip code. In contrast, the retailer may also realize that another zip code produces consistently lower returns. Research may find that these customer groups can be made more profitable with additional or alternative marketing initiatives. It is also possible, however, that this group will never bring revenue to desirable profit levels and, as such, marketing management may decide to no longer target this group (i.e., not spending any of the promotional budget on them and instead diverting those resources elsewhere).

When necessary to part ways with a client, try to make it as positive an experience as possible. For example, an ad agency might advise a client that one of your strategic partners (perhaps a smaller or newer firm) can do a better job servicing their account, since they specialize in digital media.

Customer Revenue

Marketing managers that see the real value of customers truly appreciate their business. It is no secret that it is much easier and cheaper to keep existing customers than it is to find and win over new ones. Therefore, marketers should focus their attention on improving the satisfaction levels of existing customers. Not only do existing customers require less promotion dollars than attracting new customers, satisfied customers may also purchase more frequently, purchase in higher quantities, be less price sensitive, and spread positive word-of-mouth to other potential customers. Dissatisfied customers, however, are likely to not only leave without spending additional money with the organization, but also spread negative word-of-mouth (to friends, family, and associates), thereby impeding future business opportunities.

Focusing on the Return on Investment in the Customer (ROIC), a manager can build a financial model that rewards keeping current customers satisfied and minimizes dissatisfaction. To accomplish this, one must collect some data first. John A. Goodman developed the Market Damage Model. Using data collected from the VOC, we first determine the number of customers that have problems. Second, we must estimate the number of customers that actually have made a complaint. Third, of those that did complain, it must be determined the percentage of customers that wound up satisfied, mollified, or remained dissatisfied. With this information in place, marketers are now able to account for the total number of customers at risk (of remaining a client) with the organization.[9]

Knowing the total number of customers at risk and the value of each of those customers, managers can now recognize the total financial impact of dissatisfied customers. Also, by knowing the financial impact of the potential loss of these customers, the manager can determine if selected improvements made to retain these customers are worthwhile. For example, if one solution to retaining lost customers is to implement a $2-million CRM system and that system will help in increasing CLV to an additional $5-million dollars, then this marketing decision can be seen as a positive investment. However, if the CLV calculations indicate the financial impact of the new CRM system is only $1 million, then the manager may decide to allow for their departure. It must be understood, however, that the $2-million investment may last many years, and every year it remains effective may contribute to a positive marketing return within the company.

Managers can also use data collected via VOC to determine what specific areas are causing dissatisfaction to its customers. Most organizations will have a number of areas that are causing these "pain" points with the customer. With some basic research, it can be found which problems are the most severe as well as which problems occur most frequently. Goodman also developed a model called Market at Risk Calculation. In this model, managers determine the types of problems experienced by customers, the frequency of those problems, and the severity of the problems. Armed with this knowledge, executives can determine the percentage of customers that may potentially be lost.[10] Combining this with the CLV can be a sobering experience, as it represents just how costly dissatisfied customers can be to the company.

Marketing managers should also calculate the impact of existing customers on revenue generation within the firm. Highly satisfied customers will remain loyal and not defect; many are also strong advocates for the business and attract additional customers through word-of-mouth promotion and social media. In effect, this saves the company money as delighted clients are an extension of the organization's marketing arm, reducing the need for some advertising, sales promotion, and sales force expenses.

Once again, collecting data through the VOC initiatives, managers can determine the impact of spreading goodwill. Combining this information with the CLV, management can readily see the synergistic value and opinion leadership of the top tier of customers. With additional persuasive efforts, marketers can connect closely to current clients and convince them to purchase more frequently, in higher volume, and even buy higher margin products (enhanced quality).

Communications

CLV models demonstrate that the value of the customer can be quantified. Attaching a value to a customer allows marketers to better make strategic decisions. Furthermore, putting a financial value on the customer also builds the credibility of the marketing department. The actions of the marketing manager are being held to ever higher accountability standards. In past dealings, the C-suite, the CFO, the accounting department, and other interested parties have all had issues with the "subjectivity" of reports generated by marketing. The ability to measure the customer's value in financial terms allows marketers to speak the numbers language of business.

In addition, financial accountability brings credibility to the marketing function, which leads to additional input in the boardroom. No longer is the measurement of the customer viewed only as a tactical decision. Metrics can now be made at the strategic level using a customer valuation perspective. Communications across the organization improve when all executives and staff are working from the same page in the same book.

Marketing Dashboards

Ed Koch, a former New York City mayor, had a favorite question when talking with his constituents; simply stated, it was: "How's it going?" Marketers as well as mayors need to understand whether their "customers" are happy or not.

Progressing beyond a single item to monitor the effectiveness of business performance (including customer value creation), leading organizations often use a set of key metrics called marketing dashboards to understand their critical evaluative points.[11] Just as an automobile dashboard captures critical driving information such as speed, distance, fuel levels, vehicle and engine temperatures, navigation, etc., a marketing dashboard summarizes pertinent information on branding, channels, customer contact, promotion, sales performance, service, profitability, the Web, and so forth.

According to Ogilvy and Mather, "The design of a dashboard leads to a conversation about what metrics are important, which, in turn, forces you to align your metrics to your objectives."[12] Farris and colleagues agree, stating that dashboards are one of the most vital metrics to aid executives in managing their businesses. They add: "No one metric is going to give a full picture. It is only when you can use multiple viewpoints that you are likely to obtain anything approaching a full picture."[13]

As Zeithaml et al. explain, even when batteries of items are used, the dashboard approach may yield inaccurate results, since it largely reports past (rearview mirrors) or present (KPIs) data. They propose the need to develop "headlight" or forward-looking customer metrics such as customer lifetime value and customer equity to increase customer value.[14] Arguably, rearview mirrors, dashboards, and headlights have emerged as the latest version of management information systems. Proper design, buy-in, use, and updating marketing information systems allow the leadership team to have a shared reality.

Some specific benefits of using dashboards include the following: business intelligence, trend tracking, measuring efficiencies or inefficiencies, real-time updates, visuals (charts, graphs, maps, and tables), customized reporting of performance, and aligning goals and strategies with results. Major downside considerations include the cost, time, and talent to administer marketing dashboards.

The main value of the dashboard framework is that it consists of a multitude of practical information that is current, accessible, and easy to understand. Dashboards can be designed for top C-level executives as well as the managers working in the trenches. Figure 11.1 illustrates an example of an executive marketing dashboard. This dashboard features the following metrics: sales levels and

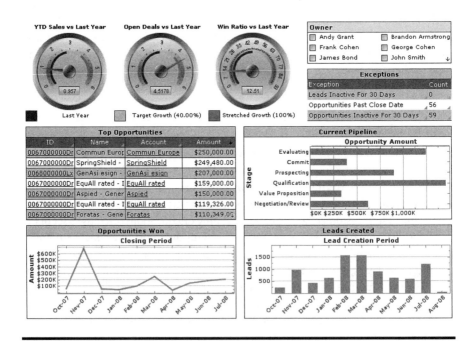

Figure 11.1 Executive dashboard. (Reprinted from InetSoft Technology, Piscataway, NJ. www.inetsoft.com. 2011. With permission.)

growth targets, the decision makers, exceptions, key accounts including revenues, the marketing pipeline (status of marketing activities throughout the buying cycle). It also tracks leads and the dollars generated over an annual period.

Summary

Doing business today requires a new level of accountability for performance. Superior customer value means knowing customers' behaviors and buying patterns. Metrics are an important part of the strategic marketing process to understand: (1) how successful the organization is now, and (2) what it needs to accomplish to become even more successful in the years ahead. This chapter discussed key CV-based metrics and offered a five-step framework for implementation. Smart customer value managers will embrace this challenge and use metrics as a sound planning tool to improve business strategies. The last part of the book provides an Appendix for analyzing business situations and a set of case studies that illustrate customer value best practices, marketing challenges, and opportunities.

Customer Value Action Items

1. Why is it important to measure customer value? To whom (within the company) is customer valuation important?

2. How does your company measure the value of customers? Does your company collect VOC data? How might CLV be utilized within your company?

3. In what ways can a Web-based company capture customer data? How should that company convert the data into CLV?

4. Many high-tech companies have a hard time getting everyone onboard with the corporate mission, vision, and goals. Marketing does not communicate well with sales, and engineering and finance are at odds. Given this situation, what should the CEO do to align business objectives? What are the implications of this scenario with respect to developing a sound customer-value-based metrics program? As a marketing consultant brought in to "fix" the business performance evaluation process, what are some of your recommendations for this firm?

5. Explain why a customer equity perspective is preferable to a brand equity perspective.

6. In the television show, *The Apprentice*, Donald Trump is known for saying, "You're fired." At times, that response is called for when dealing with unprofitable or difficult clients. How should you handle instances where separation from customers is the best strategy. Provide an example from the professional services sector.

7. In contrast to question 6, "you're hired" by a telecommunications company seeking to increase its market presence in Latin America and Asia. As one of the many hats you will be wearing, your boss, the vice-president for emerging markets, has asked you to develop a marketing metrics program. Using the 5C approach described in the chapter, develop an outline of how to proceed for your upcoming weekly managers meeting.

8. You are the owner of a small professional services firm and want to get a better handle on your customer value metrics. You heard about the idea of a marketing dashboard at a recent trade association meeting and think that may solve your problem. How should you proceed? What key performance indicators (KPIs) should be on your dashboard?

Notes

Preface

1. *2010–2012 Research Priorities* (Cambridge, MA Marketing Science Institute, 2010), http://www.msi.org/research/index.cfm?id=271.
2. C. Gronroos, A Service Perspective on Business Relationships: The Value Creation, Interaction, and Marketing Interface, *Industrial Marketing Management* 40 (2011): 240–247.
3. A. Weinstein, How to Create an Innovative MBA Course, *Marketing Educator*, 1998 (Spring): 6.

Chapter 1: Customers Want Exceptional Value

1. *Fortune*, World's most admired companies, 2011, http://money.cnn.com/magazines/fortune/mostadmired/2011/full_list/.
2. L. J. DeRose, *The Value Network* (New York: AMACOM, 1994).
3. *Random House Webster's College Dictionary*, 1992, s.v. Value.
4. R. B. Woodruff and S. F. Gardial, *Know Your Customer: New Approaches to Understanding Customer Value and Satisfaction* (Cambridge, MA: Blackwell Publishers, 1996).
5. S. MacStravic, Questions of Value in Health Care, *Marketing Health Services*, 1997 (Winter): 50–53.
6. P. Kotler, H. Kartajaya, and I. Setiawan, *Marketing 3.0: From Products to Customers to the Human Spirit* (New York: John Wiley & Sons, 2010).
7. Marketing Charts, 7 in 10 Consumers Will Spend More for Good Service, May 3, 2011, http://www.marketingcharts.com/direct/7-in-10-consumers-will-spend-more-for-good-service-17292/.
8. L. Rosencrance, Survey: Corporate Web Sites Low on Customer Respect, Computerworld, June 29, 2005, http://www.computerworld.com/s/article/102866/Survey_Corporate_Web_sites_low_on_customer_respect?taxonomyId=120&source=x51.
9. D. Fagiano, Fighting for Customers on a New Battlefield, *The American Salesman*, 1995 (February): 20–22.
10. Shop.org/Forrester Research Study, Online sales soar 48 percent in 2002, http://www.pressreleasenetwork.com/newsroom/news_view.phtml?news_id=328
11. S. Siegel, Online Retail Spending Grew by 10% in Q1 over Last Year, 2010, http://www.ecommercetrends.com/online-retail-spending-grew-by-10-in-q1-over-last-year/.

12. M. Miller, Second Quarter 2009 Online Sales Up 2.2%, 2009, http://www.suite101. com/content/second-quarter-2009-online-sales-up-22-a147716.

13. S. Murray, Service Sector Is Job-Growth Engine, *Wall Street Journal,* December 11, 2009, A8.

14. R. D. Atkinson and S. Andes, *The 2010 State New Economy Index* (Washington, DC: The Information Technology & Innovation Foundation, November 2010).

15. Amazon, 2009 Annual Report, April 23, 2010, http://www.asiaing.com/amazon-2009-annual-report.html.

16. G. Conlon, Procter & Gamble, *Sales and Marketing Management,* 1997 (October): 59.

17. R. T. Rust, C. Moorman, and G. Bhalla, Rethinking Marketing, *Harvard Business Review* 88 (January-February 2010): 94–101.

CHAPTER 2: BE CUSTOMER DRIVEN AND MARKET DRIVING

1. Several writers have said that the terms *market oriented, market driven, customer focused, customer orientation,* and so forth are synonymous. For example, see: S. F. Slater and J. C. Narver, Market Orientation and the Learning Organization, *Journal of Marketing* 59 (July 1995): 63; S. Nwankwo, Developing a Customer Orientation, *Journal of Consumer Marketing* 12, no. 5 (1995): 6; B. P. Shapiro, What the Hell Is 'Market Oriented'? *Harvard Business Review,* 1988 (November-December): 120.

2. K. Gottlieb, Attention All Passengers, e-mail sent April 7, 2000.

3. T. Jackovics, No Fees, No Problem! Airline Has No Regrets about Bag Stance, *Tampa Tribune,* July 17, 2010, http://www.allbusiness.com/marketing-advertising/marketing-advertising-channels/14824416-1.html.

4. D. E. Schultz, Study Internal Marketing for Better Impact, *Marketing News*, October 14, 2002, 8–9.

5. T. J. Brown et al., The Customer Orientation of Service Workers: Personality Trait Effects on Self- and Supervisor Performance Ratings, *Journal of Marketing Research* 39 (February 2002): 110–119.

6. A. Cheng, Best Buy Aims to Hire Human Search Engines, *Ventura County Star*, October 30, 2010, http://www.vcstar.com/news/2010/oct/30/best-buy-aims-to-hire-human-search-engines/.

7. K. Kalyanam and S. McIntyre, "The e-Marketing Mix: A Contribution of the e-Tailing Wars," *Journal of the Academy of Marketing Science* 30 no. 4 (2002): 487–499.

8. E. Sullivan, "Made for Each Other," *Marketing News*, July 30, 2009, 16–17.

9. F. F. Reichheld, *The Loyalty Effect* (Cambridge, MA: Harvard Business School Press, 1996).

10. J. Gittel, *The Southwest Airlines Way* (New York: McGraw Hill, 2003).

11. Y. Adachi, "The Effects of Semantic Difference on Cross-Cultural Business Negotiation: A Japanese and American Case Study," *The Journal of Language for International Business* 9, no. 1 (1998): 43–52.

12. A. Hartung, "Why Not All Earnings Are Equal; Microsoft Has the Wal-Mart Disease," *Forbes*, May 3, 2011, http://www.forbes.com/sites/adamhartung/2011/05/03/why-not-all-earnings-are-equal-and-microsoft-has-the-wal-mart-disease/.

13. H. Barrett and A. Weinstein, "The Effect of Market Orientation and Flexibility on Corporate Entrepreneurship," *Entrepreneurship Theory and Practice* 23, no. 1 (1998): 57–70.

14. J. C. Narver and S. F. Slater, "The Effect of a Market Orientation on Business Profitability," *Journal of Marketing* 54 (October 1990): 20–35.

15. A. K. Kohli and B. J. Jaworski, "Market Orientation: The Construct, Research Propositions, and Managerial Implications," *Journal of Marketing* 54 (April 1990): 1–18.

16. J. Dawes, "The Relationship between Subjective and Objective Company Performance Measures in Market Orientation Research: Further Empirical Evidence," *Marketing Bulletin* 10 (1999): 65–75.

17. C. R. Cano, F. A. Carillat, and F. Jaramillo, "A Meta-Analysis of the Relationship between Market Orientation and Business Performance: Evidence from Five Continents," *International Journal of Research in Marketing* 21 (2004): 179–200.

18. S. Liao et al., "A Survey of Market Orientation Research (1995–2008)," *Industrial Marketing Management* 40 (2011): 301–310.

19. P. S. Raju, S. C. Lonial, and Y. P. Gupta, "Market Orientation and Performance in the Hospital Industry," *Journal of Health Care Marketing* 15 (Winter 1995): 34–41.

20. C. P. Blocker et al., "Proactive Customer Orientation and Its Role for Creating Customer Value in Global Markets," *Journal of the Academy of Marketing Science* 39 (2011): 216–233.

21. B. Jaworski, A. K. Kohli, and A. Sahay, "Market-Driven Versus Driving Markets," *Journal of the Academy of Marketing Science* 28, no. 1 (2000): 45–54.

22. N. Kumar, L. Scheer, and P. Kotler, "From Market Driven to Market Driving," *European Management Journal* 18, no. 2 (2000): 129–142.

23. J. N. Sheth, R. S. Sisodia, and A. Sharma, "The Antecedents and Consequences of Customer-Centric Marketing," *Journal of the Academy of Marketing Science* 28, no.1 (2000): 55–66.

24. H. Barrett, "Ultimate Goal Is to Anticipate the Needs of Market," *Marketing News*, October 7, 1996, 4.

25. J. G. Covin and D. P. Slevin, "A Conceptual Model of Entrepreneurship as Firm Behavior," *Entrepreneurship Theory and Practice* 16, no. 1 (1991): 7–25.

26. R. C. Wolcott and M. J. Lippitz, "The Four Models of Corporate Entrepreneurship, *MIT Sloan Management Review*, 2007 (Fall): 75–82.

27. D. A. Garvin and L. C. Levesque, "Meeting the Challenge of Corporate Entrepreneurship," *Harvard Business Review,* 2006 (October): 102–112.

CHAPTER 3: PROCESS MANAGEMENT—BEST PRACTICES

1. E. Heard, "Walking the Talk of Customer Value," *National Productivity Review* 13, no. 1 (1993/1994): 21–27.

2. E. Deming, *Out of Crisis* (Cambridge, MA: MIT Center for Advanced Engineering Study, 1986).

3. W. Johnson and R. Chvala, *Total Quality in Marketing* (Boca Raton, FL: St. Lucie Press, 1995).

4. IBM, *Capitalizing on Complexity—Insights from the Global Chief Executive Officers Study*, white paper, IBM Corporation, Somers, NY, May 2010.

5. M. Arndt, "Creativity overflowing," *BusinessWeek.com*, May 8, 2006, http://www.businessweek.com/magazine/content/06_19/b3983061.htm

6. A. Weinstein, "Technology companies—findings," Nova Southeastern University, Fort Lauderdale, FL, September, 2010, http://www.artweinstein.com/Resources.html

7. H. Barrett, telephone conversation, June 6, 2011.

8. M. Arndt, "3M's Seven Pillars of Innovation," *Business Week*, May 10, 2006.

9. R. Brands, *Robert's Rules of Innovation* (Hoboken, NJ: John Wiley & Sons, 2010).

10. D. Boulanger, *Customer Experience Management: Is Your Entire Company Really Focused on the Customer?* (Boston, MA: Aberdeen Group, August 2008), 5.

11. L. Hunsaker, "Customer Experience: How Do Your Customers Define It?" November 11, 2008, http://www.customerthink.com/blog/customer_experience_customers_define.

12. R. King, "Sentiment Analysis Gives Companies Insight into Consumer Opinion," *Bloomberg Business Week*, March 1, 2011, http://www.businessweek.com/technology/content/feb2011/tc20110228_366762.htm.

13. R. Johnston and X. Kong, "The Customer Experience: A Road-Map for Improvement," *Managing Service Quality* 21, no. 1 (2011): 5–24.

14. J. Coffman and D. Stotz, "How Some Banks Turn Clients into Advocates," *American Banker*, May 11, 2007, http://www.bain.com/publications/articles/how-some-banks-turn-clients-into-advocates.aspx.

15. ClearAction, "Customer Experience Management Studies," ClearAction Customer Experience Optimization, Sunnyvale, CA, 2010, http://www.clearaction.biz/customer-engagement.html.

16. B. Temkin, "The 2011 Temkin Experience Ratings," Temkin Group, March 29, 2011, http://experiencematters.wordpress.com/2011/03/29/2011-temkin-experience-ratings/.

17. D. K. Rigby, *Management Tools 2009: An Executive's Guide,* Boston, MA: Bain & Company, http://www.bain.com/publications/articles/management-tools-2009-an-executives-guide.aspx

18. R. Camp, *Benchmarking: The Search for Industry Best Practices That Lead to Superior Performance* (Milwaukee, WI: ASQC Quality Press, 1989).

19. E. Sprow, "Benchmarking: It's Time to Stop Tinkering with Manufacturing and Start Clocking Yourself against the Best," *Manufacturing Engineering* 111, no. 3 (1993): 58.

CHAPTER 4: BUILDING A WINNING BUSINESS MODEL AND VALUE PROPOSITION

1. A. Osterwalder and Y. Pigneur, *Business Model Generation* (Hoboken, NJ: John Wiley & Sons, 2010).

2. Ibid.

3. M. Rappa, "Business Models on the Web," January 17, 2010, http://digitalenterprise.org/models/models.html.

4. B. W. Wirtz, O. Schilke, and S. Ullrich, "Strategic Development of Business Models: Implications of the Web 2.0 for Creating Value on the Internet," *Long Range Planning* 43 (2010): 272–290.

5. J. Hagel III, J. S. Brown, and L. Davison, "Shaping Strategy in a World of Constant Disruption, *Harvard Business Review,* 2008 (October): 1–11.

6. D. MacMillan, P. Burrows, and S. E. Ante, (2009) "The App Economy," *Business Week*, November 2, 44–49.

7. F. E. Webster Jr., "Defining the New Marketing Concept (Part 1)," *Marketing Management* 2, no. 4 (1994): 22–31.

8. eBay, "eBay Inc. Reports Strong Fourth Quarter and Full Year Results," 2011, http://prsync.com/ebay/ebay-inc-reports-strong-fourth-quarter-and-full-year-results-116689/

9. W. H. Ettinger Jr., "Consumer-Perceived Value: The Key to a Successful Business Strategy in the Healthcare Marketplace," *Journal of the American Geriatrics Society* 46 (1998): 111–113.

10. M. Treacy and F. Wiersema, *The Discipline of Market Leaders* (Reading, MA: Addison-Wesley, 1995).

11. W. C. Kim and R. Mauborgne, "Value Innovation: The Strategic Logic of High Growth," *Harvard Business Review*, 1997 (January-February): 102–112.

12. C. J. Grayson Jr. and C. S. O'Dell, "Mining Your Hidden Resources," *Across the Board*, 1998 (April): 23–28.

13. S. Crainer, *The 75 Greatest Management Decisions Ever Made…and Some of the Worst* (New York: MJF Books, 1999).

14. Blue Nile.com, 2011, www.bluenile.com.

15. F. F. Reichheld, "Loyalty and the Renaissance of Marketing," *Marketing Management* 2, no. 4 (1994): 10–21.

16. B. T. Gale, *Managing Customer Value: Creating Quality and Service That Customers Can See* (New York: The Free Press, 1994).

Chapter 5: Service and Quality—The Core Offering

1. Johnson & Johnson, "2010 Annual Report," 2011, 12.

2. L. P. Willcocks and R. Plant, "Pathways to e-Business Leadership: Getting from Bricks to Clicks," *MIT Sloan Management Review*, 2001 (Spring): 50–59.

3. C. K. Prahalad and V. Ramaswamy, "Co-Creation Experiences: The Next Practice in Value Creation," *Journal of Interactive Marketing* 18, no. 3 (2004): 5–14.

4. V. Ramaswamy, "Co-Creation of Value—Towards an Expanded Paradigm of Value Creation," *Marketing Review St. Gallen* 6 (2009): 11–17.

5. American Express, "That's Customer Focus," press release, July 7, 2010, http://www.thatscustomerfocus.com/global_service_barometer_press_release.html.

6. B. Jameson, "6 Pieces of Research Every Customer Service Pro Should Know," Customer Management IQ, October 14, 2010, http://www.customermanagementiq.com/operations/articles/6-pieces-of-research-every-cu.

7. L. Hunsaker, "Customer experience strategy: 4 overlooked competencies," May 17, 2010, http://www.focus.com/briefs/customer-experience-strategy-4-overlooked-competencies/

8. T. Hsieh, *Delivering Happiness: A Path to Profits, Passion, and Purpose* (New York: Business Plus, 2010); Zappos.com, www.zappos.com.

9. C. Kontoghiorghes and R. Gudgel, "Investigating the Association between Productivity and Quality Performance in Two Manufacturing Settings," *QMJ* 11, no. 2 (2004): 8–20.

10. K. Case, "Coming Soon: The Future," *Quality Progress* 35, no. 11 (2002): 27.

11. American Society for Quality, "Learn about Quality: Basic Concepts/Glossary—'Quality'," http://asq.org/.

12. D. Garvin, *Managing Quality* (New York: Free Press, 1988).

13. W. J. McDonald, "The Power of Customer Value Analysis," *Construction Equipment Distribution*, 2005, http://www.cedmag.com/article-detail.cfm?id=10922891.

14. Market Value Solutions, "Customer value model—market research defines customer value," 2010, http://www.marketvaluesolutions.com/value-model.htm

15. A. Velocci, "Full Potential of Six Sigma Eludes Most Companies," *Aviation Week & Space Technologies*, 2002 (September): 58.

16. S. S. Tax and S. W. Brown, "Recovering and Learning from Service Failure," *Sloan Management Review*, 1998 (Fall): 75–88.

17. V. Zeithaml, A. Parasuraman, and L. Berry, *Delivering Quality Service* (New York: The Free Press, 1990).

18. A. Parasuraman, L. Berry, and V. Zeithaml, "Refinement and Reassessment of the SERVQUAL Scale," *Journal of Retailing* 67, no. 4 (Winter 1991): 423.

19. A. Parasurman, V. Zeithaml, and L. Berry, "Alternative Scales for Measuring Service Quality: A Comparative Assessment Based on Psychometric and Diagnostic Criteria," *Journal of Retailing* 70, no. 3 (1994): 206.

20. A. Parasuraman, V. Zeithaml, and L. Berry, "SERVQUAL: A Multiple-Item Scale for Measuring Consumer Perceptions of Service Quality," *Journal of Retailing* 64, no. 1 (1988): 35–36.

21. H. N. Nasution and F. T. Mavondo, "Organisational Capabilities: Antecedents and Implications for Customer Value," *European Journal of Marketing* 42, no. 3/4 (2008): 477–501.

22. C. Gronroos, *Service Management and Marketing* (Lexington, MA: Lexington Books, 1988).

23. C. Gronroos, "A Service Quality Model and Its Marketing Implications," *European Journal of Marketing* 18 (1984): 36–43.

24. E. Naumann, *Creating Customer Value* (Cincinnati, OH: Thomson Executive Press, 1995).

25. W. Johnson and R. Chvala, *Total Quality in Marketing* (Delray Beach, FL: St. Lucie Press, 1995), 106.

26. K. Albrecht and R. Zemke, *Service America* (Homewood, IL: Dow Jones-Irwin, 1985), 31.

CHAPTER 6: PRICE AND IMAGE—THE COMMUNICATORS

1. B2B International, "The Importance of Price and Quality in the Marketing Mix," *The Market Research Blog*, September 29, 2006, http://www.b2binternational.com/b2b-blog/2006/09/29/the-importance-of-price-and-quality-in-the-marketing-mix/.

2. R. Peterson and W. Wilson, "The Perceived Risk and Price-Reliance Schema and Price-Perceived-Quality Mediators," in *Perceived Quality*, ed. J. Jacoby and J. Olson (Lexington, MA: Lexington Books, 1985), 247–268.

3. A. Biswas and E. Blair, "The Effects of Reference Prices in Retail Advertisements," *Journal of Marketing* 55 (July 1991): 1–12.

4. Thomas Nagle and George Cressman, "Don't Just Set Prices, Manage Them," *Marketing Management* 11, no. 6 (2002): 29–33.

5. T. Duncan and S. Moriarty, *Driving Brand Value* (New York: McGraw-Hill, 1997).

6. A. Cleland and A. Bruno, *The Market Value Process* (San Francisco: Jossey-Bass, 1996), 19.

7. R. Dolan and H. Simon, *Power Pricing* (New York: The Free Press, 1996), 312.

8. L. Berry and M. Yadav, "Capture and Communicate Value in the Pricing of Services," *Sloan Management Review*, 1996 (Summer): 45–47.

9. J. C. Anderson, M. Wouters, and W. Van Rossum, "Why the Highest Price Isn't the Best Price," *Sloan Management Review*, 2010 (Winter): 69–76.

10. K. Monroe and J. Cox, "Pricing Practices That Endanger Profits," *Marketing Management*, 2001 (October): 43.

11. P. Coy, "The Power of Smart Pricing," *Business Week*, April 10, 2000, 160.

12. E. Maltby, "Raising Prices Pays Off for Some," *Wall Street Journal*, October 27, 2010, B8.

13. M. Bustillo. and A. Zimmerman, "Phone-wielding shoppers strike fear into retailers," *The Wall Street Journal/WSJ.com*, December 15, 2010, http://online.wsj.com/article/SB10001424052748704694004576019691769574496.html

14. M. Marchetti, "Dell Computer," *Sales and Marketing Management* 49, no. 11 (1997): 51.

15. Starbucks Corporation, Starbucks Coffee Company—store design, 2011, http://www.starbucks.com/coffeehouse/store-design.

16. M. Rock, *Classic Queen* (New York: Sterling, 2007), 12.

17. *BrandZ Top 100 Most Valuable Global Brands* (New York: Millward Brown Optimor, 2011), http://www.millwardbrown.com/Libraries/Optimor_BrandZ_Files/2011_BrandZ_Top100_Report.sflb.ashx.

18. J. Gregory, B. Paladino, and J. Akman, "A New Brand of Value: Integrating Branding into Corporate Performance Management," *Business Performance Management*, April 22, 2009, http://bpmmag.net/mag/integrating-branding-into-corporate-performance-management-0422/index1.html.

19. A. Reis and J. Trout, *Positioning: The Battle for Your Mind* (New York: Warner Books, 1982).

20. M. Nesbit and A. Weinstein, "Positioning the High-Tech Product," in *Handbook of Business Strategy 1989/1990 Yearbook,* ed. H. E. Glass (Boston: Warren, Gorham & Lamont, 1989), 30-1–30-8.

21. Rajendran SriramachandraMurthy and Monica Hodis, "Why Is Apple Cool? An Examination of Brand Coolness and Its Marketing Consequences," *Marketing Academics*, 2010 (Fall): 1–2.

22. N. Kerner and G. Pressman, *Chasing Cool—Standing Out in Today's Cluttered Marketplace* (New York: Atria Books, 2007).

23. Doreen Hemlock, "Space Trips for $200,000 Lure South Floridians," *Sun Sentinel*, January 5, 2011, http://articles.sun-sentinel.com/2011-01-05/business/fl-virgin-galactic-sales-20110105_1_space-trips-forest-travel-unique-travel.

CHAPTER 7: E-COMMERCE—OPPORTUNITIES IN MARKETSPACE

1. M. Megna, "Cost-Cutting e-Tailers Look to Retain Customers," InternetNews.com, May 5, 2009, http://www.internetnews.com/ec-news/article.php/3818846/Cost-Cutting-Etailers-Look-to.

2. *USA Today*, "USA Today Internet 50," January 12, 2007, www.usatoday.com/money/markets/internet50.htm.

3. G. Karp, "Home Goods Click with Shoppers," *Sun-Sentinel*, January 17, 2011, 5D.

4. ATG, "Most online shoppers want live customer service," October 16, 2009, http://www.marketingcharts.com/direct/most-online-shoppers-want-live-customer-service-10712/

5. Julie Roth, "Google Provides One More Reason Why Site Speed Is Critical," April 12, 2010, www.futuremediachange.com/2010/04/google-provides-one-more-reason-why-site-speed-is-critical/.

6. DSstar, "New Scale Measures Customer Service Quality of Web Sites," *DSstar* 6, no. 10 (March 12, 2002), www.tgc.com/dsstar/02/0312/104007.html.

7. American Customer Satisfaction Index, "The American Customer Satisfaction Index," September, 2011, http://www.theacsi.org/index.php?option=com_content&view =article&id=261:acsi-sectors-and industries&catid=14&Itemid=338

8. MarketingPower.com, "Which Marketing Trend Will Be Most Significant in 2011? Here's What AMA Members Said," *Marketing News*, January 30, 2011, 6.

9. eMarketer , "Mobile ad spending up nearly 80% in 2010," October 19, 2010, http:// www.emarketer.com/Article.aspx?R=1007992

10. S.J. Campbell, Cisco study suggests Internet traffic on mobile devices will increase 26-fold by 2015, February 1, 2011, http://fixed-mobile-convergence.tmcnet.com/ topics/mobile-communications/articles/140360-cisco-study-suggests-internet-traffic-mobile-devices-will.htm

11. Forrester Research, "Q3 2010 Global Mobile Maturity Online Survey," Forrester Research, 2010.

12. Mickey. A. Khan, "Why Mobile Is a Silver Bullet for Customer Care," *Mobile Commerce Daily*, May 5, 2011, http://www.mobilecommercedaily.com/2011/05/05/ why-mobile-is-a-silver-bullet-for-customer-care.

13. P. Andruss, "Social Shopping," *Marketing News*, January 30, 2011, 22–23.

14. G. A. Westra, "e-Marketing Curriculum and Agenda," ELMAR, October 18, 2010, http://ama-academics.communityzero.com/elmar?go=2357460.

15. V. A. Zeithaml, A. Parasuraman, and A. Malhotra, "A Conceptual Framework for Understanding e-Service Quality: Implications for Future Research and Managerial Practice," MSI Working Paper, Report No. 00-115, 2000, 24.

16. Z. Yang and M. Jun, "Consumer Perception of e-Service Quality: From Internet Purchaser and Non-Purchaser Perspectives," *Journal of Business Strategy* 19, no. 1 (2002): 33.

17. A. Parasuraman, V. A. Zeithaml, and A. Malhotra, "E-S-QUAL: A Multiple-Item Scale for Assessing Electronic Service Quality," *Journal of Service Research* 7, no. 3 (2005): 213–233.

18. M. E. Rotstain, "Customer Acquisition Costs," November 23, 2002, http://www.acroterion.ca.

19. F. Reichheld and P. Schefter, "E-Loyalty: Your Secret Weapon on the Web," *Harvard Business Review* 78, no. 4 (2000): 106.

20. H-T. Tsai and H-C. Huang, "Determinants of e-Repurchase Intentions: An Integrative Model of Quadruple Retention Drivers," *Information & Management* 44 (2007): 231–239.

21. Y-S. Lii, "An Exploration of Antecedents for B2C Website Effectiveness," *Journal of Applied Management and Entrepreneurship* 10, no. 1 (2005): 40–58.

22. C. Liu and K. Arnett, "Exploring the Factors Associated with Web Site Success in the Context of Electronic Commerce," *Information & Management* 38, (October 2000): 27.

23. C. R. Allard et al., "Exploring Consumer Valuations of e-Services: A Portal Site," *International Journal of Service Industry Management* 12, no. 4 (2001): 362.

24. G. Lohse and P. Spiller, "Electronic Shopping," *Association for the Computing Machinery Communications of the ACM* 41, no. 7 (1998): 86.

25. VeriSign, "Verisign Internet Trust Index," white paper, March 2010, https://www.trustthecheck.com/assets/VeriSign_Internet_Trust_Index_March_2010.pdf.

26. G. Urban, F. Sultan, and W. Qualls, "Placing Trust at the Center of Your Internet Strategy," *Sloan Management Review*, 2000 (Fall): 40.
27. C. R. Allard, J. Semeijn, and W. Janssen, "E-Service Quality Expectations: A Case Study," *Total Quality Management and Business Excellence* 14, no. 4 (2003): 437.
28. N. Wingfield, "E-Commerce Cover Story—A Question of Trust: Online Consumers Are Buying—but Warily; Here's How You Can Minimize the Risk," *Wall Street Journal*, September 16, 2002, R6.
29. M. Mckeown, *e-Customer* (London: Financial Times/Prentice-Hall, 2001).

CHAPTER 8: IMC AND SOCIAL MEDIA

1. M. Fehrnstrom and D. M. Rich, "Using Events to Drive an Integrated Marketing Model," *Journal of Integrated Marketing Communications*, 2009: 31–37.
2. Forrester Research, "Forrester: Interactive Marketing to Hit $55B by 2014," *Marketing Charts*, July 10, 2009, http://www.marketingcharts.com/interactive/forrester-interactive-marketing-to-hit-55b-by-2014-9744/.
3. D. N. McArthur and T. Griffin, "A Marketing Management View of Integrated Marketing Communications," *Journal of Advertising Research*, 1997 (September/October): 19–26.
4. C. Krol, "Marketers embrace integrated marketing," *B to B Magazine,* June 9, 2008, http://www.btobonline.com/apps/pbcs.dll/article?AID=/20080609/FREE/142278498/1109/FREE
5. S. Reda, "The Personal Touch," *Stores*, January 2011.
6. N. Zmuda, "Retailers on Quest to Rekindle the Personal Touch of a Bygone Era," *Advertising Age*, February 14, 2011.
7. R. McKenna, "Marketing in Real Time," *Executive Excellence*, April, 3–4, 1998.
8. J. Loechner, "Tech Marketers Want to See ROI for Their Media Spend," *Media Post Blogs*, February 16, 2011, http://www.mediapost.com/publications/?fa=Articles.showArticle&art_aid=144919.
9. D. E. Schultz, "Integration Is Critical for Success in 21st Century," *Marketing News*, September 15, 1997, 26.
10. Darren Rovell, "Beer Vendor Taking Orders from Fans on Twitter," *Sports Biz*, April 4, 2011, http://www.cnbc.com/id/42415542/Beer_Vendor_Taking_Orders_From_Fans_On_Twitter.
11. Antonia Harler, "How to Successfully Use Twitter for Relationship Marketing," *Social Mouth,* March 3, 2011, http://socialmouths.com/blog/2011/03/03/how-to-use-twitter-for-relationship-marketing/.
12. C. Li and J. Bernoff, *Groundswell: Winning in a World Transformed by Social Technologies* (Boston: Harvard Business School Press, 2008).
13. ExactTarget, *The Social Profile*—Report #3, 2010, Indianapolis, IN.
14. R. Lesonsky, "Survey says: why women may love Facebook and Twitter more than shoes," *Aol Original,* July 28, 2010, http://smallbusiness.aol.com/2010/07/28/survey-says-why-women-may-love-facebook-and-twitter-more-than-s/?sms_ss=twitter
15. N. Kerner and G. Pressman, *Chasing Cool—Standing Out in Today's Cluttered Marketplace* (New York: Atria Books, 2007).
16. A. Weinstein, "Technology companies—findings," Nova Southeastern University, Fort Lauderdale, FL, September, 2010 http://www.artweinstein.com/Resources.html

17. Burson-Marstellar, *The Global Social Media Check-Up* (New York: Burson-Marstellar, 2010).
18. C. Rubin, "Why Social Media Is Really Worth Your Time," *Inc.com,* April 23, 2010, http://www.inc.com.
19. R. Duboff and S. Wilkerson, "Marketers Are Seeking to Answer 'the Greatest Question,'" *Marketing Management,* 2010 (Winter): 32–37.
20. D. L. Hoffman and M. Fodor, "Can You Measure the ROI of Your Social Media Marketing?" *MIT Sloan Management Review* 52, no. 1 (2010): 41–49.

CHAPTER 9: CREATING VALUE THROUGH RELATIONSHIP MARKETING

1. L. Berry, "Relationship marketing," in *Emerging Perspectives on Service Marketing,* ed. L. Berry, G. L. Shostack, and G. Upah (Chicago: American Marketing Association, 1983), 25–28; C. Gronroos, "From Marketing Mix to Relationship Marketing: Towards a Paradigm Shift in Marketing," *Management Decision* 32, no. 2 (1994): 4–20; A. Parvatiyar and J. Sheth, "Paradigm Shift in Marketing Theory and Approach: The Emergence Of Relationship Marketing," in *Relationship Marketing: Theory, Methods, and Applications,* ed. J. Sheth and A. Parvatiyar (Atlanta, GA: Center for Relationship Marketing, Emory University, 1994).
2. I. H. Gordon, *Relationship Marketing* (Toronto, ON: John Wiley & Sons Canada, 2000), 9.
3. B. Strothkamp et al., "Financial Services Firms Open Up about Customer Acquisition Costs," July 1, 2008, Forrester Research, Cambridge, MA, www.forrester.com.
4. R. W. Palmatier et al., "Factors influencing the effectiveness of relationship marketing: a meta-analysis, *Journal of Marketing* 70 (October 2006): 136–153.
5. W. Johnson and A. Weinstein, "Creating Value through Customer and Supplier Relationships," in *Interactions, Relationships, and Networks: Towards the New Millennium,* 15th Annual IMP Conference, Dublin, Ireland, September 4, 1999.
6. S. Ba and P. Pavlou, "Evidence of the Effect of Trust Building Technology in Electronic Markets: Price Premiums and Buyer Behavior," *MIS Quarterly* 26, no. 2 (2002): 265.
7. Les Feldman, William C. Johnson, and Art Weinstein, "Trust, Commitment, and Long-Term Manufacturer Supplier Relationships," *Research Conference on Relationship Marketing,* Atlanta, GA, June 1998.
8. A. Weinstein. Much of this material was developed and presented in the webinar entitled "Segmenting B2B Markets: From 'Big Picture' Strategy to Microtargeting," Direct Marketing Association, June 2, 2010.
9. J. Kanter, "Companies Must Improve Supply Chain Management," *Supply Management. com,* April 29, 2009.
10. Kevin O'Marah and Debra Hofman, "The AMR Supply Chain Top 25 for 2010," ID No. G00201212, Gartner Research, Stamford, CT, June 2, 2010, http://www.gartner.com/DisplayDocument?ref=clientFriendlyUrl&id=1379613.
11. QSRweb.com, "Popeyes Cuts $16 Million from Supply Chain Costs," April 18, 2011, www.qsrweb.com/article/180703/Popeyes-cuts-16-million-from-supply-chain-costs.
12. Electronic Commerce News, "Companies Often Disappointed with Supply Chain Investments, Survey Finds," May 26, 2003.
13. M. E. Porter, *Competitive Advantage: Creating and Sustaining Superior Performance* (New York: Free Press, 1985).

14. A. Weinstein and H. Barrett, "Value Creation in Business Curriculum—A Tale of Two Courses," *Journal of Education for Business* 82, no. 6 (2007): 329–336.

15. J. Rayport and J. Sviokla, "Exploiting the Virtual Value Chain," *Harvard Business Review* 73, no. 6 (1995): 76.

16. Charles Dominick, "8 Supplier Selection Criteria & the SHoCC," *PurchTips,* 209, July 27, 2010, http://nextlevelpurchasing.com/articles/supplier-selection-criteria.html.

17. *Chief Executive*, "What Customers Value Most," 1998, 8–16.

18. S. Cartwright and R. Oliver, "Untangling the Value Web," *Journal of Business Strategy* 21, no. 1 (2000): 25.

19. Bob Thompson, "Collaboration: The Cure for What Ails CRM," June 5, 2002, http://www.customerthink.com/article/collaboration_cure_what_ails_crm.

20. R. J. Baran, R. Galka, and D. P. Strunk, *Principles of Customer Relationship Management* (Mason, OH: Thomson South-Western, 2007).

21. D. Rigby and B. Bilodeau , "Management tools—customer relationship management," 2009, Bain & Company, http://www.bain.com/publications/articles/management-tools-and-trends-2009.aspx

22. Bob Thompson, "The Reports of CRM Failure Are Highly Exaggerated: An Interview with Gartner's Ed Thompson," *Customer Think*, December 7, 2004, http://www.customerthink.com/interview/reports_crm_failure_highly_exaggerated.

23. K. Cholewka, "CRM: The Failures Are Your Fault," *Sales & Marketing Management* 154, no. 1 (2002): 23.

24. B. Landau, "The Elevator Pitch for Social CRM," *CMS Wire*, October 26, 2010, http://www.cmswire.com.

25. Bob Thompson, "2011: The Year when 80% of Social CRM Projects Will Fail," *Customer Think*, January 4, 2011, http://www.customerthink.com/user/bob_thompson.

26. Jacob Morgan, "The Social CRM Process," *Social Business Advisor*, April 5, 2010, http://www.jmorganmarketing.com/the-social-crm-process/.

27. DMA Webinar, "How to track an online buyer's purchase research behavior," *The Direct Marketing Association of Northern California*, January 13, 2010. For further information, contact Frank Jamieson at frank@applieddmresearch.com

CHAPTER 10: CUSTOMER LOYALTY AND RETENTION

1. D. Mattioli, "Customer Service as a Growth Engine," *The Wall Street Journal,* June 7, 2010, B6.

2. S. M. Keveaney, "Customer Switching Behavior in Service Industries: An Exploratory Study," *Journal of Marketing* 59 (April 1995): 71–82.

3. F. F. Reichheld, *The Loyalty Effect: The Hidden Force behind Growth, Profits, and Lasting Value* (Boston: Harvard Business School Press, 1996).

4. D. Pruden, "Retention Marketing Gains Spotlight, but Does Reality Match Philosophy?" *Brandweek*, 1995 (February): 15.

5. Pete Fader, "Request—CRM Conventional Wisdom," July 10, 2001, http://www.petefader.com.

6. P. Kotler, *Marketing Management: Analysis, Planning, Implementation, and Control*, 8th ed. (Englewood Cliffs, NJ: Prentice-Hall, 1994).

7. S. Hoisington and E. Naumann, "The Loyalty Elephant," *Quality Progress*, 2003 (February): 33–41.

8. M. Seiler, P. F. Nunes, and J. D. Somers, "Marketing Mastery Matters," *Outlook* (Accenture), May 2006, http://www.CRMproject.com/15736.

9. Brand Keys, "Who Made the 2010 Brand Keys Loyalty Leaders List?" Sales & Marketing Management, October 15, 2010, http://www.salesandmarketing.com/article/who-made-2010-brand-keys-loyalty-leaders-list.

10. InsideCRM Editors, "11 Effective Strategies Apple Uses to Create Loyal Customers," *Inside CRM*, 2008, http://www.insidecrm.com/features/strategies-apple-loyal-customers/.

11. G. Brewer, "The Customer Stops Here," *Sales and Marketing Management*, 1998 (March): 31–36.

12. S. Knox, "Loyalty-Based Segmentation and the Customer Development Process," *European Management Journal*, 1998 (December): 729–737.

13. W. Reinartz and V. Kumar, "The Mismanagement of Customer Loyalty," *Harvard Business Review*, 2002 (July): 86–94.

14. T. L. Keinham et al., "A Longitudinal Examination of Net Promoter and Firm Revenue Growth," *Journal of Marketing*, 71 (July 2007): 39–51.

15. Satmetrix "USSA, JetBlue Airways, Symantec, Trader Joe's, Vanguard, & Amazon. com among the Highest in Customer Loyalty in Satmetrix 2011 Net Promoter benchmarks," *Satmetrix Press Release,* February 17, 2011, http://www.satmetrix.com/company/press-and-news/pr-archive/pr20110217/.

16. ResearchLive, "Net Promoter Score Under Attack," *ResearchLive,* July 2010, http://www.research-live.com/features/net-promoter-score-under-attack/2001829.article.

17. F. Reicheld and P. Schefter, "E-loyalty: Your Secret Weapon," *Harvard Business Review,* 2000 (July-August): 106.

18. Satmetrix, "Calculate Your Net Promoter Score," 2011, http://www.satmetrix.com/net-promoter/; R. Kahan, "Using Database Marketing Techniques to Enhance Your One-to-One Marketing Initiatives," *Journal of Consumer Marketing* 15, no. 5 (1998): 491–493.

19. M. J. Shaw et al., "Knowledge Management and Data Mining for Marketing," *Decision Support Systems* 31, no. 1 (2001): 127–137.

20. R. Dodes, "Neiman Marcus Opens Customer Door Wider," *The Wall Street Journal*, February 15, 2011.

21. R. Koch, *The 80/20 Principle: The Secret of Achieving More with Less* (New York: Currency Doubleday, 1998), 65–68.

22. R. T. Rust, V. A. Zeithaml, and K. N. Lemon, *Driving Customer Equity: How Customer Value Is Reshaping Corporate Strategy* (New York: The Free Press, 2000), 191.

23. A. Weinstein, (2002) Customer retention: A usage segmentation and customer value approach, *Journal of Targeting, Measurement, and Analysis for Marketing*, 10, 3, 265–266.

24. R. Trasorras, A. Weinstein, and R. Abratt, (2009) Value, satisfaction, loyalty, and retention in professional services, *Marketing Intelligence & Planning*, 27, 5, 615–632.

25. J. O. Fredericks, R. R. Hurd, and J. M. Salter II, (2001) Connecting customer loyalty to financial results, *Marketing Management*, Spring, 26–32.

26. S. M. Odell and J. A. Pajunen, (2000) *The Butterfly Customer: Capturing the Loyalty of Today's Elusive Consumer,* Toronto: John Wiley & Sons.

27. G. DeSouza, (1992) Designing a customer retention plan, *Journal of Business Strategy*, March/April, 24–28.

28. P. Passavant, (1995) Retention marketing needs a new vision, *Journal of Direct Marketing*, Spring, 2–4.

29. K. N. Lemon, T. B. White, and R. S. Winer, "Dynamic Customer Relationship Management: Incorporating Future Considerations into the Service Retention Decision," *Journal of Marketing*, 2002 (January): 1–14; G. H. G. McDougall and T. Levesque, "Customer Satisfaction with Services: Putting Perceived Value into the Equation," *Journal of Services Marketing*, 14, no. 5 (2000): 392–410.

CHAPTER 11: CUSTOMER VALUE METRICS

1. D. L. Yohn, "Marketing Is Losing Its Mojo," *Mediaweek*, June 6, 2010.

2. S. H. Seggie, E Cavusgil, and S. E. Phelan, "Measurement of Return on Marketing Investment: A Conceptual Framework and the Future of Marketing Metrics," *Industrial Marketing Management,* 36 (2007): 834–841.

3. A. Griffin and J. R. Hauser, "The Voice of the Customer," *Marketing Science*, 12, no. 1 (1993): 1–27.

4. P. W. Farris et al., *Marketing Metrics: 50+ Metrics Every Executive Should Master* (Upper Saddle River, NJ: Wharton School Publishing, 2006).

5. F. Kokkinaki and T. Ambler, "Marketing Performance Assessment: An Exploratory Investigation into Current Practices and the Role of Firm Orientation," Working Paper 99-114, Marketing Science Institute, Cambridge, MA, 1999.

6. Arthur M. Hughes, "ROI, Profitability, and Lifetime Value," *Database Marketing Institute*, September 15, 2010, http://www.dbmarketing.com/articles/Art129.htm.

7. J. A. Petersen et al., "Choosing the Right Metrics to Maximize Profitability and Shareholder Value," *Journal of Retailing* 85, no. 1 (2009): 95–111.

8. R. F. Dwyer, "Customer Lifetime Valuation to Support Marketing Decision Making," *Journal of Direct Marketing,* 11, no. 4 (1997): 6–13.

9. J. A. Goodman, *Strategic Customer Service: Managing Customer Experience to Increase Word of Mouth, Brand Loyalty, and Maximize Profits* (New York: AMACOM, 2009).

10. Ibid.

11. B. H. Clark, A. V. Abela, and T. Ambler, "Behind the Wheel," *Marketing Management*, 30 (2006): 19–23.

12. Ogilvy & Mather, "The Red Papers: Learning to Read the River," 2010, 12, http://www.ogilvy.com/On-Our-Minds/Articles/redpapers_june2010.aspx.

13. P. W. Farris et al. (2006).

14. V. A. Zeithaml et al., "Forward-Looking Focus: Can Firms Have Adaptive Foresight?" *Journal of Service Research*, 9, no. 2 (2006): 168–183.

CASE 1: ENTERPRISE RENT-A-CAR

1. Enterprise Rent-A-Car, about Enterprise, 2011, http://aboutus.enterprise.com/

2. Hoovers, Enterprise Rent-A-Car Company: competition, 2011, http://www.hoovers.com/free/co/factsheet.xhtml?ID=40145

3. Avis Mission and Values, 2011, http://www.avis.com/car-rental/content/display.ac?navId=T6M21S01

4. Hertz.com Car Rental, company information—Hertz firsts, 2011, http://www.hertz.com/rentacar/abouthertz/index.jsp?targetPage=CorporateProfile.jsp&c=aboutHertzFirstsView

5. R. A. Pohlman and G. S. Gardiner, *Value-Driven Management: How to Create and Maximize Value over Time for Organizational Success* (New York: AMACOM, 2000).

6. Nielsen Wire, "The State of Mobile Apps," June 2010, http://blog.nielsen.com/nielsenwire/online_mobile/the-state-of-mobile-apps/.

7. U.S. Census Bureau, "U.S. Interim Projections By Age, Sex, Race, and Hispanic Origin: 2000–2050," 2010, http://www.census.gov/population/www/projections/usinterimproj/.

CASE 2: FEDEX CORPORATION

1. M. D. Basch, *Customer Culture: How FedEx and Other Great Companies Put the Customer First Every Day* (Upper Saddle River, NJ: Financial Times/Prentice-Hall, 2001).

2. *FedEx Corporation Annual Report* 2001, http://images.fedex.com/us/investorrelations/downloads/annualreport/2001annualreport.pdf

3. United States Securities and Exchange Commission FedEx Corporation Form 10-K, 2011, http://www.sec.gov/Archives/edgar/data/1048911/000095012310065730/c03116e10vk.htm.

4. *Fortune*, 2011, http://money.cnn.com/magazines/fortune.

5. K. S. Krause, "Serious about Small: FedEx Sheds Image as Provider for Corporate Giants," *Traffic World*, April 15, 2002, 25.

6. "FedEx, UPS Face China Dispute, *JoC Week* 3 (May 6, 2002): 10.

7. "FedEx Looks at Hybrid Vehicles to Replace Delivery Vans," *Business and the Environment* 13 (April 2002): 9.

8. "Japan to Reverse Policy, Allow Narita Slots to FedEx," *Financial Times Information Limited*, March 22, 2002.

9. R. S. Dunham, "How Business Is Buckling Up: Security Concerns Pose Big, Expensive Challenges," *Business Week Online*, June 6, 2002.

10. W. Armbruster, "Going Its Own Way: FedEx Charts a Different Course from Competitors Deutsche Post and UPS, *JoC Week*, 3 (May 2002): 11.

11. FedEx Facts, "FedEx Ground," 2011, http://about.fedex.designcdt.com/our_company/company_information/fedex_ground.

12. "GE Engine Services," *Air Transport World*, 39 (June 2002): 12.

13. J. Wastnage, "Hushkits: FedEx Aids Really Quiet," *Flight International*, May 21, 2002, 31.

14. FedEx Investor Relations, Acquisition history 2011, http://about.van.fedex.com/our_company/company_information/fedex_history

15. *FedEx Corporation Annual Report* 2001, http://images.fedex.com/us/investorrelations/downloads/annualreport/2001annualreport.pdf

16. Anonymous, "FedEx Corp. (Up Front)," *Logistics Management & Distribution Report*, March 3, 2002, 41, http://www.highbeam.com/doc/1G1-84149268.html

17. The Sneeze, "The Man behind the FedEx Logo," 2004, http://www.thesneeze.com/mt-archives/000273.php.

18. "FedEx Corp. Reports Higher Fourth Quarter Results," FedEx press release, June 22, 2011, http://news.van.fedex.com/Q4FY11.

CASE 3: THE GRATEFUL DEAD

1. Barry Barnes, *Everything I Know about Business I Learned from the Grateful Dead* (New York: Business Plus, 2011).

Case 4: Harrah's Entertainment, Inc.

1. G. Loveman, "Diamonds in the Data Mine," *Harvard Business Review*, 2003 (May): 111.
2. Jonathan Barsky, "Elite Loyalty Programs: How Do They Rank with Hotel Guests," Market Metrix, November 3, 2008, http://www.marketmetrix.com/en/default.aspx?s=research&p=ElitePrograms.

Case 5: Publix Super Markets, Inc.

1. M. Moskowitz, "100 Best Companies to Work For," *Fortune* 147 (2003): 127.
2. G. W. Jenkins, personal communication to B. G. Mujtaba during Mr. Jenkins's visit to the Altamont Springs Publix in Central Florida, 1989. Note: Dr. Mujtaba (coauthor of this case) was formerly a management development specialist and department manager at Publix Super Markets.
3. Publix, "Publix Reports Third Quarter 2010 Results and Stock Price," press release, November 1, 2010, http://www.publix.com/about/newsroom/NewsReleaseItem.do?newsReleaseItemPK=4556.
4. J. Smith, "Online Grocery Shopping on Track for Rapid Growth," *Food and Consumer Packaged Goods News and Information*, September 15, 1999, 1.
5. B. G. Mujtaba and E. Franklin, "A Retailer's Steady Growth Strategy: Should Publix Stay National or Go Global?" *Journal of Business Case Studies* 3, no. 4 (2007): 33–42.

Case 6: StatePride Industrial Laundry

1. M. E. Porter, *Competitive Advantage* (New York: The Free Press, 1985).

CUSTOMER VALUE CASE STUDIES

Appendix: Analyzing Business Situations— The Customer-Value Funnel Approach*

To compete successfully, organizations must evaluate all pertinent actors and factors in a market. This briefing develops a managerial perspective featuring a four-stage customer value funnel (CVF) framework. The CVF approach is a valuable tool for understanding and assessing business dynamics and situations. You are encouraged to utilize the questions at the end of this section when analyzing the six case studies in Section V of this book.

Management's objective should be to maximize value over time, realizing that customer values have a major impact on both business processes and performance. Hence, the enhanced customer value approach offers management an alternative view of how to compete effectively in dynamic and volatile markets. This value maximization premise means that corporate success should be evaluated in a new light. We propose that business performance should be built on a dual foundation of paramount value concepts:

1. Anticipating and responding to the relevant values of all constituencies (e.g., customers; stakeholders; employees; collaborators, competitors, suppliers, and regulators; and society).
2. Value maximization—how economic value and knowledge are created and applied throughout an organization to best serve its target customers.

---

* This section builds on ideas in an article by Art Weinstein and Randolph A. Pohlman, "Customer Value: A New Paradigm for Marketing Management," *Advances in Business Studies* 6, no. 10 (1998), 89–97.

233

While the former element is largely qualitative in nature, the latter is mostly a quantitative dimension. This approach provides an insightful basis for designing a value-based model for managers to assess business situations in the 21st century. The conceptualization of the value-driven model is developed in the subsequent section.

The CVF captures and summarizes the salient attributes of the two sets of customer value concepts in action (Figure A.1). As the framework illustrates, organizations must deal with a set of macro issues as well as customer-specific concerns to excel in business. Viewing the four levels of the model—global business community, market, organization, and customers—through a broad-to-narrow lens ultimately impacts the performance of a business unit.

The values of the major players in the model must be carefully scrutinized as to value identification and congruency as well as value delivery options (these are the relevant values). From the top down, the value drivers are what: (1) society values [level I]; (2) suppliers, partners, competitors, and regulators value [level II]; (3) owners and employees value [level III]; and (4) customers value [level IV].

A realistic assessment of value creation opportunities (value maximization) throughout the funnel is the next step. Organizations consist of value providers. If the delivered value of these employees exceeds the expectations of customers (perceived value), positive net transaction experiences result. This leads to ongoing satisfaction and increased customer loyalty. In these cases, organizations are faring well in their moments of truth (points where value transfer occurs). Hence, isolated favorable transactions evolve into continued, long-term relationships.

The value over time (lifetime value) of a customer is measurable, and in many cases, substantial. For example, leading supermarkets typically generate about $50,000 from households ($100 per week for 50 weeks for 10 years), and Ford Motor Company estimates the lifetime value of an average customer at more than $300,000—and let's not forget referral business.

For the most part, the funnel model represents a downward flow, with each successive level being a component of the level above (e.g., markets are part of the global business community, organizations are part of markets, etc.). However, the feedback loops evidenced in levels I, II, and III demonstrate that gaining market intelligence and knowledge is an ongoing, iterative, interactive, and integrated process. If business performance does not meet corporate objectives, strategic or tactical changes are mandated. The organization (level III) can adjust internally via rethinking its overall direction, implementing training and development initiatives, revising business plans, etc. Often, however, external adaptations are required due to changes taking place in the macro/global or micro/market environments.

In sum, the customer value funnel offers executives and "students of the market" a tool to help achieve a competitive business edge. The long-term value of the organization is maximized by being in harmony with the relevant values in the marketplace, and the energy of value providers is harnessed to deliver excellence in all endeavors.

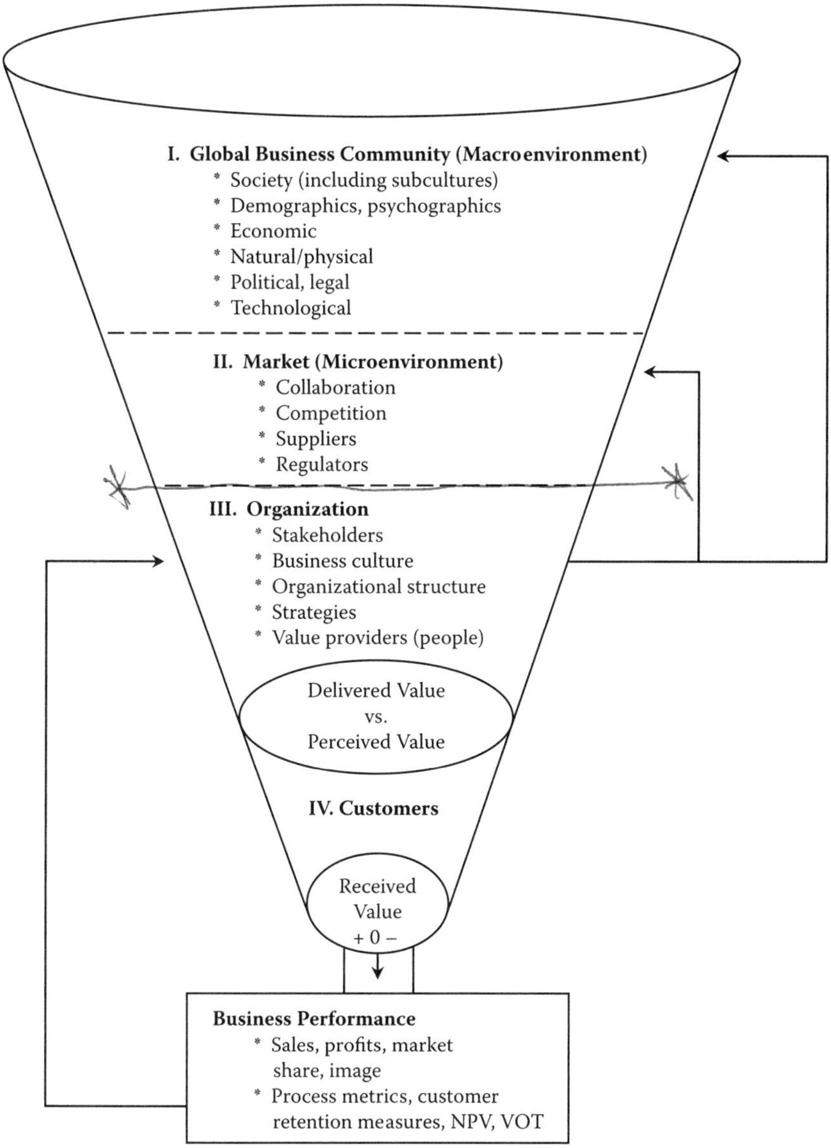
I. Global Business Community (Macroenvironment)
* Society (including subcultures)
* Demographics, psychographics
* Economic
* Natural/physical
* Political, legal
* Technological
II. Market (Microenvironment)
* Collaboration
* Competition
* Suppliers
* Regulators
III. Organization
* Stakeholders
* Business culture
* Organizational structure
* Strategies
* Value providers (people)
Delivered Value
vs.
Perceived Value
IV. Customers
Received
Value
+ 0 –
Business Performance
* Sales, profits, market share, image
* Process metrics, customer retention measures, NPV, VOT

Figure A.1 The customer value funnel.

Realize that the value paradigm is still in the formative stage. A strength of the customer value approach is that it is pragmatic and consistent with the managerial need for integrating business functional areas. The information presented in this book can provide a springboard for the creation and refinement of marketing/customer value management strategies.

Finally, think about how your organization uses competitive differentiation to take maximum advantage of market opportunities. As a framework for analysis, five guiding CVF questions are listed below to help you assess the relevant customer value issues.

Customer Value Funnel Questions

1. Identify the relevant macroenvironmental factors (level 1). What impact do these issues have on the focal organization?
2. Discuss the market factors (level 2). How do collaboration, competition, supplier, and regulators affect the performance of the focal organization?
3. Explain how the focal organization (level 3) creates value for its customers. What strategic changes are required to deliver outstanding value to its customers?
4. Do customers (level 4) perceive value as unsatisfactory, satisfactory, or superior? Why? Which attributes do customers value that are not receiving adequate attention by the organization?
5. Critique the organization's business performance based on traditional (e.g., sales, profits, market share, and image) and value-based performance criteria (e.g., process metrics, customer retention measures, net present value, value over time). What can the organization do to improve its performance?

Case 1: Enterprise Rent-A-Car—A Market-Driven Company*

Enterprise Rent-A-Car is a company that knows firsthand how responding to customer demand can create astounding progression and growth. In fact, many of the most successful and utilized services the company provides were developed because Enterprise management had the forethought to listen and respond to its customers. As can be seen from Figure A.2, Enterprise is in a great position in regard to the revenues that are generated due to its customer orientation and focus.

Enterprise, a privately held company, is the nation's largest rental car company. Begun in 1957 as an automobile leasing business, it established a niche catering to businesses.[1] Breaking current trends in the industry, Enterprise did not service airports until 1995, at the behest of customers requesting the familiar service to which they had grown accustomed. Once Enterprise responded to this demand, it moved forward aggressively, acquiring nearly 200 airport locations within 10 years.

---

* This case was prepared by Patience Rockymore-Turner and Bahaudin G. Mujtaba, Nova Southeastern University. Dr. Mujtaba can be contacted at mujtaba@nova.edu or (954)262-5045.

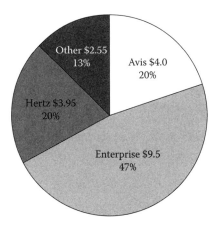

Figure A.2 Industry revenues—U.S. dollars in billions. (Note: Information was collected from corporate-owned companies and not from companies under franchise or other marketing agreements. Secondary source: *Auto Rental News*, Research and Statistics, 2011, http://www.autorentalnews.com/.)

Prior to the airport location services, Enterprise secured a hold for an untapped market: local services to community residents. The founder, Jack Taylor, responded to customer need for a short-term rental while customers' leased cars were being repaired. In fact, one of Enterprise's competitive advantages is that 90% of the United States population lives within 15 miles of an Enterprise office! In a companywide groundbreaking move, a manager responded to customer need by offering free pick-up services to his customers. This service option spread to other branches across the nation. In this example, customer demand and organizational response allowed Enterprise to develop its slogan, "We'll Pick You Up." Customer demand continues to propel Enterprise toward its mission to provide superb customer service. Enterprise continued the neighborhood concept when expanding to Europe. Although the company is located in only five countries, there are well over 300 airport branches located within those countries.

Founder Jack Taylor began with a simple concept: To provide excellent customer service knowing that profits would be sure to follow. Enterprise offers an excellent opportunity to explore the nature in which customer demand initiates organizational response, which in turn leads to organizational progress.

Customers and Environmental Factors

The environmental forces influencing the operation of Enterprise are exhibited directly and indirectly. These forces impact the firm because they present opportunities and threats. As with any organization, management's responses to these conditions largely determine the direction of profitability and sustainability of

Enterprise. Two of the direct forces include customers and competition. In addition, this section reviews economic and global influences.

Customer Expectations

Customers are the driving force behind any organization: They are the only means of realizing the firm's objective to earn revenue through the transmission of business activity. Enterprise's customers require various service needs, including replacement services, retail rental, business rentals, and fleet management.

Replacement

The vast majority of customers who rent vehicles from Enterprise are seeking "replacement" services. The crux of Enterprise's business is conducted to accommodate drivers who have been involved in vehicular accidents. Generally, insurance companies pay the cost of a rental vehicle for an insured driver, with a daily maximum amount covered. Enterprise uses this opportunity to upsell the customer into a higher class of car, or with the offering of additional insurance coverage (for the vehicle or driver). Insurance companies influence the progress of Enterprise because of the various demands and expectations placed, such as the provision of cars that fall into the covered monetary range.

Insurance companies may decide to change their internal policies, which may alter the maximum daily amount of coverage provided. If the coverage rate decreases, for instance, this may adversely affect Enterprise's profitability. The insured driver would be responsible for the cost difference, which might lead some customers to option out of a rental vehicle, or to option out of an upgraded vehicle for the duration of the rental period. Insurance companies could also change their policies to decrease the number of days an insured driver is covered, which would also decrease revenue. On the other hand, an increase in either daily coverage amount or length of coverage would have a positive impact on company revenue.

Retail Rental

Another customer type serving as a force in the organization's outcome is the drivers who rent cars from Enterprise. As mentioned previously, most customers who employ these services do so as a result of accidents, and because of this reason, most insurance companies are the direct payers of the services. There are cases, however, in which non-accident-related customers utilize Enterprise's services, whether to use rental cars for vacations, business trips, or while their cars are being repaired due to vehicular service problems. These customers may place demands on Enterprise that would lead to either positive or negative changes in profitability.

Rental car drivers cover a wide range of demographics. The drivers vary in age, socioeconomic status, professional occupations, geographical location, etc. The demands of customers may shift depending on global trends, or social and economic shifts. For instance, drivers may develop a desire for more fuel-efficient cars and for cars operating on alternative fuel sources. The expectations of customers should determine the decisions Enterprise makes. In fact, Enterprise has responded to the demand for more environmentally responsible vehicles. Enterprise advertises that its rental fleet of hybrid vehicles is the largest in the industry. These vehicles are available in over 30 metropolitan cities nationwide. Social and environmental trends have dictated the changes in customer desires and expectations, and Enterprise has appropriately responded. In fact, Enterprise has responded not only reactively, but proactively as well by challenging customers to participate in their fuel-efficient rental car opportunity. Participating customers will assist in benefiting the environment through a nominal contribution toward various carbon-offsetting projects.

Business Rental

Businesses often need short-term and long-term solutions for their transportation needs. Enterprise responds to this need by offering various services, such as all-inclusive services and packages, like the damage waiver and bodily injury/vehicle collision coverage. An added value for participating businesses is that a partnership with Enterprise will reduce the cost of owning a pool fleet, while at the same time organization members can drive newer vehicles in order to project an image of organizational success. As the global market shifts, creating changes within firms, these changes may dictate and determine the responses from Enterprise to its business rental customers. With rival rental car companies offering similar business rental services, Enterprise has had to set itself apart by offering unique services, such as fleet management.

Fleet Management

Responding to customer needs, Enterprise offers the Fleet Management program. This program is uniquely tailored to fit the specific needs of businesses. As can be seen from Figure A.3, this Fleet Management program has certainly been beneficial to Enterprise compared to the revenues generated by Avis and Hertz. In the Fleet Management program, services include vehicle license and registration management, maintenance management, nationwide usable fuel cards, and mileage reporting features, allowing for differentiation between personal and business miles driven. This detailed level of fleet management services is unique to Enterprise, and was developed from the original 1957 service of automobile leasing for the business professional.

Enterprise's present strategy for handling the force presented by its customers is to provide the best possible service. One way Enterprise has addressed the need to provide superior customer service is through the use of a customer satisfaction measurement tool, the Enterprise Service Quality index (ESQi). This measurement

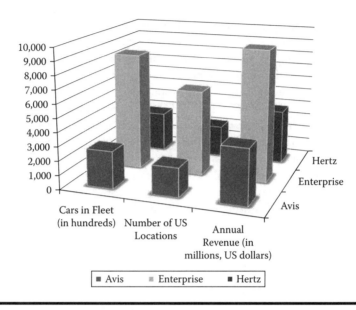

Figure A.3 Fleet, locations, and annual revenue comparison for Enterprise, Hertz, and Avis (2009–2010). (Note: Information was collected from corporate-owned companies and not from companies under franchise or other marketing agreements and from *Auto Rental News*, Research and Statistics, 2011, http://www.autorentalnews.com/.)

tool works by surveying random customers on their recent service experience. Each branch is required to maintain the companywide standard of 80% (at least 80% of customers stating they were *completely satisfied*), which impacts manager bonuses and promotions for all employees at each respective branch. Customers are a driving force influencing the company's growth, direction, and viability. Another force contributing to Enterprise's operations is its competitors.

Competitive Practices

Any firm's competitors comprise a critical force in influencing the firm's progress: Dollars spent on a competitor's goods and services are fewer dollars spent on an organization's own goods and services. According to Hoovers, Enterprise's top competitors are Avis Budget Group, Dollar Thrifty Automotive Group, and Hertz Global Holdings.[2] These competitors offer many of the same services offered by Enterprise, requiring Enterprise to stand out from the competition. Partially fueled by customer demand, Enterprise continues to set itself apart from others, capitalizing on its competitive advantages. A brief exploration of Avis and Hertz reveals why the competition is never far behind, advancing Enterprise's responses to opportunities and threats.

Avis Car Rental

A publicly held company in operation for nearly 65 years, Avis began as a rental car company designed to meet the needs of airline travelers. In fact, Avis was the first rental car company to be located at an airport. Market expansion occurred early for Avis, with its first international franchise office opening in 1953. It has since expanded to include worldwide locations in over 150 countries. Some of its locations are in lesser-known locales such as the Reunion Islands, Seychelles, and São Tomé. Avis has managed to remain a strong competitor for Enterprise because it, too, is responsive to customers' changing needs.

Avis's stated mission is to be customer oriented, and the company prides itself on "defining service excellence and building unmatched customer loyalty."[3] In 1963 it marketed the widely known slogan, "We Try Harder." Responding to customer needs, Avis has initiated a convenient self-service check-in option at airports, and has created a Customer Loyalty Program for frequent renters. In response to the changing technological demands of many of today's renters, Avis has proven to be a pioneer in the field through its inception of iPhone and iPod Touch applications, in addition to satellite radio and a handheld GPS system. These technologically advanced products and various services tout Avis as a competitive force for influencing Enterprise's progress. For instance, Enterprise does not currently have an iPhone application, but if it responds to customer demands (and industry competition), it will soon develop one.

Hertz Car Rental

Touting numerous firsts in the rental car industry, Hertz, another publicly held company, was formed in 1918. It had the first nationwide rental network due to its national franchise system. Responding to customers' need, the company began by providing railway travelers a rental car once they reached their destination. The rail location service later expanded to include airline and sailing travelers. Another first for Hertz, which started in 1933 and impacted industrywide growth, was the ability for customers to pick up cars at one location and to leave them at another location. The company eventually expanded to become the first rental car company with a European location, paralleling part of its mission statement to reinforce its worldwide position. Hertz was also first in creating a Nationwide Emergency Road Service and an On-Board Navigation System. Additional services provided due to customer demand included in-car cellular phones (introduced in 1988) and a multilingual Web site, reflecting response to growing global diversity.[4]

As a company of firsts, Hertz is in a unique position to remain a strong competitor for Enterprise: With nearly 40 more years of experience than Enterprise, Hertz is an innovator of services. If Hertz continues to market "first" services and programs, Enterprise will have to offer successful strategies as a means of keeping up with the competition.

One way Enterprise currently deals with competitive forces is by adapting successful services from its competition. The decision to service airports is a prime example. Both Hertz and Avis utilize the airport service option as their mainstay of service operations. Enterprise took advantage of this opportunity a mere 15 years ago, compared to 60 years ago for its competitors.

While customers and competitors are direct forces that sway a company's strategy and practices, indirect forces such as the economy and global conditions can also heavily influence management activities and the decision-making process of managers. Managers and employees must positively respond to all forces in a timely manner. Conditions in the economy impact all participants in the marketplace. These forces are more difficult for managers because they are often unpredictable and unexpected. Two of these indirect forces, economic and global forces, play a major role in the organizational progress of Enterprise.

Economic Influences

Within the firm, shifts in the economy require accurate response from managers. They must respond to these unexpected forces in a manner conducive to the firm's well-being. In a declining economy, changes such as an increase in the unemployment rate may lead to declining consumer spending. As can be seen from Figure A.4,

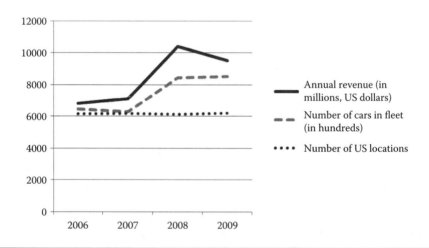

Figure A.4   Enterprise growth chart showing annual revenue, number of cars in fleet, and number of U.S. locations (2006–2009). (Note: Calculations for 2008 and 2009 annual revenue include Enterprise-Rent-A-Car as well as recently acquired National Car Rental and Alamo Rent-A-Car. Annual revenue for 2008 may be estimated slightly higher than actual amount. Secondary source: *Auto Rental News*, 2011, Research and Statistics, http://www.autorentalnews.com/.)

Enterprise has suffered a decrease in its revenues over the 2008 and 2009 years due to the general economic decline in the United States.

In the case of the rental car industry, decreased spending by retail rental customers may result in a decrease in revenue when customers choose not to rent a car; rent a car but reduce the duration of the rental period; or option out of premium cars and/or a la carte services. In terms of negative economic changes, replacement customers—insurance companies—may make changes to insurance coverage policies by reducing either the daily allowance rate or by reducing the number of days covered by the insurance policy.

Economic conditions adversely affecting Enterprise's profitability require a suitable response from managers. Adjusting to today's economic decline, Enterprise continues to offer a popular weekend rental rate, thus boosting the number of customers utilizing rental car services for recreational purposes.

Global Opportunities

Global forces are another indirect force influencing management response. For instance, seemingly obscure actions, such as a localized political upheaval in an unknown village abroad may develop, leading to global impact. Another example of global forces impacting consumers worldwide would be unexpected changes in the availability of oil. Rising fuel costs due to a scarcity of resources may negatively impact conditions for Enterprise. If customers decide to drive less by forgoing rental car services, this would have a detrimental impact on revenue. On the other hand, if Enterprise decides to tackle this particular force by turning a threat into an opportunity, the company could efficiently promote the availability of the company's flex-fuel and fuel-efficient vehicles.

Decision making involves the analysis and the determinations of managers as they respond to opportunities and threats, within the context of organizational goals, and occurs in all four stages (planning, organizing, leading, and controlling) of management functions. Recognition of the need for a decision is a key component in the decision-making process because recognition of the need propels all other steps. Learning from feedback is vital because it allows managers to reflect on the successes and failures of their actions. The decision-making process is a critical component in value creation—creating what is valued by stakeholders.

Value Creation Approach

Enterprise creates long-term value by remaining responsive to its customers. This is primarily achieved through the decentralized structure of the organization, which allows decisions to be made at the lower, local level. A case in point was the ability for a Florida branch manager to directly respond to a customer's need to receive pick-up service to the office. This concept was tremendously valued by customers, and soon spread to locations across the nation, resulting in a companywide service.

By attending to customers' needs, Enterprise works to create value over the long term. Profits are a necessary objective, but Enterprise places customer service as its driver, with profits following. In this sense, profits are steered by customer demand and organizational response. The better the customer service, the greater the amount of profits to be, and this is evidenced in Enterprise's positive growth since inception. This process has a long-term value orientation.

Another method Enterprise employs to create value over the long term is through its promotion policy. All operational positions are filled from within. Everyone on the managerial track starts from the same position as management trainee. In this way, employees work toward a future knowing their past efforts will be beneficial and are therefore valued over the long term.

Employee values are an important element of the value creation process.[5] An organization's determination of employee values is critical in the employee selection process. The interviews are structured around behavior-based questions, designed to elicit behavioral patterns. This careful selection of qualified employees is a value adder because it ensures that incoming employees will already possess a certain level of skills, which will be enhanced by intensive and relevant management training. In addition, employees are able to seek virtually any position in any area of interest to them throughout North America and Western Europe. This flexibility ensures a compatible workforce.

Another important element of the value creation process is the values of an organization's owners. Jack Taylor values the needs and well-being of others, which led him to create and incorporate various needful services for his customers; valuing others' needs also led to the creation of the promotion-from-within concept valued by Enterprise employees. Enterprise owners also value growth and profitability, which is reflected not only in companywide growth, but in the autonomy given to branch managers to become fully responsible for the branch's profits, growth, and expansion, thus allowing localized response to customer demand.

The localized decision-making process is critical to organizational success. Responding to customer demand means determining which customer demands will be responded to and developed, and then creating the desired goods and services in the most resource-efficient manner possible, in light of the benefits of long-term success. Not every customer desire is practical nor will every desire be valued by a vast majority. Aspects such as the negative and positive consequences of decision making should carefully be considered. Decisions reflecting long-term impact are also critical when deciding a course of action.

Enterprise continues to gain a larger percentage in the North American rental car industry. By enhancing its competitive advantages, it continues to be responsive to its customers, which in turn allows for tremendous positive growth, year after year. There may be a few areas in which Enterprise could improve. One suggestion is that the company should capitalize on the demands for technological features in rental cars. An increasingly popular service among today's techno-logical-savvy population is iPhone applications.[6] Avis has already responded to this demand by creating its own application; it would behoove Enterprise to fol-low suit.

Another recommendation for Enterprise is to address the needs of the disabled and the aging population—the nation's fastest growing age group.[7] Cars should feature disability-friendly technology, similar to the type provided by Hertz. Responding to these and other demands would closely fit with Enterprise's mission to provide superb customer service. After all, this type of attention to customer service is the key to Enterprise's tremendous growth.

Finally, it should be noted that social media presents an incredible opportunity for organizations because it enables them to extend to a wider audience—increas-ing their reach and visibility. The three major rental car companies in the United States utilize various social media marketing tools: Enterprise utilizes Facebook and Twitter social media sites; Hertz encourages customers to follow on Twitter, Facebook, YouTube, and Hertz Mobile; and Avis UK utilizes a blog, Twitter, and an electronic newsletter. Another advantage to social networking is that it allows increased customer participation. For instance, customers can become active par-ticipants by leaving feedback on a company's Web site. In this way, customers are presented with an opportunity to express their levels of satisfaction and loyalty.

Questions

1. Describe the organizational culture of Enterprise Rent-A-Car. How do the values of founder Jack Taylor influence the value-creation process and deci-sions made by Enterprise?

2. In terms of environmental factors, which forces (direct or indirect) have the greatest impact on an organization? Why? Use examples to support your answer. What improvements can management make to adjust to changing customer demands?

3. As observed in the case study, understanding customer desires can lead to innovative changes resulting in successful outcomes. Describe some effective marketing strategies by Enterprise. What additional changes are called for?

4. Can you think of any disadvantages to embracing a strong customer service orientation? If so, what are some of these disadvantages, and how can they be overcome?

5. Why might an organization view its competition as useful or necessary, in terms of achieving its organizational goals? How might a competitor help to improve an organization's customer-value plan?

6. How are social media platforms being used by firms to compete more effec-tively for today's technology-savvy consumers? What new initiatives should Enterprise embrace to better communicate and stay engaged with their tar-get markets?

Case 2: FedEx Corporation—A Customer Value Funnel Assessment*

"When it absolutely, positively has to get there overnight." Living up to a value proposition like "absolutely, positively"—guaranteeing great service—is not an easy task. FedEx provides a high-quality service, and has such a great image that it can charge premium prices for that service because customers know that it will deliver. The company's innovative tracking procedures, added to a corporate culture that demands excellence, gives them an edge over other overnight delivery firms.

While FedEx is a global giant today, the early days were filled with great uncertainty about the company's survival. As Michael D. Basch, senior vice president of sales and customer service at Federal Express explained, optimistic forecasts of delivering 300–3,000 packages the first night manifested itself into the gloomy reality of only six deliveries (and four were from salespeople testing the system). Imagine this nightmarish scenario as of Monday, March 12, 1973—a company with 23 airplanes, hundreds of employees, a Memphis hub/facility, no money, and two customers. By that Friday, only one package was in the system at a calculated cost of half a million dollars to ship! This situation led to an immediate mandate and vision for the company dubbed "Get The Packages."[1]

Over time, as corporate users learned about the Federal Express customer obsession, tracking system, available technology, and high-level service experience, the company's fortunes quickly turned. Today, FedEx delivers more than 4 million express air packages daily.

In August 2001, FedEx started handling Express Mail for the U.S. Postal Service. This partnership gives the Postal Service a guaranteed lift capacity for mail, and allows FedEx to gain additional daytime utilization for its air fleet—a marriage that helps both sides. This writer observed day one of the U.S. mail being loaded onto the FedEx jet prior to takeoff at the Tallahassee, Florida, airport. Amazingly, loaders sprinted across the tarmac between work stations! Here were people making just above minimum wage, but so immersed in the culture of "time is money" that they were doing everything possible to get that plane off the ground on time. In the movie *Castaway*, Tom Hanks plays a FedEx executive who goes to Moscow to convince the FedEx team there that delays are inexcusable; his "tick-tock, tick-tock," as he points to his watch, is an accurate portrayal of how important everyone in the company feels about quality and on-time service.

FedEx delivers what it promises, and communicating that promise is another area where the company shows its marketing prowess. Their first-rate promotional

---

* This case was prepared by Jerry Johnson. Mr. Johnson retired as a manager in the United States Postal Service after more than 25 years of service. He currently is the business manager for the Florida Attorney General's Economic Crimes Division in Tallahassee, Florida. For further information, contact him at jerryjohnson1@comcast.net.

initiatives feature creative advertising such as their 1981 Ally & Gargano ad featuring fast-talking John Moschitta, Jr., and their 2001 "don't worry" ad campaign by BBDO, New York, aimed at small businesses. Innovative sponsorships include supporting a team in the Simba Telecon Rally in Uganda, sponsoring the Orange Bowl football game in Miami, a NASCAR Sprint Cup car, and the PGA Tour's "FedEx Cup." Quoting from the FedEx 2001 annual report:

> During a period of challenge and change, only FedEx remains focused on a unique business model—to operate each company independently, focused on the distinct needs of each customer segment, but also to compete collectively, leveraging our greatest strengths, the power of the FedEx brand and information technology. That's why FedEx continues to deliver value for our shareholders, meaningful solutions for our customers and continued opportunity for our employees.[2]

In the May 2010 10-K report to the Securities and Exchange Commission, FedEx said, under "Strategy":

> We believe that sales and marketing activities, as well as the information systems that support the extensive automation of our package delivery services, are functions that are best coordinated across operating companies. Through the use of advanced information systems that connect the FedEx companies, we make it convenient for customers to use the full range of FedEx services. We believe that seamless information integration is critical to obtain business synergies from multiple operating units.[3]

How did FedEx achieve that perceived level of excellence? More importantly, how do they keep that perception intact? The customer value funnel (CVF) can help show how FedEx maximizes economic value while also responding to the needs of its stakeholders.

Global Business Community (Macroenvironment)

Perhaps, you have heard the classic tale about how Frederick W. Smith designed the basic idea of a "hub and spoke" delivery system for a class paper at Yale, was given a C, and told by his professor that his concept would not work. That concept is now the key building block and process management technique for every major delivery firm in the world.

When Federal Express was founded nearly 40 years ago there was not a large market for overnight delivery. The Postal Service was dominant in the delivery field at that time; there were no other national delivery firms of any size. Society moved at a little slower pace, and the CEO's "I need it yesterday" was not heard 15 times a day. Wow, how things have changed! As the speed of business changed in the 1990s, the overnight delivery business boomed, and FedEx started earning considerable profits.

FedEx's first customers were the large businesses that provided large volumes of time-sensitive mail and supplies that needed quick delivery. As just-in-time inventory strategies took off, FedEx got into the supply-chain business and succeeded so well that the firm was given "supplier of the year" awards by Dell Computer, General Motors, and Walmart. The Dell award was for superior performance in moving material between Dell's manufacturing facility in Penang, Malaysia, and distribution points in the United States. That is an example of FedEx's current growth strategy: Management believes that there is more growth potential overseas than in the U.S. market, and the firm is constantly expanding worldwide. Trade barriers have fallen in Asia, and FedEx's presence across the European continent is rising. FedEx now has customers in more than 220 countries and territories. In 2010, FedEx was ranked #13 in *Fortune* magazine's list of Most Admired Companies.[4]

Organizational demographics also show a growing small business market that is not currently having its needs met by UPS, and FedEx is working hard to grab that market niche. As an example, consider the experience of Tracy Melton, the owner of Melton Tackle:

> I sat down with UPS and FedEx and said, Here I am.… I needed to be competitive and couldn't use list rates. FedEx was willing to take a chance on me when UPS wasn't. We ship 150 to 200 packages a day— not IBM, but they aren't letters, either and that adds up. UPS wants to back up a 40-foot trailer, load it up, and drive it to a distribution center. That isn't what we are about.[5]

The economics of starting and running an enterprise like FedEx are staggering. Smith went to several cities before Memphis agreed to help him with the logistics he needed at the airport. Even now, with the firm turning big profits annually, economic downturns and events such as the September 11th Twin Towers attack can cause major economic problems.

The natural and physical problems associated with such a business are interesting. For overnight service, one major determinant is distance: How far can you go, and get back, in one night? FedEx flies the fastest cargo jets they can get, and still has to adjust clearance times on the east and west coasts to ensure that the planes can get in and out of Memphis within the sortation window at their hub. One physical problem is noise, and that ties into the political and legal issues for the firm. In the late 1980s, this case writer was sent to a business meeting in Memphis and stayed in the Sheraton Airport Hotel—a great place, until those FedEx planes started to land in the middle of the night! We ended up working all night, since none of us could sleep. FedEx has now set "mini-hubs" in several locations, including the High Point, North Carolina, airport. Residents living in close proximity to that airport continue to put up a fight against late-night noise pollution.

Another legal problem is access to markets and airports. As *JoC Week* reported in 2002, FedEx was fighting China's assertion that China Post has monopoly control over all international and domestic shipments of documents weighing less than 17 ounces and appealing Japan's decision to reverse its previous ruling allowing FedEx to obtain slots at Tokyo's Narita airport (replacing Delta).[6] It is interesting that fierce competitors UPS, DHL, Worldwide, and TNT joined with FedEx in fighting the attempt by the Chinese to monopolize intracountry jurisdiction over the international express market. Now, FedEx has basically won the Chinese distribution war. FedEx now delivers to over 400 locations in China, and in 2009 started using the new Guangzhou Baiun International Airport in southern China as a hub for their Asia deliveries. FedEx has had labor troubles with their pilots, a couple of brushes with antitrust investigations, and tax liability inquiries from the IRS. In most cases FedEx has come through these potential troubles unscathed.

The technological aspect of the global business community is one area where FedEx really shines. The firm has always been a leader in the business of tracking packages, using optical scanners and barcodes long before those were industry standards, and now even partnering with AT&T Wireless to track shipments. FedEx started purchasing the Airbus A380-800 high-capacity, long-range aircraft, with delivery of the new planes starting in 2008. Now the firm has added a contract for 38 Boeing 777 freighters, a high-capacity, long-range plane for use between major markets (think Paris to Singapore). FedEx is also experimenting with various hybrid diesel-electric delivery vehicles to replace the current 40,000 vans used by the firm. FedEx has partnered with the Alliance for Environmental Innovation to help develop the new delivery vehicle, which is targeted for a 50% improvement in fuel mileage and a 90% reduction in exhaust emissions.[7] Another very impressive FedEx technology is what employees call their "secret decoder rings"—a pinkie ring that scans and records a package barcode as the employee picks it up for sortation.

Market (Microenvironment)

FedEx is constantly seeking collaborative relationships to help grow the firm, as previously noted in the discussion of the U.S. Postal Service and AT&T. According to the *Financial Times*, another example is a partnership with Kodak, where FedEx will provide express service to Kodak stores in China.[8] As Dunham reports, to help handle security issues after 9/11, Fred Smith and the other CEO members of the

Business Round Table have established a secure phone system to help improve communications in case of another emergency situation.[9]

FedEx is handling competition from its two biggest competitors—UPS and Deutsche Post World Net—by zigging when the competition is zagging. Armbruster, in *JoC Week*, explains:

> Specifically, UPS and Deutsche Post World Net have both moved aggressively and publicly into the rapidly growing third-party logistics business. FedEx, while dabbling in logistics, has spent the last few years diversifying away from its core U.S. express business, assembling a large ground transportation network in the U.S. that now accounts for 22% of its total revenue.[10]

"Ground is exceeding our expectations," according to FedEx senior vice-president Bill Margaritis. On February 5, 2002, FedEx opened an additional 31 FedEx Home Delivery centers, giving FedEx ground coverage for 90% of the country. As of 2011, FedEx has over 500 ground facilities and 32 hubs around the country, allowing for 100% coverage of the United States and nearly 100% of Canada.[11] FedEx grew the ground delivery business by buying regional ground delivery services around the country and consolidating services. FedEx has laid off some people as these consolidations took place, increasing profitability.

With FedEx being given awards for being such an integral part of other supply-chain networks, is it any wonder that FedEx is very picky about its own suppliers? In June 2002, FedEx awarded a 20-year contract to GE Engine Services to perform engine maintenance on FedEx's fleet of planes.[12] GE Engine is known in the industry as the best contract maintenance firm of its kind. And with the night-flying noise issue, FedEx has contracted with Really Quiet, Inc., for "hush kits" for FedEx's plane engines.[13]

In the United States, there is not much regulation of the package delivery business. The Department of Commerce and the Department of Transportation ensure that FedEx meets the minimal safety requirements for transporting cargo. Overseas, there are customs issues that have to be overcome as well as the previously mentioned political and legal issues.

With the Postal Service cutting window service personnel over the last few years due to shrinking revenue, long lines started building at USPS retail units. As a result, small shipping centers started springing up across the landscape, and FedEx saw another growth opportunity. In February 2004, FedEx closed on the purchase of Kinko's, renaming the new subsidiary FedEx Kinko's. This increased customer access to FedEx products by adding 1,200 new locations in the United States.[14] This filled an obvious gap in the FedEx marketing plan, giving FedEx physical locations to help connect with their customers. In June 2008, the retail-chain subsidiary was renamed FedEx Office, dropping the Kinko's name.

Organization

FedEx knows that the way to remain profitable is to take care of its customers, and it does this in many ways: keeping guarantees in place during the holiday season, wining and dining best customers, and bundling services to create value. FedEx has won several Web Marketing Association's best Transportation Web Site awards, and eWeek has ranked FedEx number two in an annual list of e-business innovators. According to Laurie A. Tucker, senior vice-president of Global Product Marketing at FedEx,

> FedEx leads the industry in developing valuable interactive services that help customers access, manage, and secure transportation services. We are proud of the team of professionals that continues to develop the innovative technologies that enhance the customer experience on FedEx.com.

The business culture at FedEx has already been discussed to some extent. Any firm that can motivate its lowest paid employees to run between work stations, just to ensure that a plane leaves on time, and can get over 10,000 volunteer hours from employees at St. Jude's Hospital in Memphis every year, knows how to instill the firm's mission in its employees. The company encourages innovation and rewards employees handsomely for suggestions that are adopted. Since employees are treated well, it is easy to understand how the attention to needs is carried over to the treatment of FedEx customers. FedEx is a regular entry on *Fortune*'s list of Best Places to Work.

FedEx's organizational structure is fairly typical for a firm of its size, with a board of directors, VPs handling functional areas, and station managers in charge of each remote hub site. The firm likes to promote from within, and turnover amongst white-collar employees is very low (and only a 10% annual turnover of all employees). Fred Smith likes to quote President Franklin D. Roosevelt, "Find good employees, and turn them loose."

Smith discussed growth strategies in recent annual reports. The basic five-point growth plan is to grow: (1) the core transportation business, (2) internationally, (3) the logistics and supply-chain offerings, (4) e-commerce, and (5) new services or alliances.[15] FedEx is also growing through acquisitions. FedEx acquired American Freightways and Viking Freight, and has rebranded them as FedEx Freight.[16] American Freightways serviced most of the country east of the Rocky Mountains, and Viking covered 17 western states, giving FedEx additional freight firepower across the country.

FedEx obviously provides superior customer value, and that means excellent people, dedicated to delivering value. FedEx customer representatives have a $2,000 allowance that they can spend on any customer, at any time, to make that customer happy (anything from dinner to shipping refunds). As an example, this case writer went to the airport to observe the plane being loaded and was offered a jump-seat ride to Memphis to watch the hub operation; the offer shows the pride that these employees have in their company. In sum, FedEx's delivered value meets and, at times, exceeds its perceived value. FedEx is truly a value winner because it has a strong value proposition based on service, quality, image, and price components.

Branding

FedEx has consolidated all of its segments under the FedEx brand: FedEx Express, FedEx Ground, FedEx Freight, etc. All of the subsidiaries share the same FedEx logo, with all of the logos having the "FED" in purple and the "Ex" in a different color, depending on the operating company. For example, the original FedEx logo (for the overall company) has the "Ex" in orange, and that logo is the overall firm's workmark. Those colors are also used for FedEx Express. FedEx Ground has a green "Ex"; FedEx Freight has a red "Ex"; and FedEx Office has a blue "Ex."

One thing all of the logos have in common is the arrow in the design (hint: look between the second E and the X). The arrow was deliberately designed into the logo by Lindon Leader of Landor Associates, San Francisco, in 1994. He told *The Sneeze* blog in a 2004 interview that when the logo was revealed to the top FedEx staff, Fred Smith was the only person to spot the arrow![17] The arrow subliminally represents the speed and forward thinking of FedEx. The matching logo idea over all the FedEx companies helps to emphasize the brand, and that imprint is one of the best recognized brands in the world. But not everyone knows FedEx well. Ken Jenning's winning streak on *Jeopardy* ended when he asked the question "What is FedEx?" to the answer: "Most of this firm's 70,000 seasonal white-collar employees work only four months a year." The correct question was, "What is H&R Block?"

Customer Value and Business Performance

FedEx is a customer-focused company that believes in making it simple for users to do business with them. Whether it is via its telephone number (1-800-GOFEDEX), its Web site (www.fedex.com), or its corporate name (Federal Express repainted its trucks to read "FedEx" because that is what its customers called them), a "customer first" mindset dominates. This approach has contributed to top-of-mind awareness for the company as millions of customers daily say, "Let's FedEx this package." Customers appreciate their easy-to-use forms and package-tracking procedures, as well as their commitment to high quality and excellent service.

Do FedEx's customers receive superior value? The firm's business performance indicates that it is successful in execution. FedEx reported net income of $1.45 billion, up 23% from 2010. Revenue reached $39.3 billion, an increase of 13% over 2010.[18] And, the company expects a strong 2012, too. These are impressive financial results fighting off the effects of the worldwide economic slowdown. FedEx has found ways to maintain and grow market share in a volatile express market, expand to other market niches (small-business logistics, supply-chain operations, and ground-freight transportation), and become a technological leader in the package-tracking field.

Stumbling Blocks

FedEx has made a few mistakes over the years, but the firm has almost always moved quickly to change directions when necessary. In 1989, FedEx spent $883 million for the Flying Tiger Line, giving the firm additional overseas capacity and landing rights in some major European airports. However, FedEx then discovered that most of the Flying Tiger planes needed extensive repairs, and FedEx's international operation lost money in the years leading up to 1990. Service scores dropped to near 80% after the Flying Tiger takeover, but climbed back to a more normal 96% by early 1990.

One interesting stumble involved one of the latest FedEx television ads, where office workers are explaining to one of their own that he is always wrong: Steely Dan is a band, not a person; we don't get "French" benefits, we get fringe benefits; and Jimmy Dean makes sausage, James Dean was an actor. The catch is that the band Steely Dan named themselves after a steam-powered dildo that was a part of William Burroughs's book *Naked Lunch*. How that little fact got past the executives at FedEx was a subject of discussion around the company for some time!

Strategic Changes

What can FedEx do to improve in the second decade of the 21st century? While the steps toward bundling services and cobranding are a move in the right direction, additional efforts need to be made in those areas. The firm needs to do a better job of differentiating and marketing the quality level of its services, i.e., stress the fact that the FedEx value proposition is not just a tag line from an ad. And, they need to use their technological firepower to work more toward individualizing the services available to their customers. Individualized service is the wave of the future, and FedEx needs to ride that wave (and the Internet) into increased value, added care for customers, and increased profitability.

Questions

1. Critique the FedEx value proposition. How does this VP lead to customer satisfaction, loyalty, retention, long-term relationships, and enhanced business performance?
2. What marketing/business strategies should FedEx pursue to improve its market position in e-commerce?
3. What lessons can another organization (identify a specific company) learn about customer value based on the FedEx business model?
4. What are the critical success factors for FedEx and the industry? How likely are these to change in 3–5 years? The next 10 years?

Case 3: The Grateful Dead—Creating Deadheads by Providing Drop-Dead Customer Service*

What does it take to retain customers and create loyalty in them? This critical question faces all organizations today, as customers have a multitude of choices for satisfying their needs and wants. Perhaps we can learn some valuable lessons not from a *Fortune 500* company, nor a company with considerable public data. Perhaps, instead, we can learn something valuable from an unlikely organization in an unlikely industry, the legendary rock band the Grateful Dead. This choice is made because of the volatility of the music industry, an industry where bands come and go on a daily basis, an industry where response to rapid change is a requirement and has been for many years. The Grateful Dead was also chosen because the author has been actively observing this band for more than 30 years and is well acquainted with its unique history and customer service.

Throughout their career starting in 1965, the Grateful Dead grew in popularity until 1995, when they disbanded after the death of lead guitarist, Jerry Garcia. They started out playing in a pizza parlor in Palo Alto, California, for $50 a night, and by 1973 they played to the largest crowd in U.S. history (estimated at 600,000) at Watkins Glen, New York. This is nearly twice as large as the crowd at Woodstock four years earlier. In 1991, total attendance at their concerts was 1.8 million, with an over 99% occupancy rate. Demand for tickets was always strong, and sales reached $52.5 million in 1994, the band's last full year of touring.

While these numbers are impressive, they do not capture the remarkable fan loyalty that lies behind them. The bond between the Grateful Dead and the Deadheads (as their fans came to be known) was often a *lifetime relationship*. Some Deadheads even changed their lifestyles to better match the Sixties values of music, peace, and harmony. Many Deadheads moved to the San Francisco Bay area, where more concerts were played each year than anywhere else. Others planned vacations to match the band's touring schedule. As many as 2,000 Deadheads ordered tickets for *every* concert during the summer tours of 20 to 25 shows. Over the years, a virtual community of friends developed among the Deadheads as they moved from concert to concert year after year and became a "professional audience." Many fans saw *hundreds* of Dead concerts over the years. Bill Walton, former basketball great and sportscaster, saw more than 600!

What could lead to this level of customer loyalty? What were the expectations of the Deadheads? How did the Dead match or exceed those expectations with the concert experience? Deadheads, like all consumers, have a set of expectations that

---

* This case was prepared by F. Barry Barnes, Ph.D. Dr. Barnes is professor of management in the H. Wayne Huizenga School of Business and Entrepreneurship at Nova Southeastern University, Fort Lauderdale, Florida, and author of *Everything I Know about Business I Learned from the Grateful Dead*.[1] He can be reached at barry@huizenga.nova.edu.

determines their level of satisfaction with any product or service and the process of obtaining it. This set includes such things as the reliability or consistency of the product/service, its availability and accessibility, standards regarding tangible aspects of the product/service, concerns about the empathy and understanding shown regarding the process of obtaining the product/service, and responsiveness to customer needs and wants. How this set of expectations is met initially determines whether a customer is satisfied and retained, and over time it determines how loyal the customer will be for the long haul. If we examine each of these expectations held by Deadheads for the Grateful Dead, perhaps we can begin to understand the remarkable bond that developed between them.

Reliability

Deadheads were looking for more than a canned performance that sounded just like the most recent record of the Grateful Dead. They wanted live, improvisational music, music that required their attention in the here and now, music that was adventurous. The Dead were happy to oblige. Their music was an amalgam of folk, bluegrass, blues, reggae, country, jazz, and rock that had been born in the heart of the Sixties hippie revolution, yet continued to develop and grow through the years. No two concerts were ever the same, and the songs they played never followed a predictable sequence. Their active musical repertoire was 150 songs at any one time. Each song performance was different from every other performance due to the improvisational nature of their playing. In 1991, this author attended six concerts in seven nights and saw more than 100 different songs performed, with only two songs being repeated. Thus, the live Grateful Dead concert experience could always be relied on to offer a unique product, one that continued to keep demand high and fans coming back for more.

Reliability for Deadheads was also concerned with the quality and consistency of the performances. When things went just right at a Dead concert, there was a remarkable synergy between the band members as they played, and between the audience as well, that created a feeling of joy and ecstasy that's difficult to describe. This was often referred to as the X-factor. The band was always seeking this special synergy or X-factor, and although they didn't always find it, Deadheads wanted to be there when they did. As concert promoter Bill Graham said, "The Grateful Dead aren't the *best* at what they do, they're the *only* ones who do what they do."

Reliability of performances was also demonstrated by the attitude of the band members, who were dedicated to playing as well as they possibly could at every performance. During an interview in 1988 (after playing together for more than 20 years), band members said, "We're just now starting to get good at this. We're just now where we wanted to be musically 20 years ago. Even an off-night it isn't too bad these days, but in the past it could be really bad." And rhythm guitarist and vocalist Bob Weir said, "We chase the music just as hard and as fast as we can." Fans knew this was true and respected the continual effort by the band to excel in every concert.

Finally, reliability was demonstrated by the constancy of the musicians in the band. When the band was formed in 1965, the founding members were Jerry Garcia, lead guitar and vocals; Bob Weir, rhythm guitar and vocals; Ron "Pigpen" McKernan, keyboards and vocals; Phil Lesh, bass and vocals; and Billy Kreutzman, drums. A second drummer, Mickey Hart, was added in 1968. During their 30-year career, the personnel of the band stayed remarkably constant. Only on keyboards did they have any turnover in personnel. In 1995 during their last concert tour, five of the musicians had been playing together for 27 years, a remarkable achievement for any organization, and a further guarantee of consistency and reliability of performance.

Availability

Because their music was so varied and each performance unique, many Deadheads were not content to simply see the Dead perform once every few years and then fill in the time between by listening to their records. They wanted the live experience and the possibility of the X-factor, and they wanted lots of it! The Grateful Dead again obliged them. For 30 years the Dead played an average of 77 concerts a year, more than 2,300 in all. This is completely unlike other successful rock bands of the 60s, 70s, 80s, and 90s that toured only every few years to support a new album. Moreover, Dead concerts were typically two and a half to three hours long, with some performances running four hours or more. On a few occasions, they played all night long, and breakfast was served to the audience at dawn!

Recognizing that their fans were spread across the country and around the world, the Dead concert schedule typically included three tours across North America every year. They also toured Europe several times and even played at the Great Pyramid in Egypt. With this kind of availability and accessibility, it's easy to see why fans could see so many shows.

Tangibles

In order to continue to satisfy customers, tangible aspects of any product or service must improve over time. This is another aspect of customer satisfaction where the Dead excelled; they believed that if they were charging money for their performance, then the quality of the sound at the back of the venue should be just as good as at the front, since the price paid was the same. Thus, their aim was to create the best possible sound at every concert, to reproduce their music as faithfully as possible, and to minimize listener fatigue produced by noise and distortion in concert sound systems. As a result, the Dead always had the most technologically advanced sound system in the world. In 1968, they helped establish a research and development group, Alembic, which constantly pushed the sonic envelope, and created many innovations now used in all concert sound systems. In the early 1970s, the Dead pioneered the first stereo concert sound system, the "Wall of Sound," which used no stage monitors. The Wall of Sound weighed 38 tons, took as many as 40 employees to maintain, and required four tractor-trailers to transport. It was so cumbersome and expensive to maintain ($100,000 per month) that the band took their only extended break and did not tour in 1975. In 1991, the Dead pioneered the first fully digital concert sound system. The result of their efforts was the best concert sound in the world and the establishment of new industry standards. Deadheads quickly came to expect this high level of sound quality from all concerts but were often disappointed at concerts of other bands.

Another tangible aspect to the Grateful Dead concert experience was the lighting. The Dead were never concerned with creating a show or spectacle in their performances. There were no costumes, smoke, explosions, or giant props that might distract from the music. But with their roots in the Psychedelic Sixties, light shows were always a part of their concerts. The lighting effects were always subtle and sensitive to the music.

Another unique characteristic of the tangibles associated with the Dead was their tickets. When they began selling tickets via mail order (see Responsiveness section), the Dead began to add artwork to their tickets. Each concert bore a different Grateful Dead symbol, ranging from roses to dancing bears to skeletons. Each ticket thus became a piece of memorabilia for the fans. New Year's Eve concerts with the Grateful Dead became an annual party for Deadheads in San Francisco, hosted by concert promoter Bill Graham. The tickets for the New Year's Eve shows evolved over the years into spectacular pieces of art (see Figure A.5).

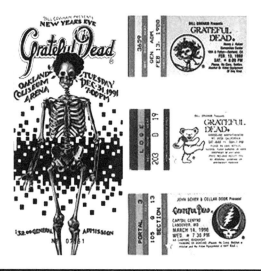

Figure A.5   New Year's Eve Grateful Dead concert tickets.

Empathy

A unique situation with their fans arose very early in the career of the Grateful Dead. Due to the improvisational nature of their music and the quest for the X-factor, fans began to clandestinely record their performances and then share the recordings with friends. Although the band recorded their songs on record albums, the studio never managed to capture the dynamics of their live performances. The band recognized this, and for many years turned a blind eye to the covert taping. Finally, in 1984, the Dead officially recognized the "taping community" and set aside a "taping section" at each concert with the stipulation that "Audio taping is for noncommercial home use only." As lead guitarist Jerry Garcia said, "When we're finished with the music, they can have it."

The sanctioned (and unsanctioned) recording of their performances led to tapes being available for nearly every one of their concerts and made them the most recorded band in history. It is not uncommon for fans to have tape collections of hundreds or even thousands of their concerts. A huge community of tape traders has arisen through the years, which trades the recordings with no money involved. This embodies the values of the Grateful Dead and the San Francisco psychedelic scene of the Sixties, as they gave away their music despite a recording career that included only one top-ten hit single in 1987, "Touch of Grey." This customer-friendly taping policy is a clear indication of their empathy toward Deadheads, again strengthening customer loyalty. It has been adopted by a growing number of bands starting in the 1990s, and also became the precursor for the huge amount of online music downloading today. The Grateful Dead trading scene has changed dramatically with the advent of music downloads, where access to the Dead's concerts is easier than ever, yet even today more Grateful Dead music is downloaded than any other band.

Another example of the Dead's empathy for fans was the Trouble line, which gave Deadheads a real person to talk to about problems with tickets, venue security, or any problem related to the band. This understanding by the Grateful Dead organization of the trials of getting tickets and traveling to see the band showed a special degree of empathy and was another element that strengthened the bond between Deadheads and the Dead. Remember, this is long before the Web, where today online service is only a click away

One decision by the Dead intended to be empathetic to Deadheads led to extremely challenging situations for the band as the number of fans grew. When there were fewer fans before their hit single in 1987, the band allowed Deadheads to sell food and T-shirts in the parking lots before and after shows. Fans freely used Grateful Dead logos and icons without paying royalties for these copyrighted symbols. One unintended consequence was the loss of tens of thousands of dollars in merchandise sales and licensing fees to the band. A second unintended consequence of their hit single was the growing number of people who would come to the concerts with no intention of seeing the show but merely to hang out in the parking lot vending area. This created logistical nightmares for the band and local officials who had to manage and police the crowds. Members of the Dead organization worked closely with local officials to minimize problems with the crowds and urged fans not to come to concerts without tickets. And in 1992, they began to carefully protect their trademarks and logos and began an ambitious licensing program, often enlisting vendors from the parking-lot scene, all with a concern for Deadheads in mind.

Responsiveness

As the Dead's popularity increased over the years, it became more and more of a challenge for Deadheads to obtain tickets. This was especially true if you wanted to see a concert in a city other than your own. In response to the concern expressed by many traveling Deadheads regarding purchasing tickets, the Dead set up a telephone hotline and established Grateful Dead Ticket Sales (GDTS) in 1984 (years before the Internet!). The hotline was a recording of information about upcoming concert tours, special events, and band member information. This allowed Deadheads to easily determine when and where the Dead would be playing next and how to obtain tickets. GDTS quickly became responsible for selling up to 50% of the tickets for each venue directly to Deadheads via mail order, usually a month or more before they went on sale at the local venue. The hotline and GDTS combined to allow Deadheads to find out when the band was playing and then easily order tickets in advance, a very responsive move by the band.

The Dead was also responsive to fans in many other ways. Many Deadheads believe that the music itself and even the X-factor were elements of responsiveness to the fans at concerts. Sometimes the music itself was clearly changed in response to Deadhead requests. One particular song, "Keep Your Day Job," just wasn't well liked by fans, and after four years it was dropped from the repertoire in 1986 at the request of Deadheads!

The Grateful Dead continue to be responsive to their fans even today, years after they disbanded. They continue to release live recordings from their concert archive at the unprecedented rate of three or four albums every year. These live performances from their 30-year career continue to be in great demand, and one ongoing series of recordings is *Road Trips*. For this series, the Grateful Dead tape archivist seeks considerable input from Deadheads, then chooses three or four concerts from the tape vaults to release each year. The *Road Trips* series is sold only through mail order from Grateful Dead Merchandising at Dead.net. Sales estimates for these albums range from 30,000–50,000 copies each, demonstrating an ongoing desire by the fans to continue listening to the music. In a very bold move of responsiveness, a limited-edition 72-CD boxed set chronicling the much-loved Europe 1972 tour was announced in the spring of 2011. The 7,200 copies were sold out in less than 48 hours at a price of $450.

Recent Developments

In 2002, the four surviving original band members reunited after seven years apart, and in early 2003 they adopted the name "The Dead." They toured again briefly and attempted to reestablish the phenomenal bond of loyalty with their fans. But interpersonal issues among the surviving members ended their efforts in 2004. They tried again in 2008 but again failed to find the interpersonal magic that was so dependent on Garcia. Since 2010, however, two surviving members (Bob Weir and Phil Lesh) have been touring as "Furthur" and have begun to follow the same tour schedule as the good ol' Grateful Dead. This may be no easy task, however, since many new "jam bands" have emerged to fill the void left by the original Grateful Dead. Bands such as Phish, Dave Matthews Band, String Cheese Incident, moe., Railroad Earth, and Leftover Salmon learned many lessons from the success of the Grateful Dead. These bands play improvisational music, tour frequently, allow taping, and sell tickets via the Internet and are well on their way to creating a high degree of customer loyalty like the Dead in their heyday.

Summary

Today more than ever, retaining customers and gaining their loyalty is the key to business survival and profitability in the 21st century. We often look to large organizations like Microsoft, Ford Motor Company, Google, Facebook, or Southwest Airlines when we seek models for loyal, satisfied customers. But one organization that at its peak employed only 70 full-time employees had a level of retention and loyalty in its customers that is only dreamed of by most organizations. Deadheads, like all customers, weighed their experiences and compared them to their expectations. What they found for 30 years was a continually surprising level of reliability, availability, tangibles, empathy, and responsiveness in their dealings with the Grateful Dead. Jerry Garcia once said, "I'd like to see what can be created from joy." Having attended 194 Dead concerts over 21 years, this author believes the Grateful Dead consistently created superior customer value and memorable performances for their fans. Whether or not Furthur can reestablish this same level of customer loyalty remains to be seen.

Questions

1. How would you rank order the importance of the five service quality characteristics exhibited by the Grateful Dead? Why?
2. How can these characteristics be used effectively by other organizations?
3. Visit the new Web site for The Grateful Dead at http://dead.net/ or Furthur at http://www.furthur.net/. Examine the various links and assess how well you think the Grateful Dead or Furthur are now exhibiting: (a) reliability, (b) availability, (c) tangibles, (d) empathy, and (e) responsiveness. Based on

your assessment, do you think Furthur will be able to reestablish the remarkable level of customer loyalty with the Grateful Dead? What steps will they have to take?

Case 4: Harrah's Entertainment—Loyalty Management*

Harrah's Entertainment, Inc., is one of the most recognized and respected brand names in the casino entertainment industry. Harrah's was founded in 1937, when Bill Harrah opened a bingo parlor in Reno, Nevada. Harrah's grew quickly, building and acquiring properties throughout Nevada and beyond. In 1973, Harrah's became the first casino company listed on the New York Stock Exchange.

Gambling is very big business in the United States. Between 1993 and 2003, total gambling revenue in the United States more than doubled, from $34 billion to $72 billion. As Table A.1 shows, Harrah's Entertainment, Inc., is a major player in the industry, with 52 casino locations (37 are in 12 U.S. states and 15 are international). Harrah's tripled the number of casinos it opened between 1990 and 1997, due in part to changes in state and federal gaming laws. Over the last 60 years, the Harrah's name has become synonymous with customer-focused, high-quality casino entertainment in more locations than any other competitor in its industry.

With the $9.4-billion acquisition of Caesar's Entertainment Inc., in 2005, Harrah's today is a $9-billion company and has been recognized by *Forbes* and *Business Week* as a market leader, due in large part to its mission to "build lasting relationships" with its customers. Largely on the strength of its new tracking and data-mining system, Harrah's has emerged in recent years as the country's largest and most geographically diverse casino company. (Note: A 2008 leveraged buyout that took Harrah's private doubled its debt to more than $20 billion. It now has more debt than any other gaming company.) Harrah's achieves its mission through operational excellence and technological leadership, which enables Harrah's to manage each customer relationship individually. While less flashy than its competitors, the company has turned personalized customer service into a science that induces people to play longer and spend more money.

Harrah's Strategy

Traditional casino marketing meant spending big money to lure "whales," or extremely wealthy gamblers. Harrah's, on the other hand, has compiled a vast customer database and sends targeted offers and come-back-soon inducements to millions of people with the desired (gambling) probabilities. Harrah's data-mining

---

* This case was prepared by William C. Johnson, president, Marketing Know-how, LLC. Dr. Johnson may be reached at (850) 893-6813, billyboy@nova.edu, www.marketingknowhow.org.

Table A.1   Harrah's Worldwide Locations

Select a casino from the list below.	
U.S. and Canada	
Arizona Casinos • Harrah's Phoenix Ak-Chin Casino	Nevada Casinos • Bally's Las Vegas • Caesars Palace (Las Vegas) • Flamingo Las Vegas • Harrah's Lake Tahoe Casino • Harrah's Las Vegas Casino • Harrah's Laughlin Casino • Harrah's Reno Casino • Harveys Lake Tahoe Casino • Imperial Palace • O'Sheas Casino Las Vegas • Paris Las Vegas • Planet Hollywood Resort • Rio All-Suite Hotel & Casino
California Casinos • Harrah's Rincon Casino	
Illinois Casinos • Harrah's Joliet Casino • Harrah's Metropolis Casino	
Indiana Casinos • Horseshoe Southern Indiana • Horseshoe Casino Hammond	
Iowa Casinos • Harrah's Council Bluffs Casino • Horseshoe Council Bluffs	
Louisiana Casinos • Harrah's Louisiana Downs • Harrah's New Orleans Casino • Horseshoe Casino Bossier City	New Jersey Casinos • Bally's Atlantic City • Caesars Atlantic City • Harrah's Resort Atlantic City • Showboat Casino • Wild Wild West Casino
Mississippi Casinos • Grand Biloxi • Harrah's Tunica • Horseshoe Casino Tunica • Tunica Roadhouse Casino & Hotel	
	North Carolina Casinos • Harrah's Cherokee Casino
Missouri Casinos • Harrah's North Kansas City Casino • Harrah's St. Louis Casino	Ontario, Canada Casinos • Caesars Windsor
	Pennsylvania Casinos • Harrah's Chester
International	
Egypt Casinos • London Clubs Casinos	South Africa Casinos • Emerald Casino Resort
Europe Casinos • London Clubs Casinos	Uruguay Casinos • Conrad Punta del Este

program has driven gaming revenue—far more profitable than food or hospitality—to 80% of Harrah's $9-billion business versus an industry average of 45%.

Harrah's differentiates itself from its competitors by generating loyalty in customer gambling behavior. Rather than competing on the traditional casino attributes of location and facilities alone, it focuses on providing assurance to gambling customers that they will enjoy an experience they have come to know, trust, and appreciate. With this brand identity, it strives to provide consistent value and a reliable, predictable experience. Harrah's derives the lion's share of its revenue from its casinos, where slots (representing 80% of their profits) is still the game of choice for the majority of its customers. Harrah's focuses on creating lasting relationships with its core customers, leading to more sustainable profit growth.

Using a multimarket strategy, Harrah's focuses on those customers who visit more than one market annually. Harrah's targets the 70% of its customers who play in more than one market per year. These multimarket players have higher budgets than single-market players, and they make more trips to casinos. To implement the strategy, Harrah's invests significant time and resources in learning who its best gaming customers are and what they want in order to give them a more customized and satisfying gaming experience.

For example, a high roller at a Harrah's casino in Las Vegas walks into a Harrah's casino in Lake Tahoe and expects to be recognized as a good customer. Harrah's can easily handle this situation with its huge database that links all of its casinos. Using its vast database, Harrah's identifies customers who gamble regularly and lose a lot of money, because a casino's success depends on how much money the average guest leaves behind. The ability to track this data and develop very targeted offers includes, for example, direct mailings to those customers who visited one of its casinos in the last 30 days. Harrah's then invites them back with special offers. It can also sort players by earning potential, which is about how much they spend and lose, and create a marketing campaign to lure them back. The database can also identify someone who has visited Harrah's casino in the past year and lost a lot of money each time.

A culling of Harrah's customer base showed that 26% of the gamblers who visited Harrah's generated 82% of its revenues. Harrah's discovered that these "heavy users" were not the gold-plated, high rollers, but doctors, bankers, and machinists with discretionary time who enjoyed playing slot machines (see Table A.2, which provides demographic characteristics for gamblers). The majority of these individuals did not stay in a hotel, but visited the casino on the way home or during a weekend night out.

Harrah's also came to understand how the lifetime value of its customers would be critical to its marketing strategy. Instead of focusing on how much people spent during a single visit to a casino, Harrah's recognized the need to focus on their potential over time. Harrah's also discovered that happy customers are more loyal. In fact, customers who indicated that they were happy with their experience at Harrah's increased their spending on gambling by 24% per year; those who were disappointed with Harrah's decreased their spending by 10% per year.[1] Encouraged

Table A.2 Demographics: National Average vs. Casino Gamblers		
Demographic Variables	*U.S. Population*	*U.S. Casino Gamblers*
Age, income, gender		
Median age	45	46
Median household income	$48,997	$56,663
Male/female ratio	48/52%	48/52%
Occupation		
White collar	42%	45%
Blue collar	27%	25%
Other—military, homemakers	17%	17%
Retired	15%	15%
Education		
No college	47%	44%
Some college	25%	28%
College graduate	18%	18%
Postgraduate	10%	10%

Source: Harrah's Survey: Profile of the American Casino Gambler, Harrah's Entertainment, p. 18. http://www.caesars.com/images/PDFs/Profile_Survey_2006.pdf

by these results, Harrah's now links employee rewards to customer satisfaction. In fact, Harrah's staff, who are given points based on customer satisfaction surveys, can redeem them through a Web site for products. Now, even Harrah's C-suite executives have their compensation pegged to customer service scores.

Harrah's expects that competitors will have difficulty duplicating its strategy because its many locations give it more opportunities to build relationships with customers. Beyond its strategy based on geographic distribution, Harrah's has the technological tools, knowledge, relationships, and experience with customers to offer a fundamentally different value proposition than competitors. That gives customers a unique reason to choose Harrah's, not just in one market, but across its entire network of casinos.

Creating Loyal Patronage

Prior to 1997, Harrah's operated and marketed itself separately from its other properties, creating a system of "fiefdoms" according to John Boushy, Harrah's senior vice president, Information Technology and Marketing Services. Then, in 1997, Harrah's introduced its Total Gold (later renamed Total Rewards) system for tracking, retaining, and rewarding its 25 million slot players, regardless of which casinos they visit over time. For example, a frequent guest at Harrah's Atlantic City, New Jersey, casino will be immediately recognized upon presenting a Total Rewards card in the company's Las Vegas casino—and is duly rewarded for his or her repeat business.

Casino operators have traditionally attempted to lure high rollers—gamblers who wager the most. Harrah's focuses instead on frequent rollers, who play the odds over and over again. Traditionally, casinos have treated customers as though they belonged to the single property they visited most often. However, Harrah's has found that customers who visit more than one of its properties represent a fast-growing segment of its revenue. "We want to encourage and reward these customers," said Boushy. He added, "Repeat customers at any one of our Harrah's properties should be recognized and rewarded for their loyalty."

This patented Total Rewards program entitles Harrah's repeat customers to free entertainment, vouchers for food and accommodation, and points redeemable for merchandise. These rewards encourage customers to remain loyal to the Harrah's brand across the country, and over time. The Total Rewards program has increased traffic and retention for Harrah's (where just a 1% increase in retention is worth $2 million in net profit annually). Harrah's also places touch-screen kiosks at each of its casinos, where customers can check on their points or print vouchers redeemable for cash or other goods.

Harrah's is borrowing from the airline industry's frequent-flier model to reward loyalty. Loyalty cards are swiped on the casino floor to monitor the sums gambled and time spent at slot machines and card tables. Players can earn gold, platinum, and diamond status based on their gambling levels. Platinum and diamond cardholders receive higher levels of service, such as not having to wait in lines and instant check-in at the front desk.

Harrah's also introduced its own Visa card, which funnels points, as a percent of purchases, directly into a member's Total Rewards account. By using the card, the customer provides Harrah's with a detailed record of gambling and purchasing preferences, enabling it to solicit that person in more sophisticated ways with its databases.

"Many of our customers have an opportunity to visit our properties just once or twice a year. To find important trends and measure repeat business, we must maintain and analyze a large amount of detailed data over a long period of time," Boushy said. Using the magnetic strips on these Total Rewards cards, Harrah's is able to build records for an unlimited number of customers, and offer "comps" and other incentives based on the amount of money inserted into machines, not the amount won.

Harrah's customers have grown extremely accustomed to their loyalty cards, where they would typically swipe them at the slot machines to play and the cards registered wins and losses. These cards have been used for years to allow customers to accumulate points for playing that can be redeemed for various gifts as well as hotel stays. Harrah's has the capability of analyzing hundreds of customer attributes to determine likelihood to visit, predicted spending, opportunities for cross sell, and much more. This allows Harrah's to target promotions and mailings to individual customer preferences. For example, Harrah's might award hotel vouchers to out-of-state guests, while free show tickets would be more appropriate for customers who make day trips to the casino.

A new pilot program that Harrah's is introducing goes even further in tracking and responding to individual user behavior. The casino now has the ability to maintain real-time data on the actions of every cardholder and uses those data to determine individuals' financial "pain point," i.e., how much money they are willing to spend before leaving the casino. The casino then uses that pain point to stage strategic interventions during real-time play. When players comes close to their limit, a staff member on the casino floor receives an alert from a dispatcher, greets them, and offers a free meal, a drink, or a bonus gift of money added to their loyalty card. Harrah's cleverly mitigates the bad experience of losing at the right moment with a gift. In so doing, Harrah's extends people beyond their pain points and they stay and play longer! Harrah's loyalty program has evolved far beyond simply a response mechanism, now allowing it to immediately intervene and turn bad experiences into good ones.

Today, Harrah's network links more than 40,000 gaming machines in 13 states and Canada. The company operates on the belief that customers will, given the right inducements, become brand loyal to Harrah's. In just two years after introducing the Total Rewards program, the company saw a $100-million increase in revenue from customers who gambled at more than one Harrah's casino. At the time, Harrah's was receiving 36 cents of every dollar that its customers spent in casinos. Harrah's current share-of-wallet now stands at 42%. Since 1998, each percentage-point increase in Harrah's share of its customers' overall gambling budgets has coincided with an additional $125 million in shareholder value.

Harrah's loyalty program is the envy of the travel and entertainment industry, rating the highest on "Program Effectiveness," a measure that identifies the amount of influence a loyalty program exerts in hotel selection ("How important was this loyalty program in your decision to stay at <hotel name>?"). Based on this metric, Table A.3 shows how the Harrah's brand compares with some of the major hotels and their loyalty programs.[2]

Migration to the Web

Initially, Harrah's Web presence was dull and static and did little more than house communications and financial investment information. Furthermore, several of the company's individual properties had developed their own marketing-oriented sites, leaving the company without a unified face on the Web.

Table A.3   Hotel Loyalty Programs (Selected List)

Rank	Brand	Program	Elite Level	Program Effectiveness (%)
1	Harrah's	Total Rewards	Diamond	86
2	Intercontinental	Priority Club	Gold	69
3	Westin	Preferred Guest	Gold	67
20	La Quinta Inns	La Quinta Returns	Elite	47
21	Holiday Inn	Priority Club Rewards	Platinum elite	44
22	Best Western	Rewards	Platinum	44

Source: Market Metrix, 2008.

All that has changed, as the company's relaunched Harrahs.com site features Harrah's eTotal Rewards program, which offers customers at the company's Harrah's, Showboat, and Rio properties comprehensive account information, benefits, and complementary offers in real time. They updated their site further by enabling customers to log on and find out how to earn a higher level "rewards card" that entitled them to various privileges at the company's properties.

Harrah's seeks to lure business away from competing casinos by personalizing relationships with customers online. By integrating with its Web site, a yield-management system used by call-center agents, Total Rewards members will be able to take advantage of various benefits based on their gambling and spending patterns.

Harrah's wants to discourage gamblers from patronizing other casinos, said David Norton, vice president of loyalty marketing. "Our competitors focus on branding, but our strategy is to extend the relationship with our best customers, using the Web site," he said. "Basically, it's bringing a lot of our Total Rewards functionality, i.e., the offline customer benefits program, to the Web," says Norton.

The revamped site also leverages the company's internal call-center environment and enables hotel customers to access their information on the Web site. Part of Harrah's Web efforts involved linking its call center—used for making hotel reservations—to the new Web site. Web visitors can now send e-mail to the call center, edit customer profiles, provide information such as physical and e-mail addresses, request nonsmoking rooms, and receive special offers at the casinos.

"What we really wanted was to use our CRM back-end technology to integrate that onto the online channel," says Tim Stanley, vice president of IT development at Harrah's, in Las Vegas. Now the company boasts of having some of the more leading-edge CRM management capabilities and providing a single view of the customer for more than 25 million Total Rewards participants.

Online Gaming

Although still in its infancy, the Internet gaming sector is expected to continue to grow. At the end of 2006, estimates were that the Internet gambling industry topped $12 billion. Much of that wealth came from bets placed by American gamblers.

In a bold move, MGM Mirage, Harrah's major competitor, recently announced a deal with Silicon Gaming to create a new subsidiary called WagerWorks. Silicon Gaming specializes in the design and manufacture of real-world gambling machines, and the new venture aims to launch an online site promoting MGM Mirage brands such as the Bellagio, Treasure Island, and New York–New York casinos. However, it will pull up short of taking wagers online, since that would violate Nevada law. Instead, company officials said WagerWorks will be a free hub where visitors can vie online for cash and coupon prizes based on the length of play.

For now, the online casino sector is in a rough-and-tumble phase of evolution that is taking place largely outside the United States. Various Caribbean countries play host to cyberparlors, including Casino-On-Net and Golden Palace Online Casino. Australia is also experimenting with licensing and regulating online gaming companies. That leaves marquee U.S. gambling houses such as MGM Mirage, Harrah's Entertainment, and Park Place Entertainment with their foundations firmly stuck in the sand: The Nevada Gaming Commission frowns on Internet-based wagering, since it violates state law against placing bets over the telephone. Regulators are particularly worried about minors gambling, and aren't convinced that any safeguards exist in the Internet arena to verify age. For that reason, the leading U.S. gambling houses have largely avoided partnering with Australian gaming companies for fear of antagonizing state regulators in Mississippi, Nevada, and New Jersey.

A Harrah's spokesman observed that "Cyberspace is simply another venue, like Vegas or Atlantic City. We think that it will be very difficult to prohibit Americans from participating in online gambling. Every major gaming operator, including Harrah's, is looking at it closely."

In May 2009, Harrah's Interactive Entertainment, Harrah's new online gambling arm, was launched. The new online venture, which promotes the World Series of Poker (WSOP), is also consistent with Harrah's strategy to explore a European interactive strategy (e.g., Caesars Bingo Online available now only in the United Kingdom) and to be one of the leading global operators by optimally leveraging its brands.

Questions

1. How does the Pareto Principle relate to Harrah's market situation? (The Pareto Principle was in play during the 2008 presidential election, where Senators Obama and McCain devoted 98% of their TV advertising spending and campaign time to 15 states.)
2. How does Harrah's practice customer relationship management (CRM)?

3. Visit Harrah's Web site (www.harrahs.com). How can the company use its Web site to more effectively practice CRM?
4. Suppose you were hired as a consultant to Harrah's. How would you advise them in terms of their presence and activity online?

Case 5: Publix Super Markets— Achieving Customer Intimacy*

Publix Super Markets, Inc., is a Florida-based grocery chain that has over 140,000 employees in 2011. Furthermore, Publix serves over 1 million customers every day. There are no immediate international expansion plans at this time. Publix, named after a chain of motion picture theaters, is one of the largest employee-owned companies in the world, with annual sales of over $25 billion. It was the first supermarket chain to install electric-eye doors, Muzak, fluorescent lighting, and air conditioning in its stores. Publix was also one of the first companies to have water fountains, self-service shopping, shopping carts, and computerized scanning technology. Since 1997, Publix has been rated as one of the best companies to work for in America, as reported by *Fortune* magazine.[1]

At Publix, everything revolves around pleasing the customer, which is why it has enjoyed the kind of success it has had since the 1930s. Publix's goal is to make every customer feel personally valued in such a way that they see themselves as one in a million. This profile focuses on the company's customer intimacy philosophy and how Publix satisfies and delights its customers daily to help it become the "premier quality food retailer in the world."

Background and Company Philosophy

By 2010, Publix was operating over 1,000 stores in Florida, Georgia, South Carolina, Alabama, and Tennessee, which makes it the largest employee-owned supermarket chain in the United States. According to Publix managers, over 25,000 of their employees have been working with them for 10 or more years. Also, for many years over the past few decades, Publix has outperformed the S&P 500 Index and the customer Peer Group Index with regard to return on investment. The Peer Group includes A&P, Albertson's, American Stores, Bruno's, Food Lion, Giant Foods, Hannaford Bros., Kroger, Safeway, Smith's Food & Drug, Weis Markets, and Winn-Dixie.

A key differentiating factor in Publix's success formula can be attributed to the philosophy of its founder, Mr. George W. Jenkins who stated that

---

* This case was coauthored by Dr. Bahaudin G. Mujtaba, Nova Southeastern University, and Dr. William C. Johnson, Marketing Know-how LLC. They may be reached at mujtaba@nova.edu and billyboy@nova.edu.

some companies are founded on policy. This is wrong. Philosophy, the things you believe in, is more important. Philosophy does not change frequently...and is never compromised.... We attempt to adapt a philosophy in such a way as to allow ordinary people to achieve the extraordinary...to reach higher...to look upon average with disdain.

The philosophy of caring for people has been embedded in Publix's corporate culture throughout its stores in the four states. Publix associates understand that they are not just in the grocery business but also in the people business. Therefore, taking care of associates, customers, suppliers, and community members is important to Publix people and the communities that they serve.

George Jenkins once said that "Publix will be a little better place to work or not quite as good because of you."[2] A philosophy of employee appreciation has been embedded in the culture of the organization; so when the upper echelon visits retail stores, especially during appreciation week, they make it a point to personally see and thank every associate. They understand that people need recognition and sincere thanks for their hard work and commitment to the company. According to Howard Jenkins, member of the Publix board and retired CEO, "growth is the end result of a simple equation. As each of us continues to please our customers, more customers will look to Publix for their shopping needs. We must never lose sight of exactly what those needs are." Table A.4 presents some of the highlights in the evolution of Publix's growth.

Publix associates are encouraged to interact with their customers on a daily basis. Publix associates constantly attempt to keep their fingers on the pulse of the customer in order to get immediate and local feedback. One of the district managers in the Central Florida region used to encourage, and in some cases require, his department managers to learn at least two customer's names every day through face-to-face introduction and interaction. This is important because Publix employees serve their own communities, and through this face-to-face interaction they can better determine customers' needs, wants, and desires faster than any research firm could ever do. Also, research shows that nearly 75% of supermarket shoppers shop and visit supermarkets on a weekly basis. So, building a relationship with customers is a necessity as opposed to a luxury in order to stay aware of their needs and expectations.

It is through these types of programs and committed people that Publix is able to offer its employees an environment "where *working* is a pleasure" and its customers an environment "where *shopping* is a pleasure." Publix associates' success with customers originates from their belief that no sale is final or complete until the meal is eaten and fully enjoyed. Then, they have made a positive and lasting impression. Publix's guarantee, which every associate is aware of, reads that "we will never, knowingly disappoint you. If for any reason your purchase does not give you complete satisfaction, the full purchase price will be cheerfully refunded immediately upon request." These are not just words to live by, but they are moral imperatives for retailers that have made Publix the successful and innovative giant it is today.

Table A.4 Publix Spirit over the Years

Year	Accomplishments
1930	First Publix supermarket opens in Winter Haven, Florida
1940	First store known as the "marble, tile, and stucco food palace" is built in Winter Haven, featuring such revolutionary retail concepts as air-conditioning, wide aisles, and electric-eye doors
1944	Publix buys the 19-store chain of All American Food stores in Lakeland, FL, and moves the headquarters to Lakeland
1950	New 70,000-square-foot grocery warehouse is built in Lakeland; today this warehouse occupies over 2,000,000 square feet
1957	Publix Employee Federal Credit Union opens in a Lakeland warehouse
1959	Publix opens its first store in Miami and buys seven stores
1963	Publix opens the Southeast Coast Headquarters and Distribution Center in North Miami
1971	Two stores open in Jacksonville
1973	Publix opens the Bakery Plant and constructs the Produce Distribution Center in Lakeland
1974	Publix sales pass $1 billion annually; Publix opens distribution center and division office in Jacksonville
1975	Publix Employee Stock Ownership Trust (ESOT) starts this year
1980	Publix celebrates 50 years of shopping pleasure; dairy processing plant opens in Lakeland; checkout scanning is implemented chainwide; Publix starts opening on Sundays during the early 1980s.
1984	Publix sales pass $3.23 billion; according to *Progressive Grocer*, Publix's 2.36% before tax net is the highest of top-ten supermarket chains, 2½ times better than Safeway, the industry leader
1986	Publix opens its first food and pharmacy stores in Orlando and Tampa
1987	Publix opens its dairy processing plant in Deerfield Beach
1990	Publix has 400 stores and 74,000 associates in Florida
1992	Publix announces its expansion plans to Georgia and South Carolina
1993	Publix implements companywide Quality Improvement Process (QIP) and Work Improvement Now (WIN) tools for fact-based decision making and employee empowerment

Continued

Table A.4 (continued)   Publix Spirit over the Years

Year	Accomplishments
1994	Sales are $8.66 billion; Publix implements a chainwide Customer Intimacy program
1998	Publix has sales of over $12 billion and 120,000 associates; almost 600 stores in four states
2000	Publix is ranked 132 on the *Fortune* 500
2001	Charlie Jenkins Jr. replaces his cousin Howard as CEO of the company
2002	Publix begins opening stores in Nashville, Tennessee
2005	Publix celebrates its 75th anniversary
2008	Ed Crenshaw becomes the new CEO; Todd Jones becomes Publix's sixth president
2009	Publix opens its 1,000th store at Murabella, St. Augustine (St. John's County), Florida
2010	On February 18, 2010, for the 16th consecutive year, Publix is ranked as the highest-ranking supermarket for customer satisfaction

Key Success Factors

There is strong competition in the supermarket industry. For example, Walmart, now the number one retail grocer in the world, has opened major supercenters throughout Florida and across the globe. However, Publix is not willing to concede its customers to the competition. Bill Fauerbach, vice president of the Miami Division, said, "Only we can give our customers a reason to shop elsewhere. As long as we take care of our customers better than anyone else, we will defeat our competition." The new generation of Publix leaders understands that complacency is their number one enemy; therefore they continue to focus and improve on the factors that have made them successful in the past.

Publix demonstrated its commitment to this principle when entering the highly competitive Atlanta market in 1991. Publix took the lead over both Kroger and Walmart by emphasizing less clutter, more consistent product placement, and faster checkout experiences, along with intensive customer service training.

They further understand that delivering superior customer value is a race without a finish line in today's fast-paced world. Therefore, they never lose sight of caring for people, delivering quality products and service, and excellence in everything they do. A previous president of Publix, Ed Crenshaw, in 1995 during his first year in the office introduced four success drivers for the company: *knowing the business*, *knowing the product*, *knowing the customer*, and *continuously training people*. Therefore, every department has implemented different means of doing a better job with these four success drivers.

Publix has instituted a world-class training program for its perishable departments like deli, bakery, produce, and seafood. The goal of getting to know the customer has made Publix better than ever with regard to understanding customers and fulfilling their needs in a timely fashion. Publix's customer intimacy program has enabled managers to keep their fingers on the pulse of the customer on a daily basis. This focus on customers has encouraged management to gather feedback not only from their own customers, but also from their competitors' customers. They gather data and feedback from satisfied as well as dissatisfied customers because they understand that using biased data to make generalizations regarding all customers is more dangerous than not using them at all.

Publix continuously collects data from its store associates using a program called Associate Voice Survey (AVS). For example, during 1997, over 90,000 retail and support associates completed this survey and, as a result, Publix learned that communication was the dominant factor in associate satisfaction, while customer service, loyalty, and positive coworker attitude ranked as the next top-three satisfaction drivers. Another positive outcome of AVS was that many departments and stores created cross-functional and ad hoc teams to discuss opportunities for improvement. Furthermore, Publix has invested heavily in developing an internal professional development curriculum to develop associates' skills and help them assume greater responsibility and leadership roles at Publix. Howard Jenkins once said to employees:

> We envision Publix as a world player. And there will be bumps in the road as we grow larger and spread further. I need each of you to help me uphold our mission to be the premier quality food retailer in the world.

This type of a statement from a top company representative can be very influential and encouraging with regard to teamwork, taking personal responsibility for results, and overall financial performance.

A major factor contributing to Publix's ongoing success is their loyalty and commitment to employee training. Most employees begin working for Publix at a young age and tend to stay there after college as well. There is a story about a young man who had recently graduated from college and was hired by a supermarket. On his first day on the job, the manager greeted him with a warm handshake and a smile, gave him a broom, and said, "Your first job will be to sweep out the store, and then we will begin mopping." "But I'm a college graduate," the young man replied indignantly. "Oh, I'm sorry. I didn't know that," said the manager. "Here, we do have on-the-job training, so give me the broom. I'll show you how!"

Industry Trends and Rankings

Industry Trends

Although U.S. food spending is on the rise, supermarkets are not capturing their fair share. Alternative formats, such as supercenters, warehouse clubs, extreme value grocers, natural/organic and specialty/upscale food markets, and nontraditional channels, e.g., dollar stores and drug stores, are all increasing their grab for the food dollar.

The major players in the industry are also embarking on store-based rationalization. Lackluster financial performance has plagued some supermarket players in recent years, so to turn things around, some supermarket operators are focusing on their most profitable units and exiting noncore markets, divesting their unprofitable units and nonvital operations to hone in on geographic areas where they typically are first- or second-place market-share players.

Alternatively, the focus is beginning to shift to differentiation and performance improvement vs. size. Conventional supermarket operators are finding it difficult to compete on price vs. Walmart and other value-oriented grocers at the low end and shopping experience vs. natural/organic and specialty/upscale markets at the high end.

Private-label branding continues to grow, with grocers now getting close to 25% of their sales from their own brands. According to a 2008 Nielsen release, private labels account for more than $81 billion in sales in the United States, a 10.2% increase from 2007 that continues to rise. Nearly one in four items in supermarkets is of a store brand, representing $88 billion in sales. The Food Marketing Institute found that in 2008, some 64% of shoppers said they often or always buy a store brand rather than a national one. That was up from 59% the prior year. Today's cost-conscious shoppers are turning away from premium-priced goods produced by name-brand labels such as General Mills and Kraft to individual store brands.

Industry Rankings

A customer satisfaction survey conducted by *Consumer Reports* revealed that Publix Supermarkets was ranked third among 46 chains, nationwide. Publix scored an 82 out of a possible 100, meaning that customers were very satisfied, on average, according to the magazine. *Consumer Reports* surveyed more than 25,000 of its readers during 2001 and early 2002, asking them to rate the various chains on prices, checkout speed, service, and cleanliness. Raley's, an 83-store chain in the West, and Wegmans, a 65-store chain in the Northeast, topped the survey. Raley's scored an 84, while Wegmans had an 83. Differences of fewer than four points are not meaningful, according to the survey, so the top three chains essentially are even. Raley's, Wegmans, and Publix each received neutral ratings on prices but excelled in checkout speed, service, and cleanliness. Many customers say they do not mind paying a little more to shop in Publix's clean stores staffed with well-trained and friendly employees. "Service is what Publix built its reputation on," said Chuck Gilmer, editor of The Shelby Report, an industry newsletter based in Gainesville, Georgia.

Publix is consistently ranked the highest among its competitors in the *American Customer Satisfaction Index* or ACSI (see Table A.5). The ACSI, which was established in 1994, consists of uniform and independent measures of how households rate various consumption experiences. ACSI tracks trends in customer satisfaction and provides valuable benchmarking insights of the consumer economy for companies, industry trade associations, and government agencies. The ACSI is produced through a partnership of the University of Michigan Business School, the American Society for Quality (ASQ), and the international consulting firm, CFI Group. The ASCI questions also assess perceptions of value and how well the products or services lives up to customer expectations and whether customers are willing to pay more for them.

The National Quality Research Center polled more than 50,000 customers on 200 companies. The University of Michigan measured the responses according to six quality indexes and scored the companies on a 100-point ACSI Index (see Table A.5). Publix has consistently scored higher than its industry competitors since the ACSI index scores for the supermarket industry were first compiled in the mid 1990s. In another ranking by *Fortune*, Publix moved up to the number two spot in the Food and Drug Store Industry for America's Most Admired Companies. Walgreens took first place. While Publix has had its share of success and recognition as a tough competitor, the fact remains that it is still relatively small compared to other supermarket giants with regard to the number of stores and yearly revenues (see Table A.6).

Publix continues to lead in the highly competitive supermarket industry, where its annualized sales per square foot is $548, just behind Whole Foods's $820. Rivals Supervalu and Safeway Inc. all had sales figures at their supermarket-format stores between $460 and $490.

Publix has received various rankings and awards for being a caring employer, an industry leader, and for being socially responsible in the community. Publix, as a caring employer, has received numerous accolades:

- Named by *Child* magazine as one of the Top 10 Child-Friendly Supermarkets
- One of the top companies in *Fortune*'s list of 100 Best Companies to Work For
- One of *Jacksonville* magazine's top 25 family-friendly companies
- One of the nation's Outstanding Employers of Older Workers, according to Experience Works
- One of BestJobsUSA.com's "Employers of Choice 500"
- One of *Central Florida Family* magazine's top companies for working families
- One of the top 10 companies to work for in America in the book, *The 100 Best Companies to Work for in America* (Currency/Doubleday)
- Won United Way's Spirit of America award

Table A.5 American Customer Satisfaction Index Scores

YEARS	Base-line	97	98	99	00	01	02	03	04	05	06	07	08	09
Publix	82	79	79	82	77	81	81	82	81	81	83	83	82	86
All Others	76	73	72	71	74	73	75	75	76	77	75	77	79	78
Kroger	78	74	73	74	71	75	75	71	73	74	76	75	77	78
SUPERVALU	77	74	77	75	75	76	77	77	75	77	74	74	74	77
Whole Foods	NM	NM	NM	NM	NM	NM	NM	NM	NM	NM	NM	73	75	76
Supermarkets	76	73	73	74	73	75	75	74	73	74	75	76	76	76

Source: The American Customer Satisfaction Index. http://www.theacsi.org/fourth_quarter.htm#sup

Table A.6   Publix and Competitors—A Comparison

Company Name	# of Stores in 2009	Revenues in 2009 ($ billion)	Revenues in 1996 ($ billion)
Kroger Co.	2,468	76.1	25.2
Safeway, Inc.	1,712	44.1	13.2
Publix	1,029	24.3	9.0
Whole Foods	284	8.0	1.7

Company Earnings

As of November 2010, Publix's sales for the third quarter of 2010 were $6 billion, which represents a 3.5% increase from the previous year's $5.8 billion. Similarly, comparable-store sales for the third quarter of 2010 increased 2.7%. Net earnings for the third quarter of 2010 at Publix were $283.2 million, compared to $254.9 million in the previous year, which shows an increase of 11.1%. Similarly, earnings per share at Publix increased to $0.36 for the third quarter of 2010, which is up from $0.32 per share in 2009. Overall, the company's sales for the first nine months of 2010 were reported to have been $18.8 billion, which represented a 3% increase from the previous year's $18.2 billion. Similarly, net earnings for the first nine months of 2010 at Publix were $996 million, compared to $877.3 million in the previous year, which shows an increase of 13.5%. Earnings per share at Publix increased to $1.27 for the first nine months of 2010, up from $1.11 per share in 2009. As a sign of its prosperity, the company announced (effective Nov. 1, 2010) that Publix's privately held stock price actually increased from $18.45 per share to $19.85 per share. Publix's current chief executive officer, Ed Crenshaw, said, "I'm very pleased that our good operating performance and improvements in the stock market resulted in an increase in our stock price. Our associate owners continue to deliver exceptional customer service, the key to our success."[3]

According to Howard Jenkins, these positive results come as no real surprise to the people of Publix. He further stated that

> Publix people have been working hard, preparing for an even grander vision of our future. Earlier in this decade, we committed ourselves to a mission to become the premier quality food retailer in the world. We introduced our own quality improvement process and later adapted a discipline of *Customer Intimacy*, which is helping us to listen more effectively to our customers. All of these initiatives have engaged the resourcefulness of thousands of associates from every area of our company. Together we are discovering powerful new methods for delivering customer value.

These successful results actually make Publix an attractive place for employment. As of 2010, Publix reported on its Web site that the average income earnings for various management positions in the retail stores are as follows:

- $44,300 per year for assistant department managers
- $64,600 per year for department managers
- $76,400 per year for assistant store managers
- $110,700 per year for store managers

Nonmanagement employees who work part time or full time can actually earn average salaries up to $25,000 annually, depending on their expertise, hourly salaries, and longevity in the company.

Service with a Smile: The Publix Style

The author of the slogan "Where shopping is a pleasure," the late Mr. William (Bill) Schroter, became a legend within the Publix culture as the spirit of the statement spread throughout the company and became part of the Publix culture. Mr. Schroter started working for Publix in 1949 and served the company for over 40 years, retiring in the early 1990s. Publix's slogan "Where shopping is a pleasure" replaced an older slogan, "Florida's Finest Food Stores," which according to Mr. Schroter was self-congratulatory, offering no promise to customers. The current slogan or value proposition tells Publix employees that its customers want more than just groceries. Publix people know that customers want good quality, excellent prices, and a good shopping experience. While quality products and good prices are very important to creating customer value, they are not enough to keep customers coming back to their stores. Therefore, Publix associates have always been receiving training on relationship-building techniques to better understand customers and quickly take care of their needs.

Publix's mission statement very clearly states that Publix is passionately focused on customer value. Publix is committed to satisfying the needs of its customers as individuals better than their competition. While its competitors can offer good prices and quality products, Publix wants to stand out in the customer's mind for providing *delightful* customer service in every shopping experience. Competitive prices and quality products must exist for a business to be successful and are easily duplicated; however, providing delightful customer service comes from the culture of an organization that creates superior customer value. This is why Publix associates closely align their daily work habits to stay focused on customers.

Publix people understand that they cannot be casual about achieving *customer intimacy*. They realize that customer intimacy needs an intimate, professional, thorough, consistent, and disciplined method of serving customers that will become a normal way of doing business.

In fact, the goal at Publix has been to build customer intimacy in all of its stores by creating an environment that is both sensitive and responsive to the wants and needs of all customers. Publix spends considerable time studying the best practices of other companies and incorporates a practical and comprehensive plan for developing customer intimacy in all Publix stores.

Developing customer intimacy means working through four phases again and again. Each phase is critical for success of the program and feeds the next phase.

1. *First*, you must understand your customers' wants and needs (with respect to food acquisition).
2. *Second*, you need to understand your customers' perceptions of your company and your competitors' perceptions of your company.
3. *Third*, you need to establish and maintain a strong customer intimacy program throughout the company.
4. *Fourth,* continually improve the customer intimacy relationship program.

The philosophy of Publix is not just to satisfy and delight customers one time; customers must be satisfied, delighted, and excited every time they visit or shop at your store. Publix associates are taught that customers are their most valued assets who must be welcomed, cherished, and appreciated for choosing to shop at their stores. Associates are often asked to reflect on some of the following facts about customers:

■ The average customer spends $5,000 on groceries each year and lives in one geographic area for about 10 years (total spending or lifetime value [LTV] = $50,000).
■ Attracting a new customer costs companies five to six times more than keeping one who already shops with them.
■ Ninety-five percent of complaining customers will continue to do business with the company if you take care of their problems properly and resolve those problems on the spot.
■ One dissatisfied customer tells eight to ten potential customers about a problem or bad experience that was not addressed in the store. It has been said that each of the eight to ten potential customers are likely to tell at least five more people about the problem or bad experience.

Publix associates understand that if they cannot satisfy customers' requirements and meet their demands, the customer will cease to do business with them and shop with other retailers. They remember that if they, as Publix associates, do not offer a great shopping experience for their customers, then someone else will. Therefore, all retail associates are taught the *10-Foot* and *10-Second Rules* to help them quickly acknowledge customers. The 10-foot rule states that one must acknowledge all customers who are within 10 feet of one's surroundings, and the 10-second rule states that these customers must be acknowledged within 10 seconds of entering into the service counter area or the 10-foot zone. Research in the supermarket industry indicates the factors that affect customer loyalty:

■ The largest percentage of customers (68%) leave if they perceive an attitude of indifference.

■ Some customers (14%) leave because they feel they can find better quality products and services elsewhere.

■ Customers (9%) shop elsewhere because they think your prices are higher than your competitors.

■ A few of the customers (5%) become friends with people who work for a competitor and take their business there.

■ Some customers (3%) leave because they move to a different area.

Publix associates are also encouraged to use their daily observations, customer feedback, survey evaluation, and other data to improve their jobs, better serve their customers, and make Publix a better place "where shopping is a pleasure." Associates can use Publix's Quality Improvement Process (QIP), Work Improvement Now (WIN), or other such tools and continuous improvement concepts to improve their jobs based on fact-based decisions and data. These statistical tools are available for everyone to learn and use during their work hours in order to deliver more than what they promise.

Publix teaches the principle of "deliver plus 1%," which states that you must consistently meet your customers' shopping needs and then exceed their expectations by improving your service by 1%. They believe in positively surprising the customer by overdelivering on what customers value. This principle further states that when you make a promise to a customer, you must be consistent and deliver *all* the time. It means before exceeding your customers' *expectations*, make sure you are satisfactorily meeting their *needs*. And if you promise any extra services, make sure you deliver as promised.

Finally, Publix rewards top-notch service by implementing an awards program that shows associates how much management values their efforts to provide *delightful* service to customers. Delightful Service Awards are given for customer service that is over and above the minimum standards listed on the *Observation Sheet* for the area. Associates are expected to provide great customer service as part of the job requirement. The awards are given to associates who make the extra effort to delight customers who shop at Publix. To receive a Delightful Service Award, associates must provide delightful service to a customer in a way that is formally recognized by either the customer, by a "mystery shopper" who is purposely appointed by district management, or by a member of the store management team. Associates are trained and encouraged to set personal goals for themselves with regard to better serving customers and exceeding their expectations. They are asked to find out what they can do to increase and improve their personal commitment to customer intimacy. They are encouraged and rewarded for setting goals to increase their awareness of customers as well as customers' wants and needs. For instance, associates may set goals like:

- Learning the names of two or more "regular" customers every week.
- Identifying new or unusual products in the store, noticing when a customer has selected the product for purchase, and using the new item as a conversation starter.
- Noticing at least four customers in a week's time who may need help locating a product and taking them to it.
- Volunteering to demonstrate a new product in the store so they can develop or improve their people skills with customers.
- Conducting their own unofficial mystery shopper evaluation when they shop at a Publix store. This will help them become aware of how they define delightful customer service when *they* are the customer.

Publix Goes Online (and Off)

An industry study revealed that by 2007, about 20 million households in the United States will purchase groceries, food, and other household items online. They will spend approximately $85 billion dollars for mainly food items.[4] However, to date none of the major grocery chains have mastered the online arena. Peapod, Inc., was the first one. Peapod began as a startup with no money. Peapod took phone calls and faxes for orders. Employees filled them at local supermarkets and delivered them to the homes of customers. Peapod was initially profitable, but eventually began to fail when, by 1999, it had incurred losses of $29 million dollars on sales of $73 million. (Peapod was acquired outright by the Dutch giant retailer Royal Ahold NV in late 2001.)

California-based Webvan entered the scene in 1999 with much fanfare and was going to revolutionize grocery retailing. Webvan utilized a "central fill" model, where large distribution centers costing $35 million each were dedicated to fill online grocery orders. Customer demand never reached anywhere near the levels required to recoup its huge fixed-cost investment, and Webvan was losing from $5 to $30 on every order it handled. Webvan filed for bankruptcy protection in early 2001 and ceased operations later that year.

Profits for Internet grocers were scarce, affected primarily by high shipping costs and regular distribution centers that were not well suited to handle order fulfillment. Not a single online grocer in the United States has been able to turn a profit. (Note: Tesco, based in the United Kingdom, has reported a profit in its online operations.) Tesco, as well as Safeway and Albertsons, utilizes a "store pick" model (see Figure A.6), where orders placed online are simply drawn from the same goods that are on their store shelves, and delivery costs are tacked on to the cost of the groceries (as opposed to Webvan's emphasis on central warehouses). While the warehouse system can be cheaper in the long run, it requires a huge amount

Figure A.6   Store pick model.

of initial capital and a well-developed infrastructure to get the goods from the warehouse to the shopper. Distribution logistics are a make-or-break proposition in online grocery retailing.

Publix was one of the late comers to enter the online grocery business when it launched PublixDirect in September 2001. Publix, unlike competitors Safeway and Albertsons, followed a centralized or "direct fill" fulfillment approach. PublixDirect served online customers over a 35-mile radius in the South Florida market from a 140,000 square foot distribution center, which was more than twice the size of many of its stores.

The warehouse was divided into areas for frozen foods, vegetables, meats, and poultry. PublixDirect also operated its own bakery, which was devoted solely to its online business. For a $7.95 fee and a minimum $50 order, PublixDirect would pick up the groceries and deliver them to a customer's doorstep. Average order size was approximated $120 per customer. PublixDirect took 18 months to develop a strategy for the Internet venture, hoping to succeed where many others had failed. For the Internet venture, it stocked only 12,500 items, selecting those that move most quickly off store shelves, whereas the typical Publix carries 40,000 stock-keeping units or SKUs.

The company benchmarked earlier grocery online operations to fine-tune and perfect its processes, including order taking, order fulfillment, and outbound logistics and payment. Orders placed at the company Web site would be downloaded at midnight to a central computer, which organized them for pick-up in the warehouse and for delivery by truck. Orders, which could be made seven days in advance, were filled starting at 6 a.m. Each order was distilled into a bar code and attached to a plastic box. When a PublixDirect employee scanned the bar code, a shopping list came up on a tiny computer attached to his or her wrist. The order also appeared on a handheld computer given to each truck driver. When the goods were delivered, the customer signed for the delivery on the computer screen using a stylus. Payment was made in advance at the Web site, using a credit card. Customers were issued a paper receipt and were sent a back-up via e-mail. If a customer had ordered beer or wine, the driver would be prompted on the computer screen to check his/her age. Drivers were even asked to cover their shoes with footsies when they entered a house.

PublixDirect believed that the average income of its online target customer would skew higher than its regular store shoppers. Although initially anticipating that its primary target market would be dual-income families with household incomes exceeding $75,000, much to their surprise, the typical shopper attracted to PublixDirect turned out to be single-income households with stay-at-home moms.

PublixDirect strongly felt that its prospect for survival in the online grocery business would be based on a well-conceived value proposition that includes the following:

■ Convenient solution to grocery shopping
■ Prices similar to local supermarkets
■ Superior product quality
■ Superior customer service

The company benchmarked earlier grocery online operations to fine-tune and perfect its processes, including order taking, order fulfillment, and outbound logistics as well as payment. Despite a well-conceived business plan, PublixDirect ceased operations in August 2003. Charlie Jenkins (CEO of Publix) explained, "We regret that our online grocery shopping business did not meet our expectations. Despite many loyal customers and dedicated associates, PublixDirect simply didn't have enough volume to continue this service."

Publix is privately held and has been tight-lipped about the specific reasons leading to the discontinuation of PublixDirect. Although it is not clear as to why PublixDirect failed to meet its internal profit and revenue targets and closed its doors (portals), following are some possible contributing factors as to why PublixDirect failed to succeed.

With a few notable exceptions, what most failed Internet grocers overlooked or miscalculated was the disconnect between marketing strategy and the operations strategy. The few successful online grocery success stories (notably Tesco, Sainsbury's, Peapod, and Albertsons) treat their online services to customers as a convenience added option that will cost customers more, but that can then be supported by using the extra funds to support operations aimed at providing convenient, timely delivery. A new market such as Internet ordering for home delivery of groceries puts great pressure on the integration of marketing and operations. The need to drive markets from a marketing perspective while simultaneously keeping a tight rein on operational costs and challenges puts a great deal of pressure on this market. PublixDirect had a huge "nut to crack" due to the operational complexity and high labor costs associated with supporting such an operation. (One failed Internet-based grocery retailer is said to have required 200 employees to fill 600 orders a day.) Revenues simply never caught up with the huge upfront investment. The question is, would revenues eventually catch up and did Publix pull the plug too soon?

Cost control in online operations is crucial to success. Companies need *scale* and PublixDirect never achieved the scale necessary to "crack the cost nut." The U.K. food retailer Tesco benefits from high population densities whereby logistical costs can be spread over a larger and more serviceable volume of customers. PublixDirect operated over the length and breadth of Broward County, a sprawling metropolis, where traffic patterns made delivery difficult and expensive.

Internet ordering with store pickup rather than home delivery seems to be the most cost-effective business model. This "store-pick" (Tesco, Albertsons, and Safeway) rather than the "direct fill" (PublixDirect) approach has turned out to be the most viable fulfillment approach.

The keys to success for online grocer retailing are: convenient solution for grocery shopping, prices similar to local supermarkets, comparable quality to products purchased in the store, and superior service. Publix was able to largely achieve three out of four of these objectives, but given the large number of conveniently located Publix stores, convenience was not overwhelming in this case. (Note: As a postscript, PublixDirect discontinued operations in August 2003, just short of two years after it was launched. Its Broward County, Florida, and surrounding area pilot program failed to meet management's projected revenues and profit levels for the business.)

Current Trends

Online technology is certainly going to play a major role in every retailer's efforts to offer more value for their customers. New forces in the environment, such as technology, are likely to bring about many changes and new procedures. Change is constant and ubiquitous throughout the supermarket industry because customers are becoming more knowledgeable and demanding. In today's market-based economy, customers want a variety of ethnic foods that are made with quality ingredients and represent their culture; therefore quality service must be aligned accordingly with the best prices in order to deliver superior value.

Over 20,000 new items are hitting the market every year, and understanding the value of each product to each customer is no easy task. Therefore, the value of understanding, anticipating, and determining consumer preference cannot be overestimated. Changing effectively is a matter of keeping up with the demands of consumers, offering more value for the customer's dollar, being competitive, and creating raving fans.

Food safety is becoming a major issue in the grocery industry. According to a *Better Homes and Gardens* panel study, only 20% of the panelists were very confident that the food they buy is safe to eat. Global activist group Greenpeace has joined two other coalitions—True Food Now and GE-Free Markets—that are trying to convince two supermarket operators in California to stop using genetically engineered ingredients in their private-label food lines. According to an *NBC Dateline* investigation, seven of the nation's largest grocery store chains, operating more than 7,000 stores in nearly every state, admitted to redating meats and fish after they had reached their original "sell-by" date. In the food retailing industry, leaders are paying more attention to ensuring that food products are safe and produced in a clean environment. According to Todd Rossow, corporate quality assurance lab coordinator at Publix, their associates are constantly looking at all the risk factors associated with food quality as well as food safety while attempting to eliminate them.

Today's customers are increasingly more concerned and vocal about the quality and nutrition of the food they purchase. According to research, 70% of women and 54% of men say they consider nutrition to be an important factor in their consideration of food purchases. Once a niche category, organic foods are becoming increasingly mainstream as small, regional organic food–producing companies have been acquired by major manufacturers. Demand for organic is growing 20%–24% annually as Americans spent $460 billion on groceries and $9.4 billion on organic items in 2001, per the U.S. Department of Agriculture. Today's nutrition-conscious supermarket shoppers are checking labels as never before. The Food and Drug Administration started requiring that trans fat content appear on all food labels as of January 1, 2006. (Trans fats are found in foods ranging from partially hydrogenated oils to fried foods, cookies, pastries, dairy products, and meats.) Finally, some manufacturers are considering the idea of offering "functional foods," which are fortified with a growing number of popular herbs, vitamins, hormones, and other healthy additives.

Technology that allows customers to be their own cashiers and check out their own groceries has been around for many years. However, it is only recently that some food retailers are toying with its implementation as a strategic tool to enhance their competitive position and offer better service to the time-impoverished customer. This is because self-checkout technology, which allows shoppers to scan their own items, offers savings to both the shopper and the retailer along with an added convenience. Self-checkouts can serve only a segment of the market comprising customers who want to scan their own groceries and have a debit or credit card to pay for the purchase. Check-out efficiency has also been improved by the widespread use of debit and credit card payment systems.

The days of preparing complete meals at home are becoming a distant memory. Today's time-impoverished shoppers are opting for prepared foods such as precut produce, cooked dinners, and prepared takeout foods. According to a *Better Homes and Gardens* consumer panel survey, 37% of respondents buy prepared products at least once each week, compared with 27% in previous years. About 22% of the panelists use more convenience foods than two years ago, and 76% buy convenience products such as salad mixes and precut vegetables. Also, 77% of the respondents purchase prepared foods to eat at home, and 49% of those who eat at home said they do so because they are more careful about what they eat. It has been said that over 40% of all consumer spending on food is for meals that are eaten away from their homes.

Concluding Remark

Publix's history shows that it bought seven Grand Union stores in Miami in 1959 and 19 All American stores in 1945 to expand its market share. According to Publix leaders, currently there are no plans for major mergers or acquisitions. They believe in a careful and steady growth strategy in order to maintain the Publix culture.[5] However, they are not against the idea of acquiring another company that fits Publix's culture and philosophy. "If the right opportunity came up we could acquire another company.... We may or may not find another company we like.... We believe in internal growth, building our own stores." The supermarket industry is becoming increasingly concentrated as large regional chains such as Kroger, Safeway, and Albertsons dominate their markets. The rapid growth and development of "supercenters," as evidenced by Walmart's grocery industry ascendancy, is testament to the viability of hybrid formats (i.e., grocery and general merchandise). Therefore, more companies are being forced to grow faster, partner, or merge in order to survive in the long term.

Questions

1. What factors are currently involved in successfully competing in the supermarket industry, and how will these factors change in the next five years?
2. What factors are currently influencing a customer's decision to shop at Publix? Why haven't competitors been able to successfully duplicate the Publix success formula?
3. What can Publix do to strengthen its market position with regard to its suppliers, customers, competitors, and employees?
4. What are the values of Publix's organizational culture, employees, customers, shareholders, suppliers, and competitors? Which ones do you consider to be value-adders and which ones do you see as value-destroyers? Can Publix become the premier quality food retailer in America?
5. What were the factors that led to the demise of PublixDirect? In hindsight, what should they have done differently to keep PublixDirect a viable business model? What does it take to create a successful online grocery operation

in the United States? It is a decade later—is the time right to reintroduce PublixDirect? Explain.

Case 6: StatePride Industrial Laundry— Value Chain Analysis[*]

The rental laundry industry is highly competitive and in the midst of consolidation. Laundries generally rent industrial uniforms and entrance mats along with the service of periodically (once or twice a week) picking up the dirty uniforms and mats, which are then laundered and returned clean. To survive and generate a reasonable profit, locally owned StatePride Industrial Laundry must outperform the larger national chains. The general manager, Davis McDonald, wants to develop a market advantage. He believes that value chain analysis is the correct tool to help him provide customers the benefits they want at prices that are reasonable. If StatePride can do this analysis effectively, the firm will discover the basis for a competitive edge.

What Is Value?

McDonald first needs to understand how customers such as the local Ford dealership, dairy plant, or plumbing supply firm perceive the value of StatePride's offerings. These companies purchase goods and services on the basis of the value they believe their company receives.

Let's explore the customer value created in more detail. The potential customer looks at the benefits he or she receives from products—not the physical characteristics. The customer does not rent a uniform or a mat. The customer pays a service fee to reduce the maintenance costs of keeping the workers and workplace clean, healthy, and presentable. The entrance mat fiber description "Nylon 6,6" has little or no meaning to the customer, whereas the words "clean," "presentable," and "healthy" have a great deal of meaning. If the mat is at the entrance to a laboratory, the customer receives little additional benefit from a mat with the company's logo, but if the mat is at the front door of a car dealership, the customer may perceive a large additional benefit from the positive image generated from a logo mat. Thus, increasing the benefits increases the value—if it helps the customer. However, simply providing more product features does not necessarily mean the customer places an increased value on the additional offering. The objective is to meet customer requirements or needs. The customer will expect to pay for benefits that satisfy needs, but nothing more.

The product is more than the mat itself. It includes the mat's cleanliness, timeliness, and service delivery as well as StatePride's response to requests for additional

---

[*] This case was prepared by Dr. Hilton Barrett, professor of business, Elizabeth City State University, Elizabeth City, North Carolina. He may be contacted at hbarrett@mail.ecsu.

mats or replacement of dirty mats in an emergency. Furthermore, "product" also means office functions such as invoicing and flexibility in regard to contract responsibilities. It also includes the attitude and helpfulness of the laundry's customer service representatives and the clarity of communications between these people and the customer.

The emphasis today is on total costs and long-term relationships. This is more than simply the price paid to StatePride. It includes associated costs. Associated costs are costs incurred by the customer using this service. For example, these costs may include the square footage within the customers' facility required for uniform lockers. After all, the area devoted to lockers cannot be used for production machinery or related profitable activities. Associated costs include normal business functions such as personnel time needed to check in product and account for returns, accounting department time to process invoices, or workers' time to fill out repair tags. Often neither the customer nor supplier recognizes the various associated costs. StatePride should communicate to the customer any ways in which StatePride reduces the customer's associated costs. This should also be communicated to all potential customers. The key to success is to drive down the total costs. If a customer's total costs over the long term are reduced, the resulting value to StatePride's customer is increased.

Price can be confusing. The uniform rental price may be quoted per change, but normal pricing within the rental laundries can include loss and abuse charges, wastewater surcharges, name and emblem charges, or setup charges. The customer is relatively unconcerned about StatePride's costs. He simply wants a viable, profitable supplier who can provide a long-term, ongoing solution to his needs. He is concerned only about the invoiced price coupled with his company's associated costs and the supplier's continuing ability to provide the required quality level of service.

The value concept is simple and straightforward: Increase the benefits and increase the value, or decrease the price paid and/or associated costs and increase the value. The customer will pay up to the perceived value and not a penny more! And, if the price paid is less than the perceived value received, so much the better for the customer!

Creating Value: The Value Chain Analysis

Value chain analysis is a powerful management tool used to understand how to drive down costs, provide greater benefits to the customer, and understand the generation of value. This technique is the most useful weapon in the marketing arsenal for increasing the value of StatePride's products to its customers. A value chain follows the generation of value in an organization from design through operations to the final product (goods and services) delivered to the customer and even the invoicing and payment options. It can then be expanded to include development of StatePride's suppliers and delivery of its goods/services, and finally into the

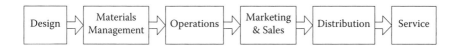

Figure A.7   Generic value chain.

customers' systems as the products are used. Each phase of the chain provides an opportunity to increase a customer's benefits or to decrease costs. As mentioned previously, either increasing benefits or decreasing costs or both can increase the relative value (especially related to a competitor) for the customer. Remember that value, quality, and beauty are in the eye of the beholder (the customer)! Michael E. Porter, an economics professor at Harvard Business School, discusses the value chain concept in his book *Competitive Advantage*.[1] A generic value chain is shown in Figure A.7. At this stage, the core question to be answered is, "What activities add value within your firm?" To use value chain analysis fully, the generic chain needs to be expanded and redefined to include your suppliers, firm, and customers. Let's follow the value chain for a StatePride Laundry uniform rental program for a regional plumbing company, DownEast Plumbing.

Three separate levels of activity are depicted in Figure A.8. In value chain analysis, the middle phase is always the analyst's firm. If a uniform manufacturer performs the analysis, the suppler might be a textile mill and the customer might be a rental laundry. By tracing the activities of each phase and the generation of value, management can evaluate possibilities for increasing benefits and lowering costs within each of the phases. These possibilities are shown in the figure by the comments given under the various activities.

The more the analyst understands the processes and real needs within the customer's internal value chain, the easier it is to develop products and related support services that increase the benefits or drive down the associated costs. Value chain analysis is a multipurpose tool. It can be used in numerous applications, as shown here:

1. Cost reduction through reengineering your processes (changing the way you run the business)
2. Cost reduction through reengineering processes with suppliers
3. Cost reduction through reengineering processes with customers
4. Developing a competitive advantage by restructuring the value chain (supplier–firm–customer) to offer greater benefits, lower total costs, and increase the value of your goods and services
5. Including benchmarking in your value chain (for example, FedEx is often benchmarked for its world-class logistics systems)
6. Analyzing strengths and weaknesses of key competitors: competitive analysis—a learning experience that can help you find a unique market advantage
7. Objectively critiquing the performance of business strategies and tactics: evaluation and control

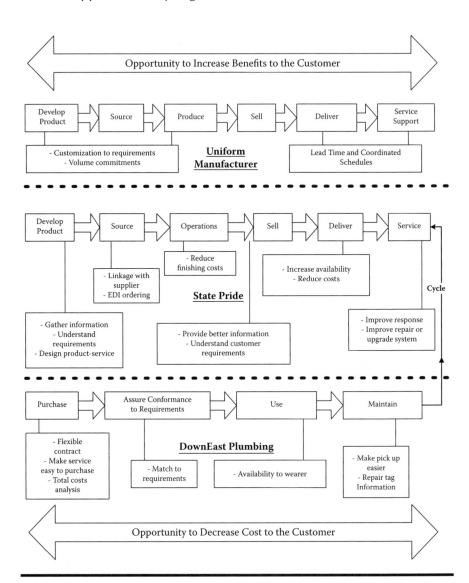

Figure A.8 Value chain analysis.

Applying Value Chain Analysis

DownEast Plumbing is a large regional firm with many service vehicles. Its major competitor is a national franchised firm with a similar number of vehicles in the targeted market. Competition is intense (where is it not today?). DownEast's marketing tactics emphasize the professionalism of its people and its service response time. Management wants company personnel to wear appropriate uniforms and to wear them appropriately to enhance the company image. StatePride's salesperson is working with DownEast on developing an image-oriented program. The uniform will be basic navy pants and a striped workshirt that is unique for DownEast Plumbing. The uniform program is an important part of DownEast's marketing activities. A series of local cable television commercials is built around their friendly and professionally uniformed plumbers. (As an aside, note that the automotive firms have "professionalized" their earlier-named "mechanics"—through the use of image-oriented uniforms featured in television advertisements—into "technicians" fully capable of conducting the high-tech maintenance needed for the 21st-century automobile. Each brand [e.g., General Motors, Ford] has its own apparel program and often features their uniformed technicians in the advertisements.)

McDonald's initial use of value chain analysis is to examine the activities within his firm. This evaluates the intrafirm or horizontal linkages between value-generating activities. The first step is to review possible alternatives for increasing value by increasing benefits or lowering costs. For example, more-durable uniforms will increase StatePride's initial purchasing costs but will lower the replacement, repair, and average weekly costs.

Next, McDonald assesses the interfirm or vertical linkages between the uniform supplier, StatePride Laundry, and the customer, DownEast Plumbing. What are the requirements of each within the process? The greater the understanding of buyer needs and requirements as well as the uniform supplier's capabilities and requirements, the better is the ability to generate greater value for customers. A working relationship with both supplier and customer will allow evaluation of capabilities and requirements and provide possible alternatives with the objective of increasing benefits and reducing costs—a win-win for StatePride and DownEast.

DownEast wants to emphasize comfort as much as appearance for its personnel. It anticipates redefining the image of its workforce in about 18 months. On the basis of StatePride's salesperson's knowledge and support from the uniform manufacturer, this could lead to a proposal for 100% cotton shirts and pants. While these garments do not last a long as 65/35 fabrics, the plumbing firm does not need the longer wear life, nor does such a fabric increase the benefits of StatePride's products for them. Further discussion may indicate that wrinkle-resistant cotton shirts and pants provide an acceptable appearance with excellent wearer comfort. The laundry can then forgo pressing, thereby decreasing labor and energy costs. Such savings can be passed on to its customers or shared between customers and StatePride (the more likely scenario).

StatePride can work with the uniform manufacturer on a shirt unique to DownEast, possibly using a base fabric already in stock by the manufacturer. McDonald can work with the manufacturer to look for ways to reduce his costs while still meeting the objectives of DownEast Plumbing. Good manufacturing suppliers welcome the opportunity to work with their customers on this objective. Hence, value chain analysis helps the manufacturer in the same way it assists StatePride. A shirt that is overengineered may be a great shirt, but remember that StatePride, as well as DownEast, will only pay for a shirt that meets its requirements, and nothing more.

McDonald can easily use value chain analysis to evaluate his marketing options. It is typical for a manufacturer to require a volume commitment and a lead-time commitment. The value chain shows once again that this is an area of opportunity. Working with the customer, StatePride can develop forecasts for the customer's uniform needs. This benefits the production planning for the manufacturer and leads to a delivery schedule agreed to in advance by all participants. It also reduces inventory vulnerability by all concerned—another cost reduction. These win-win collaborative solutions benefit all parties.

Communication is the key to success in the development of any value chain analysis program. What are DownEast Plumbing's requirements for the uniform and servicing? What are the uniform manufacturer's requirements for volume and lead time? What are the laundry's requirements for receiving garments so as to provide adequate time for preparation for initial placement into DownEast? Every participant in the transaction has its own requirements and capabilities. Armed with value chain analysis knowledge and understanding, the process of supplying uniforms, from uniform manufacturer through laundry to customer (and the service cycle back through the laundry) can be evaluated. Properly assessed, the opportunities for increasing benefits, lowering costs, and increasing value are readily apparent. Successfully implemented, satisfied customers receive greater value, and StatePride builds customer loyalty and retention and increases profits.

The StatePride and DownEast relationship is an example of industrial marketing (also called B2B). In consumer marketing, the consumer's value chain is the actual use of the product. This is the reason that consumer marketers (e.g., Procter & Gamble) often visit households to see how products are used. This provides the needed insights to develop better products to increase value for the consumer.

Questions

1. What are some ways that StatePride can reduce the price paid without changing its regular list prices for services?
2. How can StatePride's advertising campaign affect a customer's perceived benefits and resulting perceived value?
3. Explain how service firms should apply value chain analysis to create, deliver, and maximize customer value.

Index